토익 EDGE 실전

1000 제

LR 5 SET + 해석 해설

토익EDGE실전
1000제
LR 5 SET +해석 해설

초판 1쇄 인쇄 2018년 1월 26일
초판 1쇄 발행 2018년 2월 5일

지은이	박영수
펴낸이	임충배
편집	양경자
디자인	여수빈
홍보/마케팅	김정실
영업	김요한
펴낸곳	도서출판 삼육오 (PUB.365)
제작	(주)피앤엠123

출판신고 2014년 4월 3일
등록번호 제406-2014-000035호

경기도 파주시 산남로 183-25
TEL (031)946-3196 FAX (031)946-3171
홈페이지 www.pub365.co.kr

ISBN 979-11-86533-79-6 13740
© 2018 PUB.365 & 박영수

이 도서의 국립중앙도서관 출판예정도서목록(CIP)은 서지정보유통지원시스템 홈페이지(http://seoji.nl.go.kr)와
국가자료공동목록시스템(http://www.nl.go.kr/kolisnet)에서 이용하실 수 있습니다. (CIP제어번호: CIP2018001962)

토익EDGE실전

1000제

LR

5 SET + 해석 해설

머리말

토익의 변화!

현재 한국에서는 토익이 약 300회 이상 실시되었다. 이 과정에서 2006년 5월과 2016년 5월에 2번의 형식의 변화가 있었다. 2016년 5월 29일 개정된 토익이 처음 시행되었고 현재까지 시행되고 있다.

신토익 사전 준비!

2015년 11월에 토익을 개정하겠다는 ETS의 발표가 있었다. 저자는 그 이전이 이미 토익 개정에 대한 정보를 입수해 많은 정보를 수집해 가지고 있었다.

최신 분석 자료!

2016년에는 13회, 2017년에는 24회의 신토익이 시행되었다. 2018년에도 총 24회가 예정되어 있다. 현재까지 ETS는 12회의 신토익 유형의 문제를 공개했다. 이 중 먼저 공개한 6회 분의 문제는 실제 시험에서 사용하지 않는 문제이다. 나중 공개한 6회의 문제는 실제 시험에서 사용한 문제이다.

기출문제!

ETS는 토익의 문제를 Item Pool(문제은행) 방식으로 관리한다. 이 과정에서 한 번 사용한 문제는 절대 다시 사용하지 않는다. 그래서, 기출문제를 공부하는 것은 오히려 나오지 않을 문제만을 골라 공부하는 것이다. 다만, 기출문제는 출제 경향과 유형을 파악할 수 있는 기본적 자료로서의 가치만 있을 뿐이다.

토익 적중!

저자인 토익 예언자 박영수는 ETS가 어떤 방식으로 토익의 문제를 출제하고 관리하는지를 알아냈다. 그리고, 이를 바탕으로 향후 어떤 문제가 출제될지를 예측할 수 있게 되었다. 본 〈신토익 엣지 실전 1000제 LR〉의 문제 하나하나는 이런 저자 토익 예언자 박영수의 결과물이다. 〈신토익 엣지 실전 1000제 LR〉로 공부하고 시험을 보는 토익커는 〈신토익 엣지 실전 1000제 LR〉의 정답이 실제 시험에서 정답과 일치하는 기적을 경험하게 될 것이다.

이 땅의 모든 토익커들이 본 〈신토익 엣지 실전 1000제 LR〉로 공부해 신토익에 대해 정확한 이해를 하고, 최단 시간에 최고의 점수를 획득하길 기원한다.

본 〈신토익 엣지 실전 1000제 LR〉의 출간을 흔쾌한 허락하신 도서출판 Pub.365 임직원 여러분들에게 깊은 감사를 드린다.

토익 예언자 **박영수**

목차

* 특별 부록

신토익 OMR 카드 5장

고사장의 다양한 상황에 대비한 총 4종류의 L/C mp3 무료 제공

➡ 정상, 스피커 불량, 외부 소음, 스피커 불량 및 외부 소음

토익 EDGE 실전 1000제 LR SET 1~5 정답 / 스크립트 / 해석 / 해설 무료 제공

➡ 홈페이지(www.pub365.co.kr) 도서 자료실

EDGE [ed3] 엣지

www.pub365.co.kr

무료제공

QR코드   자동채점

1

모바일 자동 채점 방식 제공

정답 + 해석&해설 확인 (다운로드 : 홈페이지 ⇒ 도서자료실)

실제 시험에 출제될 수 있는 핵심 표현 정리

Part 5, 6, 7 선택지의 상위 개념부터 하위 개념으로 정확하게 분석

OMR

실전에 대비하는 토익 OMR 카드 5장

4종MP3

미국, 영국, 호주 남녀 원어민이 참여하여

실제 시험과 동일한 방식의 깨끗한 음질 제공

[단계별 악조건]   **2**

Normal ver. 일반 시험용

Speaker Noise ver. 방송실 불량

External Noise ver. 기침 소리, 교통소음 등 주변 환경소음

Speaker & External Noise ver. 방송실 불량과 함께 실생활 속 소음 환경

단어장   받아쓰기

홈페이지 www.pub365.co.kr ⇒ 도서 자료실 무료 다운로드

§ 4종 MP3, 자동채점, 해석&해설 확인 방법

매 세트 앞면 QR코드를 스마트폰 어플로 찍으면 해당 모의고사의 LC MP3를 들을 수 있으며, 모의고사 정답을 입력하면 바로 성적을 확인할 수 있고, 해석&해설을 볼 수 있습니다.

1

1 각 모의고사 세트 QR코드를
스마트폰으로 찍어보세요.
본인의 실력을 즉시 자동 채점되며,
토익 예상 성적까지 제시합니다.

2

2 각 고사장의 방송실 상황 및 주변 소음 환경을 고려
한 총 4가지 Type의 원어민 mp3 음성 제공합니다.

* Type 1. 미국, 영국, 호주 남녀 원어민이 참여하여
실제 시험과 동일한 방식의 깨끗한 음성 제공

* Type 2. 수험장 스피커 불량인 상황의 음성 제공

* Type 3. 여름철 매미 소리와 함께 기침 소리, 자동차 소리 등
주변 소음이 들어간 상황의 음성 제공

* Type 4. 비 오는 날 천둥과 함께 유난히 기침 소리도 많고,
다양한 주변 소음까지...
게다가 수험장 스피커 상태도 안 좋은 최악의 상황

§ 4종 MP3, 해석&해설, 단어장, 받아쓰기 노트 다운로드 방법

홈페이지 www.pub365.co.kr ⇒ 도서자료실에서 「토익 EDGE 실전 1000제 LR」을 클릭!

MP3와 해석&해설 및 단어장, LC 받아쓰기 노트를 다운로드할 수 있습니다

Old TOEIC vs. New TOEIC

		Old TOEIC 문항 수			New TOEIC 문항 수
1 LC	Part 1 Photographs	10		2	6
	Part 2 Question & Response	30		3	25
	Part 3 Short Conversation 10	30		4	39
	Part 4 Short Talk 11	30		5	30
RC	Part 5 Incomplete Sentences	40		6	30
	Part 6 Text completion 12	12		7	16
	Part 7 Reading Comprehension 13	단일 지문	28		29
		이중 지문	20	8	10
		삼중 지문	0		15
	Total	200		9	200

1 LC 전체의 Speaker가 다변화되었다. 미국, 캐나다, 영국, 호주 등 4개국의 남녀가 speaker로 총 8명이 등장한다.

2 Part 1이 10문항에서 6문항으로 축소되었다.

3 Part 2가 30문항에서 25문항으로 축소되었다.

4 Part 3이 30문항에서 39문항으로 증가했다. 발화의 수가 3~9번 발화까지로 다변화되었고, 3명의 화자가 등장하는 대화가 추가되었다. 신유형의 문제로 Intention Question과 Graphic Question이 추가되었다.

5 Part 4가 30문항으로 유지되었다. 신유형의 문제로 Intention Question과 Graphic Question이 추가되었다.

6 Part 5가 40문항에서 30문항으로 축소되었다.

7 Part 6가 12문항에서 16문항으로 증가했다. 신 유형의 문제로 Sentence Selection 문제가 추가되었다.

8 Part 7이 48문항에서 54문항으로 증가했다. 단일 지문에 새로운 지문 형식인 Text Message Chain과 Online Chat Discussion이 추가되었고, 삼중 지문도 도입되었다. 신유형 문제로 Intention Question과 Sentence Location 문제가 추가되었다.

9 시간과 배점은 동일하다. 시간은 LC 약 45분, RC 75분이다. 배점은 LC와 RC 각각 495점이다.

Part별 신유형 분석

[10] Part 3

▶ 발화의 수 다변화 : Old TOEIC에서는 2명의 화자가 3번 또는 4번 발화했으나,
  New TOEIC에서는 3번, 4번, 5번, 6번, 7번, 8번 9번 등 발화의 수가 다변화되었다.

▶ 3명 화자의 대화 도입 : 3명의 화자가 최소 6번, 최대 9번 발화하는 대화가 1set 또는 3set 등장한다.

▶ Intention Question 도입 : 완전한 문장 또는 불완전한 문장을 다시 한번 들려주고 이것의 의도를
  묻는 문제가 2문항에서 3문항 정도 등장한다.

▶ Graphic Question 도입 : 도표, 그래프 등 시각적인 정보를 주고 이를 보면서 정답을 찾아야 하는
  문제가 2문항에서 3문항 출제된다.

[11] Part 4

▶ Intention Question 도입 : 완전한 문장 또는 불완전한 문장을 다시 한번 들려주고 이것의 의도를
  묻는 문제가 2문항에서 3문항 정도 등장한다.

▶ Graphic Question 도입 : 도표, 그래프 등 시각적인 정보를 주고 이를 보면서 정답을 찾아야 하는
  문제가 2문항에서 3문항 출제된다.

[12] Part 6

▶ Sentence Selection 도입 : 지문의 흐름 상 빈칸에 들어갈 알맞은 문장을 고르는 문제가 출제된다.
  1 지문당 1문항으로 총 4문항 정도가 출제된다.

[13] Part 7

▶ Text Message Chain 또는 Online Chat Discussion의 도입 : 2명 또는 3명 이상의 writer가 등장하는
  휴대전화 문자 메시지가 2set 정도 등장한다. 2문항 1set와 4문항 1set로 등장한다.

▶ Sentence Location 도입 : 지문의 흐름 상 주어진 문장의 알맞은 위치를 묻는 문제가
  2문항에서 3문항 정도 출제된다. 3, 4문항짜리 지문에서 출제된다.

▶ 삼중 지문 도입 : 어떤 연관 관계가 있는 3개의 지문을 하나의 set으로 묶여 출제한다.
  1set 당 5문항으로, 3set 15문항이 출제된다.

① 10문항에서 6문항으로 축소된다.

② Part 1은 이제까지의 출제 경향이 그대로 유지될 것으로 예상된다. 즉, 1인이 등장하는 사진, 2인 이상이
등장하는 사진, 사람이 등장하지 않는 사진 등 3가지로 분류할 때 10문항일 때와 거의 같은 비율로
출제될 것이다.

아래는 New TOEIC에 대한 총 8회 시험의 Part 1 문항 통계이다.

	1회	2회	3회	4회	5회	6회	7회	8회	평균
1인	1	3	2	1	3	3	3	2	2.3
2인	4	2	4	4	2	2	2	3	2.9
사물	1	1	0	1	1	1	1	1	0.9

* 기본 점수를 높이기 위해서는 인물이 등장하는 사진을 중점적으로 공략하되, Part 1 만점을 위해서는 사물에
대해서도 명확히 학습해야 한다.

③ 토익의 주제인 일상생활과 비즈니스 분야로 분류할 때 역시 10문항일 때와 같은 비율로 구성될 것이다.

아래는 New TOEIC에 대한 총 8회 시험의 Part 1 문항 통계이다.

	1회	2회	3회	4회	5회	6회	7회	8회	평균
일상생활	5	6	4	3	4	5	5	4	4.5
비즈니스	1	0	3	3	2	1	1	2	1.6

* 기본 점수를 높이기 위해서는 일상에 대한 문제를 중점적으로 공략하되, 고득점을 목표로 두고 있다면
비즈니스 상황에 대한 내용까지 공략하여야 한다.

Part 2 기출 분석 및 시험 공략법

① Part 2 Direction에서 예시 문제가 삭제되어 Direction 시간이 약 1분에서 약 30초 정도로 축소된다.

② 문항 수가 30문항에서 25문항으로 축소된다.

③ Part 2는 이제까지의 출제 경향이 그대로 유지될 것으로 예상된다. 즉, 의문사로 시작하는 의문사 의문문, Be동사와 조동사로 시작하는 일반 의문문, 기타 의문문 (평서문, 부가 의문문, 부정 의문문, 간접 의문문, 선택 의문문, 청유 의문문) 등 3가지로 분류할 때 30문항일 때와 거의 같은 비율로 출제될 것이다.

아래는 New TOEIC에 대한 총 8회 시험의 Part 2 문항 통계이다.

	1회	2회	3회	4회	5회	6회	7회	8회	평균
의문사	10	11	10	13	13	10	12	9	11.0
일반	9	6	6	5	6	9	7	7	6.9
기타	6	8	9	7	6	6	6	9	7.1

* 기본 점수를 높이기 위해서는 의문사로 시작하는 의문문에 대해 중점적으로 공략하면 Part 2의 50% 이상은 맞출 수 있다. 하지만 고득점을 위해서는 비중이 비슷한 일반 의문문 및 기타 의문문까지 학습하여야 하며, 학습 순서는 의문사 의문문, 기타 의문문, 일반 의문문 순으로 진행하는 것이 좋다.

④ 토익의 주제인 일상생활과 비즈니스 분야로 분류할 때 역시 30문항일 때와 같은 비율로 구성될 것이다.

아래는 New TOEIC에 대한 총 8회 시험의 Part 2 문항 통계이다.

	1회	2회	3회	4회	5회	6회	7회	8회	평균
일상생활	8	8	9	10	8	8	8	8	8.4
비즈니스	17	17	16	15	17	17	17	17	16.6

* 일상생활과 비즈니스의 문제 출제 비율은 거의 2배가 된다. 즉, 기본 점수를 위해서는 비즈니스 상황을 먼저 공략하는 것이 바람직하며, 그다음 일상생활 주제에 맞는 문제를 중점적으로 풀어보는 순으로 학습하자.

① 문항 수가 30문항에서 39문항으로 증가한다.

② 대화 1set 당 3문항은 유지된다. 총 13set, 39문항으로 출제된다.

③ 2명의 화자가 최소 3번에서 최대 8번까지 발화할 것으로 예상된다. 4번 발화하는 것이 가장 많을 것으로 예상된다. 3번 발화하는 대화가 1~5set 정도, 4번 발화하는 대화가 2~7set 정도, 5번 발화하는 대화가 1~2set 정도, 6번 발화하는 대화가 1~2set 정도, 7번 발화하는 대화가 0~2set 정도, 8번 발화하는 대화가 0~1set, 9번 발화하는 대화가 0~1set 정도로 출제될 것으로 예상된다.

④ 3명의 화자가 등장하는 대화가 1~2set 출제된다. 3명의 화자가 최소 5번에서 최대 8번 발화한다.

아래는 New TOEIC에 대한 총 8회 시험의 Part 3 문항 통계이다.

		1회	2회	3회	4회	5회	6회	7회	8회	평균
2명	3회	3	4	1	1	2	2	5	3	2.6
	4회	6	2	6	7	4	5	5	4	4.9
	5회	1	2	2	2	2	2		2	1.6
	6회	1	2	1	1	2	1	1	1	1.3
	7회		1	1	1	1	1		2	0.9
	8회		1	1						0.3
	9회		1							0.1
3명	5번	2		1	1	1		1		0.8
	6번					1			1	0.3
	7번		1				1			0.3
	8번						1			0.1

* 화자 2명일 경우 11.6회, 3명 1.4회로 8배 이상 차이가 발생한다. 기본 점수를 높이고자 한다면 화자 2명 중에서도 4회, 3회를 집중적으로 공략하여야 하며, 그다음으로 5, 6회까지 학습하면 중간 이상 점수를 확보할 수 있다. Part 3 고득점을 위해서라면 3명 5번 발화를 중점적으로 하되, 그 이외 다수 발화도 신경을 써야 한다.

⑤ 3명의 화자가 등장하는 대화는 2명의 화자가 등장하는 대화의 중간에 위치할 것이다.
2명의 화자가 등장하는 대화 set의 발화 횟수와 맞춰 3명의 화자가 등장하는 대화 set이 위치할 것이다.
즉, 3명의 화자가 6번 발화하는 경우 2명의 화자가 6번 발화는 대화 set에 비슷하게 53번 대화 정도에, 3명의 화자가 8번 또는 9번 발화하면 59번 또는 62번 정도에 위치할 것이다.

⑥ 3명의 화자가 등장하는 대화에서 질문에 복수 주어가 등장할 수 있다. 즉, the men, the women이 주어인 질문이 등장할 수 있다. 두 명 화자의 공통점을 묻는 질문이다.

⑦ Intention Question이 신유형으로 출제된다. 불완전하거나 완전한 문장의 문맥적 의미를 묻는 문제가 출제된다. 불완전한 문장을 Fragment라 한다. 2문항 또는 3문항 정도일 것으로 예상된다.

아래는 New TOEIC에 대한 총 8회 시험의 Part 3 신유형 문항 통계이다.

	1회	2회	3회	4회	5회	6회	7회	8회	평균
Intention	3	3	2	3	2	2	2	2	2.4

아래는 New TOEIC에 대한 총 8회 시험의 Part 3 출제된 표현들이다.

1회 ⇨ that's a good question ⇨ I've been really busy with the inventory ⇨ Cajun cafe	2회 ⇨ I work until 3 o'clock in Tuesday ⇨ I volunteered last year ⇨ Didn't Hiroshi work on this project
3회 ⇨ I really can't say ⇨ I think we can do better	4회 ⇨ It's easy to miss ⇨ I am interviewing someone in here in five minutes ⇨ I get paid early once a month
5회 ⇨ Mr. Lehmann's in a meeting with clients right now? ⇨ That's a big increase from last year	6회 ⇨ And who can do that ⇨ There's a policy against that
7회 ⇨ look at all these cars ⇨ Tell me about it	8회 ⇨ Dena, this is your area of expertise ⇨ most reports have an executive summary in the beginning

* 총 19개의 Intention Question이 출제되었다. 이 중 2개는 3명의 화자가 등장하는 대화에서 출제되었다.

⑧ Graphic Question이 신유형으로 출제된다. 도표, 그래프, 지도 등의 시각적 요소를 보고 푸는 문제가 출제된다. 대화 세트로는 2set 내지 3set일 것으로 예상되며 실질적으로 각 set에서 1문항 정도가 Graphic을 보고 푸는 문제일 것으로 예상된다. 그러므로, 2문항에서 3문항 정도의 출제가 예상된다.

또한 Graphic이 포함된 대화 set은 마지막에 위치할 것으로 예상된다. 즉, 2set면 65번, 68번으로 시작하는 대화에, 3set면 62번, 65번, 68번으로 시작하는 대화 set에 위치할 것으로 예상된다.

Graphic Question의 Pause 시간은 12초일 것이다.

아래는 New TOEIC에 대한 총 8회 시험에 출제된 Graphic들이다.

1회 ⇨ building directory ⇨ floor plan (chart) ⇨ list	2회 ⇨ map ⇨ invoice	3회 ⇨ chart ⇨ room schedule ⇨ list
4회 ⇨ chart ⇨ sign	5회 ⇨ packing slip (전표) ⇨ flight schedule ⇨ chart	6회 ⇨ seat map ⇨ schedule ⇨ pie chart (원 그래프)
7회 ⇨ seating chart ⇨ invoice ⇨ train schedule	8회 ⇨ receipt ⇨ weather forecast ⇨ table	

* 총 23개의 Graphic Question이 출제되었다. 일반적인 표에 해당하는 Table에 속하는 것이 12개로 가장 많이 출제되었고, 간략한 지도에 해당하는 것이 4번 출제되었으며, Invoice가 2번 출제되었다. 나머지 유형들은 1번씩 출제되었다.
3명의 화자가 등장할 때는 Graphic Question이 출제되지 않았다.

⑨ 1개의 대화 set에 Intention Question과 Graphic Question이 동시에 출제되지는 않고 있다.

Part 4 기출 분석 및 시험 공략법

① 기존과 동일하게 30문항으로 유지된다.

② 기존과 동일하게 1set 당 3문항으로 출제된다.

아래는 New TOEIC에 대한 총 8회 시험의 Part 4 문항 통계이다.

	1회	2회	3회	4회	5회	6회	7회	8회	평균
Advertisement				1		1	1		0.4
Announcement	2	2	1	3		3	2	2	1.9
Information		1	1				1		0.4
Excerpt	2	3	3	1	2	2	1	4	2.3
Telephone Message	3	2	2	2	3	1	3	2	2.3
Recorded Message						1			0.1
Broadcast			1	1	1		1		0.5
Introduction	1	1		1	1			2	0.8
Talk	1		1	1	3	2	1		1.1
News report	1	1	1						0.4

* 위의 통계를 근거로, 회의 중 발췌에 해당하는 "Excerpt from a meeting"과 "Telephone Message"가 18번으로 가장 많이 출제되었고, "Announcement" 15번, "Talk"가 9번, "Introduction"이 6번, "Advertisement"가 3번, "Information"이 3번, "News Report"가 3번, "Recorded Message"가 1번 출제되었다.

③ Intention Question이 신유형으로 출제된다. 불완전하거나 완전한 문장의 문맥적 의미를 묻는 문제가 출제된다. 불완전한 문장을 Fragment라 한다. 2문항 또는 3문항 정도일 것으로 예상된다.

	1회	2회	3회	4회	5회	6회	7회	8회	평균
Intention	3	2	3	2	3	3	3	3	2.8

아래는 New TOEIC에 대한 총 8회 시험의 Part 4 출제된 표현들이다.

1회	2회
⇨ the store's already been open for these months ⇨ five thousand unit a lot ⇨ I know what you're thinking	⇨ I know it's a long trip ⇨ this isn't formal inspection

3회	4회
⇨ Can you believe me? ⇨ another conference is scheduled to begin here at 1:00? ⇨ This will be a big event	⇨ It'll only take a minutes ⇨ We already have a lot volunteers signed up for this event
5회	6회
⇨ it isn't what I was expecting ⇨ who knows when that will be ⇨ this is a very popular building	⇨ the grand opening is in two months ⇨ the user's manual currently about 20 pages long ⇨ this might take some tine
7회	8회
⇨ it's blocking the road from a factory ⇨ many people have that problem ⇨ Hartford Sweet Shop's ice cream is delicious	⇨ You can't miss it ⇨ I'll let Dr.Castillo tell you all about it ⇨ I'll have access card by tomorrow

④ Graphic Question이 신유형으로 출제된다. 도표, 그래프, 지도 등의 시각적 요소를 보고 푸는 문제가 출제된다. 담화 세트로는 2set 내지 3set일 것으로 예상되며 실질적으로 각 set에서 1문항 정도가 Graphic을 보고 푸는 문제일 것으로 예상된다. 그러므로, 2문항에서 3문항 정도의 출제가 예상된다.

또한, Graphic이 포함된 담화 set은 마지막에 위치할 것으로 예상된다. 즉, 2set면 95번, 98번으로 시작하는 담화에, 3set면 92번, 95번, 98번으로 시작하는 담화 set에 위치할 것으로 예상된다.

Graphic Question의 Pause 시간은 12초일 것이다.

	1회	2회	3회	4회	5회	6회	7회	8회	평균
Graphic	2	2	2	3	2	2	2	2	2.1

1회	2회	3회	4회
⇨ expense report ⇨ graph (막대)	⇨ map ⇨ floor plan (map) ⇨ Tuesday schedule	⇨ chart ⇨ map	⇨ time schedule ⇨ survey
5회	6회	7회	8회
⇨ coupon ⇨ flowchart	⇨ order form ⇨ graph (막대)	⇨ schedule ⇨ weather forecast	⇨ seating chart ⇨ graph (막대)

* 총 17개의 Graphic Question이 출제되었다. 일반적인 표에 해당하는 Table에 속하는 것이 6개로 가장 많이 출제되었고, 간략한 지도에 해당하는 것이 4번 출제되었으며, 막대 그래프가 2번 출제되었다. 나머지 유형들은 1번씩 출제되었다.

⑤ 현재까지 노출된 정보를 근거로 1개의 담화 set에 Intention Question과 Graphic Question이 동시에 출제되지는 않고 있다.

Part 5 기출 분석 및 시험 공략법

① 40문항에서 30문항을 축소된다.

② 문법 문제는 조금 감소하고 어휘 문제가 많이 감소할 것으로 예상된다. 문법 문제와 어휘 문제는 아래와 같을 것이다.

- 문법 문제 : 18~23 문항, 평균 20.5 문항
- 어휘 문제 : 8~13 문항, 평균 9.5 문항

③ 문법 문제를 구체적으로 살펴보면 아래와 같다.

아래는 New TOEIC에 대한 총 8회 시험의 문법 문항 통계이다.

	1회	2회	3회	4회	5회	6회	7회	8회	평균
품사	3	5	7	6	7	6	5	7	5.8
절 vs. 구			1	1	2	2			0.8
대등접속사		1					2		0.4
종속접속사		2	2	1	1	1	1	1	1.1
관계사	1		1	1	1	1	1	1	0.9
동사의 형태	4	5	4	3	4	5	4	3	4.0
인칭대명사	1	1	2	2	1	1	1	2	1.4
전치사	5	3	2	3	2	3	2	5	3.1
비교		1					1		0.3
한정사	1	1		1		2	1		0.8
개별 어법	1	2	1	1	1	1	3	1	1.4
도치									0.0
생략									0.0
기타	2	1		1	1			1	0.8
계	18	22	20	20	20	22	21	21	20.5

* 가장 많은 문법 문항은 품사의 구별을 묻는 문제로 평균 5.8문항, 그다음으로는 동사의 형태 4.0문항이다. 상기 출제되는 문법 문항별 평균을 보면서 시험을 준비하도록 하자.

* 도치 및 생략과 관련된 문제는 출제되지 않고 있다.

④ 어휘 문제를 구체적으로 살펴보면 아래와 같다.

아래는 New TOEIC에 대한 총 8회 시험의 어휘 문항 통계이다.

	1회	2회	3회	4회	5회	6회	7회	8회	평균
명사	7	3	3	3	3	3	3	3	3.5
동사	2	4	3	3	2	2	3	3	2.8
형용사	1		2	3	3	2	2	1	2.0
부사	3	1	2	1	2	1	1	1	1.5
계	13	8	10	10	10	8	9	8	9.5

* 명사 및 동사의 쓰임에 대해서는 명확히 알고 넘어가야 기본 점수뿐 아니라 고득점의 첫 단계가 될 것이다.

Part 6 기출 분석 및 시험 공략법

① 12문항에서 16문항으로 증가한다.

② 1set 당 3문항에서 1set 당 4문항으로 변경된다.

③ 3문항은 기존의 문법 어휘 문제이다.

④ Sentence Choice의 신유형 문제가 추가된다. 각 set 당 1문항일 것이다.

아래는 New TOEIC에 대한 총 8회 시험의 Part 6 문항 통계이다.

	1회	2회	3회	4회	5회	6회	7회	8회	평균
문장 선택	4	4	4	4	4	4	4	4	4

⑤ 문법 문제를 구체적으로 살펴보면 아래와 같다.

아래는 New TOEIC에 대한 총 8회 시험의 문법 문항 통계이다.

	1회	2회	3회	4회	5회	6회	7회	8회	평균
품사	2	2	1		1	1	1	1	1.1
절 vs. 구					1				0.1
종속접속사	1				1				0.3
관계사						1		1	0.3
동사의 형태	1	4	4	4	2	2	4	3	3.0
인칭대명사		1		1		1	1		0.5
전치사			2		1	1		1	0.6
비교	1			1					0.3
개별 어법							1	1	0.3
기타							1		0.1
계	5	7	7	6	6	6	8	7	6.5

* 가장 많은 문법 문항은 동사의 형태를 묻는 문제로 전체 평균 6.5문항 중 3.0문항을 차지한다.
  그다음으로는 품사의 구별을 묻는 문제로 평균 매회 1문항 이상 출제되고 있으니 놓치지 않도록 하자.

* 대등접속사, 한정어, 도치 및 생략과 관련된 문제는 출제되지 않고 있다.

⑥ 어휘 문제를 구체적으로 살펴보면 아래와 같다.

아래는 New TOEIC에 대한 총 8회 시험의 어휘 문항 통계이다.

	1회	2회	3회	4회	5회	6회	7회	8회	평균
명사	1	1	2	4	2	2	1		1.6
동사	3		1	1	2	1	2	2	1.5
형용사	2	2	1			1			0.8
부사	1	2	1	1	2	2	1	2	1.5
계	7	5	5	6	6	6	4	4	5.4

* 명사, 동사, 형용사의 문제가 골고루 출제되고 있다. 그에 반하여 형용사에 대한 문제는 다소 출제 횟수가
 작지만 놓쳐서는 안 될 부분이다.

Part 7 기출 분석 및 시험 공략법

① 48문항에서 54문항으로 증가한다.

② 단일지문이 28문항에서 29문항으로 증가한다. 지문당 2, 3, 4문항으로 총 10set로 출제될 것이다.

③ 이중지문이 4set, 20문항에서 2set, 10문항으로 축소된다.

④ 삼중지문이 도입된다. 3set, 15문항이다. 3개 지문을 모두 읽어 답하는 통합형 문제는 출제되지 않고 있다. 3개의 지문 중 2개 지문을 읽어 답하는 통합형 문제는 출제되고 있다.

아래는 New TOEIC에 대한 총 8회 시험의 Part 7 삼중지문의 구성이다.

	Q.186~190	Q.191~195	Q.196~200
1회	e-mail ⇨ report ⇨ e-mail	web-page ⇨ receipt ⇨ customer review	web-page ⇨ online form ⇨ e-mail
2회	web-page ⇨ e-mail ⇨ e-mail	e-mail ⇨ web-page ⇨ article	form ⇨ e-mail ⇨ letter
3회	advertisement ⇨ e-mail ⇨ web-site feedback	schedule ⇨ e-mail ⇨ review	article ⇨ newspaper editorial ⇨ e-mail
4회	e-mail ⇨ log sheet ⇨ e-mail	advertisement ⇨ e-mail ⇨ text message	advertisement ⇨ online form ⇨ review
5회	web-page ⇨ e-mail ⇨ form	e-mail ⇨ menu ⇨ comment card	e-mail ⇨ flyer ⇨ text message
6회	announcement ⇨ instructions ⇨ e-mail	schedule ⇨ e-mail ⇨ letter	e-mail ⇨ attachment ⇨ e-mail
7회	e-mail ⇨ program ⇨ information	coupon ⇨ memo ⇨ receipt	notice ⇨ e-mail ⇨ form
8회	article ⇨ information ⇨ form	web-page ⇨ list ⇨ article	article ⇨ advertisement ⇨ customer review

⑤ 단일지문에 Text Message Chain 또는 Online Chat Discussion이 도입된다. 2명의 writer가 등장하는 2문항짜리 1set, 3명 이상의 writer가 등장하는 4문항짜리 1set이 출제될 것이다.

* 세트 (문항)

	1회	2회	3회	4회	5회	6회	7회	8회
Text	1 (2)	1 (2)	1 (2) 1 (4)	1 (2) 1 (4)	1 (2) 1 (4)	1 (2)	1 (2)	1 (4)
Online	1 (4)	1 (4)				1 (4)	1 (2)	1 (2)

⑥ Intention Question이 신유형 문제도 도입된다. Part 3과 Part 4에 도입된 문제와 같은 유형의 문제이다.
Text Message Chain 또는 Online Chat Discussion에만 등장할 것이며,
각 set 당 1문항씩으로 총 2문항 정도가 출제될 것이다.

	1회	2회	3회	4회	5회	6회	7회	8회	평균
Intention	2	2	2	2	2	2	2	2	2

1회 ⇨ why wait ⇨ of course	2회 ⇨ is that it? ⇨ I hope we've kept backup files
3회 ⇨ of course ⇨ that works	4회 ⇨ Certainly ⇨ You're in luck
5회 ⇨ I'm not at my desk ⇨ We'll be working late the next few days	6회 ⇨ That's true ⇨ NNC Systems is a big client
7회 ⇨ Yes, please do ⇨ I can't believe it	8회 ⇨ That's a new one ⇨ We're working on it

⑦ Sentence Location이 신유형 문제로 도입된다. 주어진 문장의 위치를 묻는 문제이다.
단일지문에만 등장하고 해당 지문의 마지막 문제로 출제될 것이다. 3문항짜리 지문 또는
4문항짜리 지문에서만 출제될 것이고, 각 지문당 1문항으로 2문항 또는 3문항 정도가 출제될 것이다.

	1회	2회	3회	4회	5회	6회	7회	8회	평균
단락 처음					1				0.1
단락 중간	2	2	1	1		2	1		1.1
단락 마지막			1	1	1		1	2	0.8

⑧ Part 7은 지문 읽는 것도 많은 시간 할애가 된다. 홈페이지(www.pub365.co.kr)에서 제공하는 SPEED
READING 온라인 학습 프로그램으로 속독 훈련을 통해 문제 풀 수 있는 충분한 시간을 확보해 보자.

新토익 점수 환산표

	맞은 개수	환산 점수		맞은 개수	환산 점수
	96~100	485~495		96~100	465~495
	91~95	440~490		91~95	415~470
	86~90	400~445		86~90	380~425
	81~85	360~410		81~85	350~390
	76~80	330~375		76~80	320~365
	71~75	300~345		71~75	290~335
	66~70	270~315		66~70	260~305
	61~65	245~285		61~65	230~275
	56~60	220~260		56~60	200~245
Listening Test	51~55	195~235	Reading Test	51~55	170~215
	46~50	165~205		46~50	145~185
	41~45	140~180		41~45	115~155
	36~40	115~150		36~40	95~130
	31~35	95~130		31~35	70~105
	26~30	80~115		26~30	55~90
	21~25	60~95		21~25	40~70
	16~20	40~65		16~20	30~55
	11~15	25~45		11~15	20~45
	6~10	15~30		6~10	15~30
	1~5	5~15		1~5	5~15
	0	5		0	5

* 절대적인 기준은 아니며 본 실전모의고사에 대해 참고로 활용할 수 있습니다.

新토익 시험 진행 안내

❶ 시험 시간 : 120분(2시간)

오전 시험	오후 시험	시간	비고
9:20	2:20		입실
9:30 ~ 9:45	2:30 ~ 2:45	15분	답안지 작성에 관한 Orientation
9:45 ~ 9:50	2:45 ~ 2:50	5분	수험자 휴식시간
9:50 ~ 10:05	2:50 ~ 3:05	15분	신분증 확인 (감독 교사)
10:05 ~ 10:10	3:05 ~ 3:10	5분	문제지 배부 및 파본 확인
10:10 ~ 10:55	3:10 ~ 3:55	45분	듣기 평가(L/C)
10:55 ~ 12:10	3:55 ~ 5:10	75분	독해 평가(R/C) * 2차 신분확인

※ L/C 진행 후 휴식 시간 없이 바로 R/C 진행

❷ 준비물

» 신분증 : 규정 신분증만 가능 (주민등록증, 운전면허증, 기간 만료 전의 여권, 공무원증 등)
» 필기구 : 연필, 지우개 (볼펜이나 사인펜은 사용 금지)

❸ 시험 응시 준수 사항

» 시험 시작 10분 전 입실 (오전 9:50, 오후 2:50 이후에는 입실 불가)
» 종료 30분 전과 10분 전에 시험 종료 공지함
» 휴대전화의 전원은 미리 꺼둘 것

❹ OMR 답안지 표기 요령

» 반드시 지정된 필기구로 표기
※ 성명, 주민등록번호 등을 틀리게 표기하였을 경우 채점 및 성적 확인이 불가능하므로 주의하시기 바랍니다.

OMR 답안지 표기 Sample				
O	Ⓐ	Ⓑ	●	Ⓓ
X	Ⓐ	Ⓥ	Ⓒ	Ⓓ
X	Ⓐ	Ⓑ	Ⓒ	ⓧ
X	Ⓐ	Ⓑ	Ⓒ	Ⓓ
X	Ⓐ	Ⓑ	Ⓒ	Ⓓ

토익 EDGE 실전
1000제
LR SET 1

지금부터 Actual Test를 진행합니다.
실제 시험과 동일한 방식으로 진행됨을 말씀드리며,
방송 음성은 QR코드로 청취하실 수 있습니다.

준비 되셨으면 바로 시작하세요.!

LISTENING TEST

In the Listening test, you will be asked to demonstrate how well you understand spoken English. The entire Listening test will last approximately 45 minutes. There are four parts, and directions are given for each part. You must mark your answers on the separate answer sheet. Do not write your answers in your test book.

PART 1

Directions: For each question in this part, you will hear four statements about a picture in your test book. When you hear the statements, you must select the one statement that best describes what you see in the picture. Then find the number of the question on your answer sheet and mark your answer. The statements will not be printed in your test book and will be spoken only one time.

Statment (A), "Some people are paddling through the water," is the best description of the picture, so you should select answer (A) and mark it on your answer sheet.

1.

2.

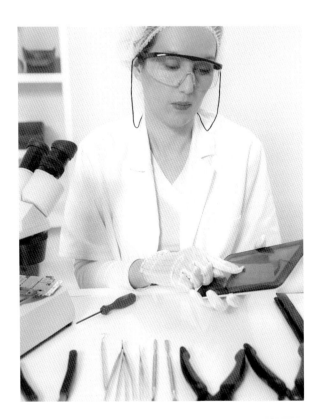

GO ON TO THE NEXT PAGE

3.

4.

5.

6.

GO ON TO THE NEXT PAGE

PART 2

Directions: You will hear a question or statement and three responses spoken in English. They will not be printed in your test book and will be spoken only one time. Select the best response to the question or statement and mark the letter (A), (B), or (C) on your answer sheet.

7. Mark your answer on your answer sheet.

8. Mark your answer on your answer sheet.

9. Mark your answer on your answer sheet.

10. Mark your answer on your answer sheet.

11. Mark your answer on your answer sheet.

12. Mark your answer on your answer sheet.

13. Mark your answer on your answer sheet.

14. Mark your answer on your answer sheet.

15. Mark your answer on your answer sheet.

16. Mark your answer on your answer sheet.

17. Mark your answer on your answer sheet.

18. Mark your answer on your answer sheet.

19. Mark your answer on your answer sheet.

20. Mark your answer on your answer sheet.

21. Mark your answer on your answer sheet.

22. Mark your answer on your answer sheet.

23. Mark your answer on your answer sheet.

24. Mark your answer on your answer sheet.

25. Mark your answer on your answer sheet.

26. Mark your answer on your answer sheet.

27. Mark your answer on your answer sheet.

28. Mark your answer on your answer sheet.

29. Mark your answer on your answer sheet.

30. Mark your answer on your answer sheet.

31. Mark your answer on your answer sheet.

PART 3

Directions: You will hear some conversations between two or more people. You will be asked to answer three questions about what the speakers say in each conversation. Select the best response to each question and mark the letter (A), (B), (C), or (D) on your answer sheet. The conversations will not be printed in your test book and will be spoken only one time.

32. What will Logan go to America for?
    (A) To attend a meeting
    (B) To meet Keith's family
    (C) To live there permanently
    (D) To visit his parents

33. When did Logan originally intend to go to America?
    (A) In January
    (B) In February
    (C) In November
    (D) In December

34. Why was Logan's trip postponed?
    (A) He wanted to go to Anaheim instead.
    (B) His parents were very busy.
    (C) He was too busy with work.
    (D) Keith did not allow him to go.

35. Who will contact the applicants?
    (A) Mr. Cooper
    (B) The training manager
    (C) Leigh
    (D) The personnel department

36. What problem does the man mention?
    (A) The personnel manager is not available.
    (B) They need not fill the position right away.
    (C) They don't have enough time to contact the applicants.
    (D) The candidates are not qualified.

37. What did the woman agree to do?
    (A) Tell the training manager to call the applicants
    (B) Meet the personnel department right away
    (C) Request that Mr. Cooper return next month
    (D) Ask the applicants to prepare for a presentation

38. What does the man mention about the woman?
    (A) She held a party.
    (B) She asked Jolly to bring some mobile phones.
    (C) She got a new job.
    (D) She insisted that the man receive his paycheck.

39. What did the woman ask the man to do?
    (A) Buy the vegetables
    (B) Come to a party
    (C) Interview Jolly
    (D) Give Jolly a paycheck

40. Where will Mark most likely be tonight?
    (A) In Audrey's house
    (B) In a restaurant with Audrey
    (C) In a job interview
    (D) In his office

41. Why should the woman meet Garland?
    (A) To send her notes in chemistry to him
    (B) To offer a book to him
    (C) To go with him to Milford's office
    (D) To communicate with him

42. According to the man, who did Garland meet?
    (A) Kirk
    (B) Patricia
    (C) Milford
    (D) Garland's friend

43. According to the woman, what problem does Mr. Garland have?
    (A) He misplaced his library card.
    (B) He borrowed different books for Patricia.
    (C) He missed his chemistry book.
    (D) He received a library card from Kirk.

GO ON TO THE NEXT PAGE

44. What is the woman concerned about?

    (A) She has only a few computers.
    (B) Her company spends too much.
    (C) She needs to get a new electric meter.
    (D) The photocopier isn't working.

45. What did the man ask Vicky to do?

    (A) Confirm the electric meter
    (B) See a bank official
    (C) Make a plan to minimize costs
    (D) Complete a report

46. What will the woman do next?

    (A) Tell Vicky to meet Cameron
    (B) Wait for Richard
    (C) Order a meal
    (D) Check the loans

---

47. What problem does the woman have?

    (A) She cannot ask Travis to play with her pet.
    (B) She cannot sell her old bike.
    (C) She won't rent the garage.
    (D) She has too many useless things

48. What was the man's suggestion?

    (A) She should sell her stuff.
    (B) She should renovate the garage.
    (C) She should purchase a new shirt.
    (D) She should ask for help.

49. What will the woman most likely do next?

    (A) Use her bike
    (B) Ask for Travis' help
    (C) Go outside with her dog
    (D) Buy new clothes

50. Where will the conversation probably take place?

    (A) At a box office
    (B) At a shoe store
    (C) At a post office
    (D) At a hardware shop

51. According to the man, what is included in his parcel?

    (A) Software program
    (B) Papers
    (C) Gifts
    (D) Clothing

52. What will the woman do next?

    (A) Pick up and take her colleague to Baltimore
    (B) Give a presentation at a seminar
    (C) Board a ship at the harbor
    (D) Send a package

---

53. What did the man hear about?

    (A) Ms. Evans will get a high wage.
    (B) Ms. Evans will be the director of the accounting department.
    (C) Ms. Evans will leave the company.
    (D) Ms. Evans will handle many details.

54. According to the man, why did the employees get paid late?

    (A) Mr. Jameson didn't know how to use the accounting system.
    (B) Mr. Jameson did all the work alone.
    (C) Mr. Jameson hired a small number of new employees.
    (D) Mr. Jameson listened to his dismissal.

55. What does the woman mean when she says, "I took over the job"?

    (A) She was Jameson's successor.
    (B) She updated the job information.
    (C) She didn't care what happened to him.
    (D) She changed her title.

56. What is the conversation mainly about?

(A) Designing a new product to meet the client's needs
(B) Their client's product release schedule
(C) The promotion for the new product
(D) The best way to show a new product to a client

57. What does Ms. Harden suggest them to do?

(A) To delay the event until Mr. Wallace can come
(B) To polish up the presentation after the event
(C) To make sure Mr. Wallace is at the event
(D) To tell Mr. Wallace that there won't be an event

58. What does he say about Blanton Cosmetics?

(A) Their representative will attend the event.
(B) The new product won't be useful to them.
(C) They are valued buyers.
(D) They are difficult clients to handle.

---

59. What did Mr. Sanders ask Ms. Flores to give?

(A) Yellow pages
(B) Some traffic information
(C) An electronic device
(D) A checklist

60. What does Ms. Kelly mean when she says, "In that case"?

(A) If you lost your papers
(B) If you wanted to draw attention
(C) If you were in danger
(D) If you received an apology

61. What do the women ask the man to do?

(A) Contact a colleague
(B) Send a document
(C) Cancel an appointment
(D) Find a substitute

Conference	
WHERE	**WHAT**
Memphis	Marketing
Portland	Accounting
Denver	Sales
London	Personnel

62. What is the conversation mainly about?

(A) The conference keynote address
(B) The conference location
(C) The conference agenda
(D) The conference procedure

63. Loot at the graphic. What will be discussed at the event?

(A) Marketing
(B) Accounting
(C) Sales
(D) Personnel

64. What problem does the man report?

(A) He dislikes boarding airplanes.
(B) He can't leave his office empty for a long time.
(C) He has a scheduling conflict with the conference.
(D) He has an invalid passport.

GO ON TO THE NEXT PAGE

Car Rental

12 hours	$40
24 hours	$80
48 hours	$150
72 hours	$220
96 hours	$280

Lenova Laptop $2000	Dell Laptop $1600	Apple Tablet $1000
Size: 15.6 inches	Size: 17 inches	With 24 month Internet
Lightweight aluminum case	Powerful	contract $50/month

65. What is the conversation mainly about?

(A) Traveling to a company conference in a rental car
(B) Their business plans
(C) A speech by the boss
(D) A due date

66. What is the man concerned about?

(A) They will be late for the conference.
(B) The woman will drive too fast.
(C) They won't be able to come back within seven hours.
(D) The rental car is too expensive.

67. Look at the graphic. How much will the woman likely have to pay for the car rental?

(A) $80
(B) $150
(C) $220
(D) $280

68. Why does the woman want to buy a laptop?

(A) To use in her office
(B) To replace her old one
(C) To prepare for a school class
(D) To give to her son as a present

69. What is the problem with the Dell Laptop?

(A) It's not powerful enough.
(B) It is not very portable.
(C) The design is not modern.
(D) It looks cheap.

70. Look at the graphic. How much will the woman likely spend on her purchase?

(A) $50
(B) $1000
(C) $1600
(D) $2000

PART 4

Directions: You will hear some talks given by a single speaker. You will be asked to answer three questions about what the speakers say in each talk. Select the best response to each question and mark the letter (A), (B), (C), or (D) on your answer sheet. The talks will not be printed in your test book and will be spoken only one time.

71. What is Ms. Lacy Williams majoring in?
(A) Event planning
(B) Public relations
(C) Writing reports
(D) Story telling

72. Where did Ms. Lacy Williams start her career?
(A) At a botanical garden
(B) At a law firm
(C) At a broadcasting company
(D) At a hospital

73. What happened to the zoo in the second year of Lacy's campaign?
(A) More botanical garden keepers were employed.
(B) More people came to the botanical garden than before.
(C) Plants were better taken care of.
(D) Botanical garden keepers attended more ceremonies.

74. What is Hughes' Farm going to do in 2016?
(A) Celebrate its anniversary
(B) Finish its business
(C) Reopen a franchise
(D) Relocate to another location

75. What number should be pressed for educational information?
(A) Number 6
(B) Number 7
(C) Number 8
(D) # Button

76. What is the caller advised to do to hear the telephone message again?
(A) Leave a message
(B) Stay on the line
(C) Press a certain button
(D) Hang up and call again

77. Where is the seminar being held?
(A) On a cruise
(B) At the Anderson Center
(C) At the Hudson hotel
(D) At a company

78. How long will the seminar last?
(A) One day
(B) Two days
(C) Five days
(D) Seven days

79. What has been organized for the participants?
(A) A motivational course
(B) Sightseeing trips
(C) Job counseling
(D) A formal banquet

80. Who will the speaker most likely be?
(A) A flight attendant
(B) The captain
(C) An airport employee
(D) A weather forecaster

81. Where will this announcement most likely take place?
(A) In an airport
(B) In a hotel
(C) In a plane
(D) On a bus

82. What will Ms. Sammy do next?
(A) Apologize for the inconvenience
(B) Inform the passengers of the destination of each bus
(C) Ask the captain to divert a flight
(D) Announce the next plane schedule

GO ON TO THE NEXT PAGE

83. What should the listeners do when the fire alarm is tested?

    (A) Call maintenance department
    (B) Leave the building
    (C) Listen carefully
    (D) Review the drill procedures

84. Which door should NOT be used in the North Wing?

    (A) The main gate
    (B) The front gate
    (C) The side gate
    (D) The North gate

85. Who will determine the end of the drill?

    (A) The construction workers
    (B) The department heads
    (C) The official of the city hall
    (D) The maintenance department

---

86. When will the bus arrive in Vancouver?

    (A) 1:10 P.M.
    (B) 1:40 P.M.
    (C) 2:10 P.M.
    (D) 4:20 P.M.

87. What must passengers remember to do when they get off?

    (A) Come back on time
    (B) Take their valuables
    (C) Memorize the number of their seats
    (D) Take their boarding tickets

88. What happens in Vancouver?

    (A) The bus is refueled.
    (B) There is a change in drivers.
    (C) The bus is fixed.
    (D) The lunchtime is provided.

89. Who will the speaker most likely be?

    (A) A laboratory employee
    (B) A cleaning crew member
    (C) A new equipment administrator
    (D) A company boss

90. Why does the speaker says, "here's what we'll do"?

    (A) To introduce new equipment
    (B) To summarize the lab's operations guideline
    (C) To assign research job
    (D) To provide directions

91. According to the speaker, what does the green light mean?

    (A) That the lab is being cleaned
    (B) That the lab is empty
    (C) That people may enter the lab
    (D) That people may not use the lab

---

92. What is the main purpose of this announcement?

    (A) To advertise a retirement insurance
    (B) To introduce financial support for university students
    (C) To inform a new type of loan
    (D) To hold free consultation seminar

93. What does the speaker mean, when he says, "They're the people to call for financial consultation"?

    (A) They provide discounts with students.
    (B) They ask for funding.
    (C) They are seeking for new workers.
    (D) They are the best for the job.

94. What does the speaker mention about the organization's scholarship?

    (A) It celebrates their twentieth anniversary.
    (B) The university will hire scholarship recipients.
    (C) It is only good for local students.
    (D) Livestrong Foundation will only offer tuition.

Program	
Product	Time
Vacuum Cleaner	2:00 ~ 2:30 P.M.
Microwave Oven	2:30 ~ 3:00 P.M.
Dish Washer	3:00 ~ 3:30 P.M.
Air Conditioner	3:30 ~ 4:00 P.M.

TEAM	MEMBER
Research & development	6 people
Public relations	8 people
Marketing	18 people
Sales	20 people

95. Who will most likely be interested in this speech?
(A) Event planners
(B) Attendees at an event
(C) Merchants at a trade show
(D) Job seekers

96. What did the speaker mention about the problem last year?
(A) The closing time was not decided.
(B) The presentations were loud.
(C) There was no information desk.
(D) The stage was too large.

97. Look at the graphic. What will be demonstrated in the last presentation?
(A) A vacuum cleaner
(B) A microwave oven
(C) A dish washer
(D) An air conditioner

98. According to the speaker, what is the purpose of this party?
(A) To honor a retiring president
(B) To celebrate the company's anniversary
(C) To thank Murray Stewart employees
(D) To welcome new colleague

99. How long has the product been on sale?
(A) For six weeks
(B) For eight weeks
(C) For ten weeks
(D) For eighteen weeks

100. Look at the graphic. Which team does Murray Stewart lead?
(A) Research and Development
(B) Public Relations
(C) Marketing
(D) Sales

This is the end of the Listening test. Turn to Part 5 in your text book.

GO ON TO THE NEXT PAGE

READING TEST

In the Reading test, you will read a variety of texts and answer several different types of reading comprehension questions. The entire Reading test will last 75 minutes. There are three parts, and directions are given for each part. You are encouraged to answer as many questions as possible within the time allowed.

You must mark your answers on the separate answer sheet. Do not write your answers in your test book.

PART 5

Directions: A word or phrase is missing in each of the sentences below. Four answer choices are given below each sentence. Select the best answer to complete the sentence. Then mark the letter (A), (B), (C), or (D) on your answer sheet.

101. Mr. Kingsley has been with Stone-Hedge Resources since 2005, and he was promoted to branch manager in January 2010 after five ------- years in general department.
    (A) success
    (B) successful
    (C) successfully
    (D) succeed

102. Texas meat producers currently face the challenge of minimizing ------- production costs while supplying leaner, more visually appealing meats to various consumer markets.
    (A) them
    (B) theirs
    (C) themselves
    (D) their

103. Customers Satisfaction Center will be open for a ------- time only and anyone can use without restriction.
    (A) minor
    (B) limited
    (C) partial
    (D) free

104. Ms. Nadia will be transferred to the advertisement department ------ has been separated from the sales department.
    (A) who
    (B) whom
    (C) whose
    (D) which

105. National Tax Service will bring up official apartment prices nationwide by over 15 percent from next July, a move that will force owners of apartments to pay ------- taxes.
    (A) high
    (B) higher
    (C) highest
    (D) highly

106. Those who are interested in the marketing campaign are asked to complete this ------- .
    (A) apply
    (B) applicant
    (C) application
    (D) applying

107. The doctor had her patients ------- down for about an hour after regular check-ups.
    (A) lie
    (B) lying
    (C) lied
    (D) to lie

108. Flight attendants say that they sometimes feel dizzy and nauseous ------- flights take off.
    (A) in
    (B) during
    (C) when
    (D) afterwards

109. We have been looking forward to working with your company ------- we examined the prototype of your product at the last seminar.
(A) after
(B) while
(C) because
(D) since

110. The manager of the Welfare foundation suggested that Ms. Gibbson ------- teaching the piano the disabled students.
(A) consider
(B) considers
(C) will consider
(D) considered

111. The CEO of this company appeared disappointed ------- the budget proposals that the committee had determined.
(A) in
(B) for
(C) on
(D) at

112. Ms. Scarlet has ------- a good command of Korean but also significant business experience in Korea.
(A) both
(B) either
(C) neither
(D) not only

113. ------- one of America's oldest and largest cookware manufacturers, Regal Ware World has built a reputation for producing high quality cookwares since 1911.
(A) By
(B) As
(C) Through
(D) Like

114. The large discount stores have been warned to keep better ------- of where their vegetables come from.
(A) states
(B) marks
(C) points
(D) records

115. Our newly formed committee convenes every month to discuss creative and effective ways to extend ------- to new newcomers.
(A) preference
(B) hostility
(C) hospitality
(D) fondness

116. ------- the Japanese stock market has been on the rise in the last few months, youth unemployment has been higher.
(A) Although
(B) If
(C) Because
(D) As soon as

117. A public clinic ------- at Target Mart for influenza shots for one month.
(A) holds
(B) will hold
(C) has held
(D) has been held

118. A web document with an obvious bias does not ------- imply that the information it contains is without value.
(A) barely
(B) highly
(C) gradually
(D) necessarily

119. ------- by Mr. Williams, his students could successfully finish their performance.
(A) Assist
(B) Assisted
(C) Assisting
(D) To assist

120. The staff's work has been of high quality, was delivered on -------, and we have been well satisfied with its technical competence and professional approach.
(A) schedule
(B) appointment
(C) authority
(D) condition

GO ON TO THE NEXT PAGE

121. The number of high school students who want to major in natural science ------- went down last year.

(A) signify
(B) significant
(C) significantly
(D) significance

122. ------- can understand the decision that the company will fire 200 employees; that is, we are short of workers at present.

(A) Anyone
(B) Everyone
(C) No one
(D) Someone

123. ------- they have dropped some clear hints, choosing a gift for the die-hard video gamers in the family could be overwhelming this holiday season.

(A) Unless
(B) As
(C) Without
(D) Except

124. ------- he reappear today looking hale and hearty, his long absence will have cast a shadow over his position.

(A) If
(B) Had
(C) Though
(D) Should

125. The measure is a part of the government's efforts to curb ------- real estate speculation that has become a major social issue.

(A) outstanding
(B) exclusive
(C) breathtaking
(D) rampant

126. ------- should also be made for the additional space a computer monitor and its peripheral can occupy.

(A) Account
(B) Allowance
(C) Consideration
(D) Concern

127. Thomson Electronics is now working towards a ------- to a problem that has emerged in the process of production recently.

(A) number
(B) cause
(C) result
(D) solution

128. If you are thinking of buying a home, a condominium, or a commercial building, it should be thoroughly inspected ------- the final purchase.

(A) in
(B) under
(C) before
(D) on

129. Quality products and ------- more high-risk goods require a detailed analysis of the suppliers that are willing to quote for a contract.

(A) all
(B) very
(C) any
(D) even

130. International Monetary Fund was established to provide loans to countries having temporary difficulties dealing with ------- of payment problems.

(A) deposit
(B) balance
(C) account
(D) margin

PART 6

Directions: Read the texts that follow. A word, phrase, or sentence is missing in parts of each text. Four answer choices for each question are given below the text. Select the best answer to complete the text. Then mark the letter (A), (B), (C), or (D) on your answer sheet.

Questions 131-134 refer to the following article.

The director of Libby's mine said on Friday that the state recorded its seventh coal-related

fatality there this year. ------- a safety director, Dionne Searcey was to play an important
131.

role in investigating this year's string of coal mine accidents including the March 11th

explosion at the Libby Mine that ------- in the death of 13 miners.
132.

Ms. Searcey said at the press conference Friday evening that he is ready to try something

different after more than 20 years in state government. She said she had already

approached Mayor Kevin Munsell last year about ------- the office. ------- .
133.   134.

131. (A) As
(B) After
(C) By
(D) For

132. (A) brought
(B) took
(C) occurred
(D) resulted

133. (A) quit
(B) quitted
(C) quitting
(D) quits

134. (A) So, Ms. Searcey told that she would retire her position.
(B) However, after being persuaded, she agreed to stay until the end of this year.
(C) But, Ms. Searcey didn't play an important role in investigating Libby's mine.
(D) Therefore, Mayor Kevin Munsell told us not to return to the official position.

GO ON TO THE NEXT PAGE

We have just completed negotiations to merge with Saint Furniture. Our new name will be Strongman Saint Furniture. We will make every effort not to ------- and to retain our existing
135.
staffs. Saint Furniture has been known for great customer service since we opened, so we are hopeful that sales will increase ------- after the merger of the two organizations.
136.
------- . We will be changing our bank accounts, so if you have set up an automatic transfer
137.
to your account, you will need to fill out a special form. This form, ------- is only available
138.
from Monica Tyler in personnel, should be completed by April 30th to insure no interruption to your payments.

135. (A) shorten
     (B) extend
     (C) downsize
     (D) expand

136. (A) rarely
     (B) already
     (C) barely
     (D) substantially

137. (A) Beginning on May 1, your paychecks will have the new name on them.
     (B) Once again, we will try to handle the merger.
     (C) All employment contracts are due to expire in April.
     (D) Every staff will receive the notice of dismissal by April 30.

138. (A) which
     (B) who
     (C) whom
     (D) whose

Questions 139-142 refer to the following letter.

Anri Catering

700E Anapamu Street

Santa Barbara, CA 93103

RE : Soren-Gularte Wedding, March 19, 2016

Client(s): Marie Soren and Anthony Gularte

Dear Soren and Gularte :

I would like to confirm the details for the ------------ wedding.
139.

As we discussed, in order to ------------ a little money on the appetizers, we will not provide
140.

sashimi for all of the 100 guests, but rather just prepare 50 portions. Okita Seafood is

making up those trays and I will pick them up on my way to the guesthouse. We will be

getting to the site by 4:00 P.M. to set up. ------------ .
141.

When you come back from the main hall, we can start the appetizers. We will have

everything on the main table except for the sashimi, which will be in its own special corner

------------ the soy sauce, wasabi and small dishes. If you have any questions about last
142.

minute arrangements, please give me a call.

Thank you,

Kelly Harlost

Head Caterer, Anri Catering

139. (A) former
(B) existing
(C) upcoming
(D) seasonal

140. (A) deposit
(B) save
(C) withdraw
(D) spend

141. (A) We will be cleaning the table at 6:00
P.M.
(B) While you are in the main hall, we will
arrive at the reception hall.
(C) We will pick your guests up on our
way to the hotel.
(D) We'll get everything ready while the
ceremony is going on.

142. (A) out of
(B) ahead of
(C) along with
(D) apart from

GO ON TO THE NEXT PAGE

Questions 143-146 refer to the following advertisement.

Vail Ski Resort is a place where anyone, no matter what their ability, can progress to a higher level in the sport of skiing. Register for one of our programs this winter and learn from the professionals in the best snowboard and ski camp ------- on Earth!
143.

Located on Mt. Rocky, we are the biggest winter park in America. Vail ski Resort has a staffs of 100 to give you the ultimate ski camp experience! Many of our coaches are the same well-known skiers that have been ------- in magazines and televised competitions.
144.

------- . Everyone at Vail Ski Resort, from the professionals to the service staff, is focused
145.
on making your ski camp experience superb; every single person involved ------- the camp
146.
is dedicated to making sure you have the best time of your life.

---

143. (A) refinery
(B) capacity
(C) facility
(D) complexity

144. (A) feature
(B) featured
(C) featuring
(D) features

145. (A) You can progress to a higher level in the sport of skiing.
(B) You should learn the snowboard and ski to survive.
(C) All employees will be concentrated on making your ski performance to enhance.
(D) Nowhere else in the world can you find a more qualified group of expert instructors.

146. (A) in
(B) to
(C) on
(D) for

PART 7

Directions: In this part you will read a selection of texts, such as magazine and newspaper articles, e-mails, and instant messages. Each text or set of texts is followed by several questions. Select the best answer for each question and mark the letter (A), (B), (C), or (D) on your answer sheet.

Questions 147-148 refer to the following announcement.

PROVISIONS & CONDITIONS OF MWC ENTRANCE TICKET

* Marine World California Pvt. Ltd.(MWC) has no responsibility whatever to anyone in respect to unintentional events or wounds suffered. MWC is not liable for injury and loss to belongings or commodities however sustained or originated while on the place except when the staff of MWC caused the problem, nor will compensations be offered for inconveniences or disobedience of contract due to the collapse of facilities and deficiencies outside the charge of Marine World California Pvt. Ltd.

* Bringing foods or drinks and smoking are banned within the Aquarium.
* Taking pictures is banned in the spots with "Do Not Take Pictures" signs.
* This ticket is applicable for just one entry.

---

147. What is MWC responsible for?
(A) Loss caused by the staff of MWC
(B) Injuries by accident on the place
(C) Damage by accident on the place
(D) Compensation for disobedience of contract

148. What is allowed customers to do in the Aquarium?
(A) Use a previous admission ticket
(B) Drink beverages
(C) Eat snacks
(D) Take pictures in some areas

Questions 149-150 refer to the following text message chain.

Kenji Muro / 1:24 A.M.

Louisa, the meeting with the CEO is about to start. Are you ready for the presentation on marketing of our new product? I can't see you. Where are you now?

Louisa Santos / 11:25 A.M.

Sorry, my train stopped because it's out of order. I'm only one station away from the office, but I can't move a step.

Kenji Muro / 11:27 A.M.

Why don't you take a taxi? Both the CEO and the board of directors are coming, so we've got to start on time. Our project is already on thin ice.

Louisa Santos / 11:28 A.M.

Yes, I know, but there's nothing I can do. I'm stuck between stations now.

Kenji Muro / 11:29 A.M.

If you are so, I think we have no choice but to delay the meeting. I'll text everyone and try to change the meeting to 2:00 P.M.

Louisa Santos / 11:30 A.M.

Thank you. But call the CEO instead of sending text to him. He's probably already in the building.

---

149. At 11:27 A.M., what does Kenji Muro mean when he says, "Our project is already on thin ice"?

(A) The CEO is excited about the project.
(B) The project is almost finished.
(C) The project will be difficult to succeed.
(D) The project might be cancelled.

150. What will happen at 2:00 P.M.?

(A) Louisa will arrive at the office.
(B) The rescheduled meeting will start.
(C) The CEO will arrive at the office.
(D) The train will start moving again.

Revealing Everything for the Bluff House

7 bedrooms

4 baths

5 car garage

Affords wide views of the North Calf Bay and Atlantic Ocean

This house was built in the 1790's by Chris Ratledge, and his descendants have owned it ever since. It is placed close to the edge of a rock face on half acre with a beautiful scene of South Rio Bay. The merchants area retire officers, Ethan Damitz and his sister, Cortney Damitz, an artist and an owner of a gallery. Local dealers say the residence needs considerable modernizing, including a temperature system and new piping. A brilliant position on the side – line of a cliff. Current construction policies would disallow erecting it on the lot today. Selling price : $2.25 million. Opening offer : $1.9million.

151. What condition is the house in?

(A) It requires much work.
(B) It needs no more repairs.
(C) It has been recently updated.
(D) It needs paint.

152. What would happen if someone tried to build the same house today?

(A) It would be too costly.
(B) It would be deemed unsafe.
(C) It could not be as large.
(D) It would not be allowed.

Date: August 19, 2016
From: Matthew Pentacoff
To: James Marquis, Administrator of Investigating Programs
Subject: Praising — Malcolm Thomas — Convey Requiring Project

The point of this memo is to authoritatively praise Malcolm Thomas for his excellent assistances all over his obligations to the Convey Requiring Project (CRP).

As you realized, Malcolm has been putting his efforts on special duties with the CRP group for the past five months. He will shortly be going back to your division, and I would like to be sure that he gets deserved acknowledgment for his considerable assistance to CRP.

As a young economist, Malcolm's position in the project was crucial to its well-timed and prosperous completion. It was Malcolm who spent long hours, several nighttimes and weekends, with his tiny group of investigators. The quality of Malcolm's work in documents was also outstanding.

As a group member, Malcolm was terrific. His optimistic passion for the assignment was infectious, and he appeared to motivate the whole group. He was very popular by all group constituents, and in the result he happened to be the "informal" deputy assignment manager.

In conclusion, I would like to say that I haven't seen anyone more proficient and industrious as Malcolm Thomas although I have worked with many young economists for several years. I suppose that the group as a whole should be acquainted with his incomparable involvement to an important project.

Please contact me if you have questions or commentary.

Matthew Pentacoff
Director of Econometric Research

cc: Malcolm Thomas
    Personnel file — M. Thomas

153. What does Matthew Pentacoff want?

(A) Malcolm's replacement
(B) Recognition for Malcolm's contribution
(C) Malcolm's promotion
(D) More time to work with Henry

154. How did Malcolm affect the members of CRP?

(A) He changed their personalities.
(B) He inspired them for the project.
(C) He helped them in economically bad times.
(D) He made them more proud of themselves.

155. What is going to happen in the near future?

(A) James Marquis will transfer to another office.
(B) Matthew Pentacoff will retire from her position.
(C) Malcolm Thomas will return to Mr. Marquis's part of the organization.
(D) Many economists will be out of jobs.

GO ON TO THE NEXT PAGE

FAQs

Q1. Does IGEM supply phone service?

Yes. When you require technical supply, you need to follow the solution of the problem and resolution procedures suggested by IGEM. An engineer will try to make the first diagnostication of your phone's trouble and, on the phone, inform you how to solve it.

Q2. During the contract period, how will my PC be serviced?

IGEM, or the agency, will notify you of the accessible kinds of service for PCs, depending on its nation of setting up. IGEM, at its solitary classification, may fix the computer or make it exchanged.

Q3. What should I do first prior to calling the service center?

Most problems can be resolved without an IGEM engineer. Start by looking through online description or the instruction manual which is enclosed with your computer. Most computer instruction manuals contain a list of common problems with appropriate resolutions, details of messages showing error, and information about problem-solving checks that you can make. If you get an error code, pass on to the code indicator listed in your instruction manual and follow the orders offered. If you believe there is a trouble with your software, seek advice from the documents of the OA system or application agenda.

Q4. What information would I need to give when I require a technical service?

If you didn't list your computer with IGEM, you may be obliged to present confirmation of your purchase to get technical service. To help you fast and proficiently, please get the following information prepared when you make a call:

Computer Model Number and its Serial Number
Specify the problem
Exact messages of any error
Software and hardware configuration information
Your computer must be accessible so you can enter in directions given by the engineer.

156. What is a customer required to do before making a call for technical support?

(A) Have credit card ready for payment
(B) Follow the determination and resolution procedures that IGEM specifies
(C) Make an appointment to have the computer fixed
(D) Read all of the printed documentation that comes with the computer

157. What information will the caller be asked to provide when seeking telephone technical support?

(A) Original buyer of the computer
(B) Description of the problem
(C) Place where computer was purchased
(D) Price of the item

158. How can a customer solve a problem without IGEM assistance?

(A) By reviewing online help
(B) By asking for assistance from someone else who has the same equipment
(C) By calling the store where the computer was purchased
(D) By taking the computer apart to see what's wrong

GO ON TO THE NEXT PAGE

Questions 159-161 refer to the following notice.

We are contented to inform you of a special chance to acquire excellent pianos at considerable savings. Pianos provided to the Music Department of Leonard College by Thomann Corporation, plus other famous brands, will be offered at an exceptional preview sale.

Pianos vary from grand pianos for concert to small grand, spinets, uprights, quality digital keyboards, and consoles. All of them have been carefully preserved.

The sale will be opened from 10 a.m. to 4 p.m. on Saturday, May 29, in Leonard College at the Music Department. Paying and delivery planning will be performed on the place.

2 ways to observe the instruments:
1. Starting Monday, May 24 at 11 a.m., call to arrange a personal meeting. This preview show provides you priority and guarantees the best choice and cost. These preview arrangements are highly suggested.
2. Go to the sale for the common public on Saturday, May 29, from 10 a.m. to 4 p.m. in the Leonard College at Music Department.

We, at the Music Department, wish you will take benefit of this chance to own an excellent piano at a practical charge.

159. What is significant about the pianos?
(A) They are brand new.
(B) They are damaged.
(C) They are used.
(D) They are imported.

160. What may people do on May 24?
(A) Bid on a piano
(B) Register for piano lessons
(C) Look at the merchandise
(D) Attend a piano recital

161. Who is holding the event?
(A) An educational institution
(B) A piano maker
(C) A piano repair shop
(D) A famous pianist

Test 01
Test 02
Test 03
Test 04
Test 05

December 13, 2015

The company states that Zachary Morlen will quit working as Finance Manager of this company on December 21, 2015 to get another job. The directors show gratitude to him for his great involvement in the company during the past five years and hope him well in his next job.

We are contented to publicize that Robin Welch will fill the position as a new Finance Manager on December 22, 2015. Robin Welch is a competent accountant and he graduated the Business Department in Brown University. For 16 years, he used to work in resource banking and is now with the VNT Fund Group in Manhattan.

Isabel Queller
Personnel Affairs Manager

162. What would be the best title for this notice?
(A) Job offer
(B) Strategy proposal
(C) Personnel changes
(D) The company merger

163. What is mentioned about Robin Welch?
(A) He is admired for his contribution to the company.
(B) He is working for VNT Fund Group at the moment.
(C) He will start working for this company from December 21, 2015.
(D) He is one of the most qualified accountants at VNT Fund Group.

GO ON TO THE NEXT PAGE

Dream Job: Web designer for TwinkleStar.Com

The duty of Web designer at TwinkleStar.Com is a demanding one. The Web designer is in charge of all portions of TwinkleStar.Com. The task is to build up the web-site as a world's superlative resources of homepage producers all over the place. The applicants for this job must be familiar with working for long while, mostly alone. ---[1]---.

In all aspect, the current applicant has to do a superior work than our prior Web designer. Luckily, the Directorate considers those empty positions easy to fill in. Applicants must recognize that the position oblige you to have a passionate and positive attitude although you are in unavoidable challenges. ---[2]---.

If you believe you are worthy of being our Web designer, e-mail a short summarize of your abilities and knowledge to Jobseeking@TwinkleStar. Com. All submitted applications become the assets of the Directorate and are not to be returned. ---[3]---.

Note: Please do not relinquish your current job to wait for a call scheduling an interview. We apologize that the Directorate is incapable to reply every applicants. When the suitable person volunteers for this job, the Directorate will contact him or her. Please do not call us. We will call you. You are allowed to return to this web-site to check the updates on employments of a Web designer. ---[4]---.

164. Whom is this advertisement for?

(A) Occupation seekers
(B) Interior designers
(C) Architectural engineers
(D) Photo editors

165. How can applicants apply for the job?

(A) Call the Director of Human
Resources division
(B) E-mail a short outline of experience
to the company
(C) Submit resume and required
documents in person
(D) Take advantage of an online
application tool

166. Which is suggested for applicants?

(A) Resign from your current job
(B) Wait for a call from Design Shop
(C) Call the company
(D) Prepare for a test of web design skills

167. In which of the positions marked [1], [2],
[3], and [4] does the following sentence
best belong?

"Your private information will be treated
as firmly undisclosed."

(A) [1]
(B) [2]
(C) [3]
(D) [4]

GO ON TO THE NEXT PAGE

Questions 168-171 refer to the following online chat discussion.

Online Chat	_ □ ×

Oliver Koh
09:38 a.m.

Thank you for joining us under such short notice. I think it's nightmare tonight for some of you.

Denise Matova
09:39 a.m.

As it already happened, we have to discuss the items we ordered.

Oliver Koh
09:40 a.m.

Ok, let's get it sorted.

Aaron Koskinen
09:41 a.m.

I am really sorry about the mix-up with the shipments. The Galuxy 8 series really look similar to the Anycall 5 series. We should have been more careful to prevent the error earlier.

Liz Flores
09:42 a.m.

I get that, but we have the trade fair event on the 15th, and 25 of next season's small leather goods are supposed to be on display there.

Denise Matova
09:43 a.m.

We really need to get a definite answer on the second delivery, Aaron?

Aaron Koskinen
09:46 a.m.

I understand. We'll send the designs in the morning and they should be at Flores' office by Friday.

Liz Flores
09:48 a.m.

Friday? If so, I will not have much time to examine and prepare them for showcase.

Denise Matova
09:49 a.m.

Aaron, why don't you use express cargo this time?

Aaron Koskinen
09:52 a.m.

OK, I've just confirmed that we can do that this time.

Oliver Koh
09:53 a.m.

Good. Let us know the tracking details as soon as you can.

Send

168. At 09:40 a.m., what does Oliver koh mean when he writes, "let's get it sorted"?

(A) He needs some advice about a problem.
(B) He needs to understand an issue.
(C) He wants help with organizing inventory.
(D) He wants to resolve an error.

169. In what type of industry do the people in the discussion most likely work?

(A) Textiles
(B) Fashion accessories
(C) Financial trading
(D) Event planning

170. According to the discussion, what was the problem?

(A) Oliver Koh started the meeting at an inconvenient time.
(B) Denise Matova ordered the wrong number of items.
(C) Aaron Koskinen sent a different order that requested.
(D) Liz Flores didn't manage her time properly.

171. What information has Oliver Koh requested from Aaron Matova?

(A) The latest updates on the status of the package
(B) The current amount of inventory available
(C) The estimated completion date of the project
(D) The recent changes in the product schedule

GO ON TO THE NEXT PAGE

Dear Kenneth Duncan,

A short time ago, we sent you a letter regarding a special advantage. Only for being a respected client in H. Trust Bank, you can get up to $100,000 for accidental death insurance at no charge to you. For our favored clients, we are lengthening the time limit to make an application for this insurance. ---[1]---.

We want to make sure to you that significant amounts of elective, extra protection - up to $300,000 - is obtainable from Clement Guard Life Insurance, at a very practical price. For instance, a person can receive $10,000 of extra insurance for paying only $1.00 monthly; and insurance for a whole family – in whatever size – is offered at monthly payments of $1.60. ---[2]---.

The plan is assured for all H. Trust Bank individual checking account clients of age 19 and above — no health check or questions are necessary. To apply, just write out the enclosed Application Form and send it back in the envelope given. If you prefer to take benefit of additional insurance, your payments will be automatically taken away from your checking account of H. Trust Bank. ---[3]---.

If you have any inquiries about this insurance, please make a call to Customers' Service Center at 1-700-332-5452 (toll-free), between 8:00 in the morning and 6:00 in the afternoon on weekdays. ---[4]---.

Sincerely,
Adam Torres
Insurance Professional

P.S. Kindly ignore this notice if you have already answered to this offer.

172. What is the main purpose of this letter?

(A) To remind customers about an insurance service
(B) To introduce a new banking system
(C) To attract new bank customers
(D) To reply to customer's questions about insurance

173. How can a customer apply for insurance?

(A) Visit the nearest bank branch and register
(B) Call a representative toll-free at 1-700-332-5452
(C) Register as a member on the website of the bank
(D) Complete the enclosed form and mail it in the offered envelop provided

174. How can people pay the insurance payment?

(A) It will be automatically deducted from their checking account.
(B) They should visit the bank and pay in person.
(C) They should pay the premium on-line through the Internet banking system.
(D) They should take advantage of Giro System.

175. In which of the positions marked [1], [2], [3], and [4] does the following sentence best belong?

"No fee is requisite with your Application Form."

(A) [1]
(B) [2]
(C) [3]
(D) [4]

GO ON TO THE NEXT PAGE

HELP WANTED

Our Norbert marketing team is seeking a poised and polished applicant. You possess: a bachelor's degree in English or communications; a can-do attitude; significant agency experience (5 years or more) and a vision for our clients in Japan, the United Kingdom and right here domestically. Direct inquires to Tina Samuel, The Matthew Agency.

Applicants without a complete resume and cover letter detailing expected compensation will not be considered.

July 9, 2016

I am writing about your recent ad in the Ontario Tribune. I am a marketing expert with over seven years of agency experience and extensive exposure to high level clientele and demanding deadlines. I have traveled extensively in East Asia as well as here in the United States, so I have a feel for the types of ads people in these areas would respond well to. I also have a Master's in communication form Lakehead University in Thunder Bay, and I am able to relocate at the beginning of August. My current position pays $ 70,000 a year, but given Matthew's prestige and the lower cost of living and working in Sudbury, I am willing to consider a pay scale starting in the mid 60s. Please find enclosed my resume. I look forward to hearing from you.

Clyde Meadows

176. What is NOT mentioned about
the requirements for the job in the
advertisement?
(A) A bachelor's degree
(B) Fluency in three foreign languages
(C) Experience in agency work
(D) An enthusiastic outlook

177. What should an interested applicant
submit to the company?
(A) A duplicate of his/her degree
(B) Salary requirements
(C) Letters of reference
(D) Examples of their work

178. What made Clyde apply for this position?
(A) The high status of the company
(B) The competitive salary
(C) The ease of promotion
(D) The employee benefits package

179. Where is Matthew probably located?
(A) In the United Kingdom
(B) In Thunder Bay
(C) In Sudbury
(D) In Japan

180. What is suggested about Clyde
Meadows?
(A) She is willing to accept less money.
(B) She is not qualified for the job.
(C) She has recently moved to Sudbury
(D) She has experience working in
England.

GO ON TO THE NEXT PAGE ➡

Questions 181-185 refer to the following letter and instructions.

Arikess' Games
2706 Trafalgar St, Vancouver
BC V6K 2J6

Ms. Daniela Pearce
955 Harbourside Dr, North Vancouver
BC V7P 3S4

Dear Ms. Daniela Pearce:

Thank you for purchasing the Sea Life Go Fish Game and your letter of 15 May.
To maintain a reasonable price for this card game, we have stopped including the
instructions in the box. It is played like the card game "go fish", so many people
already know how to play it. Although you did not see our notice, it states on the box
that Instructions are available at: www.norbertandsonsgames.com/rules/gofish.htm

I have enclosed a copy of the rules to that page in this letter and a coupon for a $5
discount on your next Arikess' game. I apologize for the inconvenience. I trust that you
and your family will now be able to play and enjoy the game. If you have any further
questions, please call us toll-free at 1-800-555-7200.

Very best wishes,
Marlon Ayon
Customer Service

Sea Life Go Fish Game Instructions

A set has 52 cards, and the 52 cards are composed of 4 sub-sets, and a sub-set is 13 cards.
Each of 13 cards represents a different sea animals (monk seals, bottle-nose dolphins,
humpback whales, parrotfish, moray eels, sea urchins, angelfish, tiger sharks, penguins,
sea gulls, starfish etc). Therefore, there are four cards representing each animal.

Rules: Play with 2~5 players. Shuffle cards. One player deals each player 5 cards. The
others are put in a round pile in the middle of the table. This pile represents the ocean.
Play goes clockwise starting with the person sitting to the left of the dealer. Let's call her
"Mary." Mary asks a specific player, John-"John, do you have any penguins?" If John has
penguins, he must give all of them to the player who asks for them. If he doesn't, he says:
"Go fish." If Mary gets penguins from John, she may take an additional turn. If not, play
continues to Mary's left and Mary picks a card up on the top of a round pile. Once a player
collects all four cards with the same sea animal, that player can put them on the table in
a stack called a "book." The first player who puts all of his or her cards on the table in this
way becomes the winner.

181. Why did Mr. Ayon wrote this letter?

(A) To learn how to play the game
(B) To reply to a letter from Ms. Pearce
(C) To ask how Ms. Pearce is enjoying the game
(D) To apply for a job at Arikess' Games

182. Where can someone who purchases the game find the rules?

(A) Inside the box
(B) On the back of the box
(C) At the company's web-site
(D) In a separate game book available for purchase

183. Which of the following is NOT offered to the customer in the letter?

(A) A discount on a future item
(B) An apology
(C) A copy of the rules
(D) New cards for the game

184. In the instructions, the word "turn" in paragraph 2, line 6, is closest in meaning to.

(A) change
(B) trend
(C) spin
(D) opportunity

185. How does someone win the game?

(A) By getting one each of all 13 sea animals
(B) By being the first one to get all 4 of the same card
(C) By placing all of his or her cards on the table
(D) By taking away at least one card from every player

GO ON TO THE NEXT PAGE

Product Recall

Tanner Freewalker v2 Stroller

Manufacturer : Tanner   Category : Strollers   Recall post date : May 16

The Tanner Freewalker v2 Stroller sold in all major departments and baby stores across the country has been found to pose a risk to users when attempting to fold and unfold the product due to the sharp edges of the hinges.

After long research, Tanner has created a hinge cover to ensure no further risk is posed. To receive these covers, please contact Tanner Customer Services directly using the contact information at the bottom of this notice or take your stroller back to the place of purchase and consult with the staff.

This recall applies to all Tanner Freewalker v2 Strollers with the following product numbers:

11807   11808   11809   11810   11811   11814

The product number can be found by looking at the white sticker placed on the left-hand side bar of the lower luggage part. This issue will not affect our forthcoming summer line-up of v3 and v4 models.

Phone : 053-179-5011
E-mail : tannercs@tanner.com

Daily Business Log
Babyneeds Co., Selby City
May 16 18:07

Dear Mr. Oakley,

Ms. Hall came to the store this morning and most concerned about Tanner's recall announcement today on news. She owns a Freewalker Stroller which she bought at a recent charity event of her local community, but Ms. Hall had been told it had originally been purchased here.

We were unable to make out the product number due to damage and stain to the white sticker. Her stroller is black and purple with silver wheels but when I looked up for this description, I found that this color choice was applied to both the v1 and v2 model, so we have not yet been able to confirm which model Ms. Hall has and whether she requires the hinge cover. I informed Ms. Hall that you would be back in the store tomorrow and she left you her phone number and e-mail address for further details.

Isabella Hall 077-074-9851
izzyh@chillpost.com

Thanks,
Mike

To	izzyh@chillpost.com
From	Oakley, Seb <oakseb@babyneeds.co>
Date	May 17 09:47 A.M.
Subject	Tanner Freewalker

Dear Ms. Hall,

Thank you for visiting Babyneeds yesterday. I'm sorry I was not available to discuss the matter of your stroller with you in person but my staff, Mike Blake, who tells me you are a regular customer at our store, has passed on the details of your inquiry. I understand you need to confirm which model of the Freewalker you have to decide whether you receive the hinge cover or not.

I have been in contact with Mr. Tanner directly this morning and have explained your case to him. Fortunately, he said that a representative for the company, Daniel O'Connor, is going to be on a regularly scheduled visit to our Selby City branch this Wednesday between 9:00 A.M and 11:45 A.M. And he advised me to ask you to visit the store during the last thirty minutes. Mr. O'Connor will inspect your stroller and officially identify whether yours is a v1 model or v2 model.

I realize this is a last-minute request, but if you could find the time to stop by Babyneeds, I think we can resolve this issue smoothly.

Please let me know your availability.

Sincerely,
Sebastian Oakley
Store Manager
Babyneeds Co. - Selby City

186. What did the Tanner company announce?

(A) A new design for baby strollers
(B) The discontinuation of a service
(C) An issue with an existing product
(D) The introduction of insurance coverage

187. What is indicated about Ms. Hall?

(A) She purchased her stroller at Babyneeds.
(B) She recently sold some used items.
(C) She frequently shops at the Selby City branch.
(D) She acquired her stroller after May 16.

188. What is true about Babyneeds?

(A) It sells Tanner products.
(B) It keeps sales records at the head office.
(C) It is managed by Daniel O'Connor.
(D) It donates profits to local charities.

189. What will Ms. Hall probably do next?

(A) Bring her documentation to the Tanner head office
(B) Show proof of purchase for her stroller
(C) Visit the Babyneeds store at around 11:15
(D) Buy a Freewalker in an another color

190. In the e-mail, the word "smoothly" in paragraph 2, line 8, is closest in meaning to

(A) thoroughly
(B) clearly
(C) reliably
(D) easily

GO ON TO THE NEXT PAGE

Questions 191-195 refer to the following newspaper advertisement, post and comment.

With Runaround's new cab app, you can get a taxi with the touch on a button of your smart-phone. Turn on your GPS and touch "QUICK HAIL," and one of our drivers will locate you immediately. You can also enter your current location and destination and select "ESTIMATED FARE" to get an idea of how much you will be charge before starting. Changed your mind? Simply select "SPEED CANCEL." Want a cab tomorrow or later date? Choose the "BOOK TAXI" option. Feel like wandering or going to somewhere? Put in the kind of place you want to go (e.g. a hotel, restaurant, attraction) in the "PLACE OF INTEREST" field, and our up-to-date computer system will show you the most suitable route. Want to know when your taxi will arrive? Select "MAIL ON APPROACH" and you can receive notification when the taxi is about to reach you. And the last, you can choose from a comfortable sedan to SUV with big trunk. Taking a taxi has never been so simple and useful!

* GPS must be enabled.
** A telephone number is required.
*** Gratuity included. Extra charge of 3% during late night hours (11 P.M. to 5 A.M.).

---

blog/post

I test them for you

Monday, March 14th

So today, I'm going to tell you about Runaround's new taxi app which I originally read about in an ad. I liked the "PLACE OF INTEREST" option, because it gives me an automatic recommendation about a travel destination. The fare estimate is very helpful when you are on a tight budget like me, but I'd also like to see some kind of loyalty system for regular passengers.

The "QUICK HAIL" is a great idea for when you have a load of shopping and can't put in long addresses, but for some reason the app kept turning on my GPS during the day which is not good for battery life. I was glad to have a choice of vehicle (no choice of driver gender, however) when my bike got a puncture and I could pack it in the back of one of Runaround's roomy cars.

I also hope they consider more wheelchair-friendly designs in the future. All in all, this is a very welcome addition to my set of applications. Any comments? Let me know your thoughts on the Runaround App below. (David Shaw)
March 14 at 05:07 P.M.

Hi, Dave.

It is first time for me to comment, but I have often read your blog. By the way, I was happy to learn that you saw the ad we put in last month's Daily News. And I thought I would respond to some of your points.

Runaround does have mainly male drivers, but we are going to increase female drivers to guarantee at least one per shift.

Sorry about the GPS battery's discharge, but it should be OK after yesterday's app update. If it is any help, we have been introducing smart-phone chargers into our cars which may be useful on longer journeys.

Finally, we are pleased to announce our new "Runaround" prepaid card which also offers a 5% discount on any service over 8km excluding our late night hours.

Keith Ford

Runaround, CEO

191. What is the purpose of the advertisement?
(A) To launch a new taxi company
(B) To notify customers of an increase in charges
(C) To promote local sightseeing
(D) To explain how to use a new service

192. What will a customer do to use a taxi on the following day?
(A) Pay an extra 3%
(B) Press the "BOOK TAXI" button
(C) Phone the Runaround office
(D) Enable GPS on his/her phone

193. What is indicated about David Shaw?
(A) He is the head of a company.
(B) He is being paid for his review.
(C) He rides a bicycle to work.
(D) He first found out about the app in February.

194. What did David Shaw like about the app?
(A) Reasonable price
(B) One-touch cab call
(C) Battery-charge service
(D) "PLACE OF INTEREST" option

195. What is true about Runaround?
(A) It offers three choices of vehicles.
(B) It caters to those who cannot walk.
(C) It has no women drivers yet.
(D) It has just updated its user software.

GO ON TO THE NEXT PAGE

Questions 196-200 refer to the following e-mail, invoice and response.

To	Bill Days <daysb@asaday.co.sf>
From	John Hooper <hoopcyc@wheels.com>
Date	August 9 4:43 p.m.
Subject	Delivery split

Hi Bill,

I know this letter may be a bit sudden thing to you, but I'd like to make a change in our order. It is because this year we've been asked to display our products at a sporting event on Saturday near our new location, which also happens to be close to your warehouse. So I beg you. Could you divide our order into two parts? For the first part, can you send three of the Marzini Racers (black, silver and white, one of each) to 143 Seaview Lane instead of original address? If possible, I'd like to receive them in the morning of the 15th to give me time to get them all in the display program and set them up on the stall. The second part of the delivery remains unchanged, so if you could send the rest to our head office on Gainsley as originally requested, it'd be much appreciated. Can you send me one invoice with all the updated when you are ready, please?

Many thanks,
John
Hooper's Cycles

Fisherman's Way
Carmel, California 93921
052-154-6474
Invoice number 58192
August 10 (revised)
Prepared for: Hooper's Cycles
John Hooper 915791-44XF

ASADAY DISTRIBUTORS

Description of order	Qty	Unit Price	Amount
Delivery (Split order): Marzini Racer (Blk x1/ Sil x1/ Wh x1) To: Hooper's Cycles 143 Seaview Lane, Carmel, California 93921	3	$250	$750
Delivery (Split order): Marzini Racer (Blk x1/ Sil x1/ Wh x1) To: Hooper's Cycles 1846 Gainsley Blvd, Oakland, California 93940	3	$250	$750
Delivery: Funtrike (Pink x2/ Blue x3) To: Hooper's Cycles 1846 Gainsley Blvd, Oakland, California 93940	5	$75	$375
Total Amount			$1,875

To	John Hooper <hoopcyc@wheels.com>
From	Bill Days <daysb@asaday.co.sf>
Date	August 11 8:43 a.m.
Subject	Order adjustment

Hi John,

Glad to hear you have been asked to participate in the sports event again. The additional exposure could be very helpful for you this year.

I assume you have already received the revised invoice by now. But actually, I've just heard from the Funtrike manufacturer that due to the upgrading of its factory to prepare for the assembly of a new model, they are now in limited production. So the shipment of a third blue bike will be delayed for a couple of weeks. We're sorry about that. I could give you another 10% off if you can accept this delayed shipment. Otherwise, I should search for another solution.

Thanks as ever for your business and see you at your company's barbecue party this fall!

Bill

196. Why did John Hooper contact Bill Days?

(A) To alter shipment details
(B) To update payment information
(C) To get a refund for a late delivery
(D) To investigate a new location

197. What is true about Hooper's Cycles?

(A) They deal exclusively in sports bikes.
(B) They have not done business with Asaday.
(C) Their main store is in Oakland.
(D) They are in a competitive market.

198. Which color of Funtrike will John Hooper receive on schedule?

(A) Pink
(B) Black
(C) Blue
(D) Silver

199. What does Bill Days offer to his client?

(A) An invitation to a food event
(B) A tour of a factory
(C) An adjusted price on an order
(D) A chance to pre-order a new product

200. What will Bill Days do this fall?

(A) Accept the additional solution
(B) Search for a new business model
(C) Upgrade the assembly line
(D) Take part in the party of Hooper's Cycles

Stop! This is the end of the test. If you finish before time is called, you may go back to Parts 5, 6, and 7 and check your work.

新토익 시험 진행 안내

❶ 시험 시간 : 120분(2시간)

오전 시험	오후 시험	시간	비고
9:20	2:20		입실
9:30 ~ 9:45	2:30 ~ 2:45	15분	답안지 작성에 관한 Orientation
9:45 ~ 9:50	2:45 ~ 2:50	5분	수험자 휴식시간
9:50 ~ 10:05	2:50 ~ 3:05	15분	신분증 확인 (감독 교사)
10:05 ~ 10:10	3:05 ~ 3:10	5분	문제지 배부 및 파본 확인
10:10 ~ 10:55	3:10 ~ 3:55	45분	듣기 평가(L/C)
10:55 ~ 12:10	3:55 ~ 5:10	75분	독해 평가(R/C) * 2차 신분확인

　　※ L/C 진행 후 휴식 시간 없이 바로 R/C 진행

❷ 준비물

　　» 신분증 : 규정 신분증만 가능 (주민등록증, 운전면허증, 기간 만료 전의 여권, 공무원증 등)
　　» 필기구 : 연필, 지우개 (볼펜이나 사인펜은 사용 금지)

❸ 시험 응시 준수 사항

　　» 시험 시작 10분 전 입실 (오전 9:50, 오후 2:50 이후에는 입실 불가)
　　» 종료 30분 전과 10분 전에 시험 종료 공지함
　　» 휴대전화의 전원은 미리 꺼둘 것

❹ OMR 답안지 표기 요령

　　» 반드시 지정된 필기구로 표기
　　※ 성명, 주민등록번호 등을 틀리게 표기하였을 경우 채점 및 성적 확인이 불가능하므로 주의하시기 바랍니다.

OMR 답안지 표기 Sample				
O	Ⓐ	Ⓑ	●	Ⓓ
X	Ⓐ	Ⓥ	Ⓒ	Ⓓ
X	Ⓐ	Ⓑ	Ⓒ	Ⓧ
X	Ⓐ	Ⓑ	Ⓒ	Ⓓ
X	Ⓐ	Ⓑ	Ⓒ	Ⓓ

토익 EDGE 실전
1000제
LR SET 2

지금부터 Actual Test를 진행합니다.
실제 시험과 동일한 방식으로 진행됨을 말씀드리며,
방송 음성은 QR코드로 청취하실 수 있습니다.

준비 되셨으면 바로 시작하세요.!

LISTENING TEST

In the Listening test, you will be asked to demonstrate how well you understand spoken English. The entire Listening test will last approximately 45 minutes. There are four parts, and directions are given for each part. You must mark your answers on the separate answer sheet. Do not write your answers in your test book.

PART 1

Directions: For each question in this part, you will hear four statements about a picture in your test book. When you hear the statements, you must select the one statement that best describes what you see in the picture. Then find the number of the question on your answer sheet and mark your answer. The statements will not be printed in your test book and will be spoken only one time.

Statment (A), "Some people are paddling through the water," is the best description of the picture, so you should select answer (A) and mark it on your answer sheet.

1.

2.

GO ON TO THE NEXT PAGE ➤

3.

4.

5.

6.

GO ON TO THE NEXT PAGE

PART 2

Directions: You will hear a question or statement and three responses spoken in English. They will not be printed in your test book and will be spoken only one time. Select the best response to the question or statement and mark the letter (A), (B), or (C) on your answer sheet.

7. Mark your answer on your answer sheet.

8. Mark your answer on your answer sheet.

9. Mark your answer on your answer sheet.

10. Mark your answer on your answer sheet.

11. Mark your answer on your answer sheet.

12. Mark your answer on your answer sheet.

13. Mark your answer on your answer sheet.

14. Mark your answer on your answer sheet.

15. Mark your answer on your answer sheet.

16. Mark your answer on your answer sheet.

17. Mark your answer on your answer sheet.

18. Mark your answer on your answer sheet.

19. Mark your answer on your answer sheet.

20. Mark your answer on your answer sheet.

21. Mark your answer on your answer sheet.

22. Mark your answer on your answer sheet.

23. Mark your answer on your answer sheet.

24. Mark your answer on your answer sheet.

25. Mark your answer on your answer sheet.

26. Mark your answer on your answer sheet.

27. Mark your answer on your answer sheet.

28. Mark your answer on your answer sheet.

29. Mark your answer on your answer sheet.

30. Mark your answer on your answer sheet.

31. Mark your answer on your answer sheet.

PART 3

Directions: You will hear some conversations between two or more people. You will be asked to answer three questions about what the speakers say in each conversation. Select the best response to each question and mark the letter (A), (B), (C), or (D) on your answer sheet. The conversations will not be printed in your test book and will be spoken only one time.

32. When did Clair meet Lesley?

(A) Last month
(B) This month
(C) Last year
(D) This year

33. Who is Clair supposed to meet?

(A) Lesley
(B) Emerson
(C) Jayson
(D) Denny

34. According to Lesley, where might Jayson most likely be?

(A) At Emerson's place
(B) In the auditorium
(C) In the cafeteria
(D) At Denny's office

35. Who was assigned to a new position in the company?

(A) Mr. Pino
(B) Mr. Elston
(C) Mr. Svenson
(D) Mr. Cadwell

36. What did the man do yesterday?

(A) He worked on a new proposal.
(B) He went to Singapore.
(C) He was away on a trip.
(D) He had lunch with his employees.

37. According to the woman, where did Mr. Elston meet employees?

(A) At Mr. Pino's retirement party
(B) At Mr. Svenson's office
(C) At a lunch meeting
(D) At Mr. Cadwell's office

38. What didn't Ms. Olivia bring to the conference room?

(A) Documents
(B) Food
(C) Drinks
(D) Mobile Phone

39. According to the man, who cleaned the table that Ms. Olivia used?

(A) Ms. Sydney
(B) Mr. Clinton
(C) Ms. Lindsay
(D) Mr. Irving

40. What will the man do next?

(A) Put the phone on the table in the cafeteria
(B) Go into the conference room
(C) Return the phone after the meeting
(D) Continue looking for Ms. Olivia in other places

41. What problem does the man mention?

(A) Too early departure
(B) The preparation for a contract
(C) The renovation of a road
(D) The additional terms

42. What does the woman suggest the man to do?

(A) Go to Ms. Bovorn's office directly
(B) Drive his own car
(C) Take a subway
(D) Use a different road

43. What will the woman do next?

(A) Prepare for a presentation
(B) Revise the contract
(C) Compare the cost of the construction
(D) Confirm the details

GO ON TO THE NEXT PAGE

44. What is the main topic of the conversation?
   (A) The brand of a newspaper
   (B) The relocation of television station
   (C) The promotional strategy of a new product
   (D) The released data to media

45. What will the man do next?
   (A) Go to the bank
   (B) Arrange a conference
   (C) Contact the radio stations
   (D) Revise an advertisement

46. What does the woman mean when she say, "You are always an idea bank"?
   (A) The man has presented many bright ideas.
   (B) The man has prevented a lot of trouble.
   (C) The man has been industrious.
   (D) The man has promoted a lot of products.

47. What is the main topic of the conversation?
   (A) The pets that they lost neat their house
   (B) The horse they bought yesterday
   (C) The many incidents in their workplace
   (D) The promotion of a colleague

48. What does the woman think about Todd?
   (A) He is the one who took Eric's pets.
   (B) He deserved to have his car stolen and his dog lost.
   (C) He deserves the promotion more than Eric.
   (D) He is the one who stole Eric's vehicle.

49. What will the speakers probably do next?
   (A) Watch a movie with Eric
   (B) Celebrate Todd's promotion
   (C) Steal Eric's car after work
   (D) Work overnight with Todd

50. What does the man mean when he says, "I can find out soon enough"?
   (A) He will place an order too late.
   (B) He is able to seek a solution after a little.
   (C) He may speak to someone right now.
   (D) He manages to recognize a problem.

51. What problem does the woman report?
   (A) The number of flowers
   (B) The color of the napkins
   (C) The size of the tables
   (D) The price of design

52. What does the man say about Elvin?
   (A) He is thorough at his job.
   (B) He is too careless.
   (C) He has a good manner.
   (D) He will be the best designer.

53. What is the conversation mainly about?
   (A) Their order with the paper supply firm
   (B) Lowering wastage in the office
   (C) The second quarterly conference held in June
   (D) The company's plan to hire a new accountant

54. What does the man mean when he says, "I don't support the idea"?
   (A) He thinks they didn't need to hire an accountant.
   (B) He thinks it is a good idea.
   (C) He doesn't oppose hiring an accountant.
   (D) He didn't suggest his own idea.

55. What did the man expect the accountant to do?
   (A) To decrease costs on paper usage
   (B) To adopt measures to reduce waste
   (C) To make new ideas
   (D) To forward employees an e-mail

56. What kind of industry will the speakers likely work in?
(A) Cosmetics
(B) Manufacturing
(C) Pharmaceuticals
(D) Tourism

57. What did the man like about the Mondrian's Hotel?
(A) It was close to the city center.
(B) There was a special discount package.
(C) It was good value for money.
(D) The service was excellent.

58. What problem do the speakers report?
(A) The hotels in the area will all be busy at that time.
(B) There are no cheap flights into London.
(C) There might be no hotels near the venue.
(D) It will be hard to get into the seminar.

59. Why does the woman say, "You don't say"?
(A) To announce her written report
(B) To notify the content of the announcement
(C) To inform the receipt of some bad news
(D) To express a pleasant surprise

60. What will happen in November?
(A) A new menu will be added.
(B) A cafeteria will be opened.
(C) A magazine will be issued.
(D) A survey will be carried out.

61. What do the men suggest to do?
(A) To take out an advertisement
(B) To recruit a new chef
(C) To remodel a kitchen
(D) To offer a discount

The Area's Largest stores

Location	Number of Items
Brooklyn Street	15,000
Rossette Street	17,000
Cliffside Street	14,000
Mapplewood Street	11,000

62. Where will this conversation most likely take place?
(A) At a hardware store
(B) At a grocery store
(C) At a bookstore
(D) At an electronics store

63. What problem does the man report about her order?
(A) It is flaw.
(B) It has been postponed.
(C) It has been mixed up with others.
(D) It is out of stock.

64. Look at the graphic. Where will the woman probably go next?
(A) To Brooklyn Street
(B) To Rosette Street
(C) To Cliffside Street
(D) To Mapplewood Street

GO ON TO THE NEXT PAGE

Brand Name	Available Color
Woosley's	Black
Fike's	White
Dash's	Gold
Hartsell's	Silver

4F	Art Gallery
3F	Shoe Stores
2F	Electronics Stores
1F	Clothing Stores
B1F	Food Court
B2F	Parking

65. What kind of job will the speakers likely be?

(A) A manufacturer
(B) A wholesaler
(C) A hotelier
(D) A landlord

66. What does the woman ask the man to do?

(A) To find out a new supplier
(B) To clean a room
(C) To call a repairperson
(D) To order merchandise

67. Look at the graphic. What brand will the man purchase?

(A) Woosley's
(B) Fike's
(C) Dash's
(D) Hartsell's

68. What floor are the speakers on now?

(A) B2F
(B) B1F
(C) 1st floor
(D) 2nd floor

69. Look at the graphic. What will be sold on the floor where the speakers meet the clients?

(A) Home appliance
(B) Garment
(C) Beverage
(D) Footgear

70. What does the man recommend to the woman?

(A) The fish from the Sky Restaurant
(B) The fish from the food court
(C) The steak from the Sky Restaurant
(D) The steak from the food court

PART 4

Directions: You will hear some talks given by a single speaker. You will be asked to answer three questions about what the speakers say in each talk. Select the best response to each question and mark the letter (A), (B), (C), or (D) on your answer sheet. The talks will not be printed in your test book and will be spoken only one time.

71. For whom is this telephone message intended?

(A) A consultant
(B) A book retailer
(C) An owner of bookstore
(D) A buyer

72. How many days does LittleLook Bookstore open in a week?

(A) For four days
(B) For five days
(C) For six days
(D) For seven days

73. What number can be asked to contact an adviser?

(A) 7
(B) 8
(C) 9
(D) 0

74. What can be recommended for the residents living in the east?

(A) A swim suit
(B) A rain coat
(C) A short shirt
(D) A life vest

75. According to the speaker, what kind of weather is expected for the next 3 days?

(A) Stormy and rainy
(B) Sunny but partly cloudy
(C) Cloudy and windy
(D) Warm and sunny

76. What time will the next report be broadcasted?

(A) At 5:00 A.M.
(B) At 6:00 A.M.
(C) At 7:55 A.M.
(D) At 9:55 A.M.

77. Who will appear after this introduction?

(A) A president
(B) A professor
(C) A nurse
(D) A research assistant

78. What is tonight's keynote speaker going to talk about?

(A) A characteristic of the targeted agents effect
(B) The reason of making a speech
(C) A side effect of the targeted agents
(D) The period of his research

79. What will the attendants do after the speech?

(A) Meet with Professor Hunter Douglas
(B) Enjoy free meal on the fifth floor
(C) Attend another speech
(D) Have a group discussion

80. For how many years has Aaron Spencer been working in the psychological field?

(A) 3 years
(B) 30 years
(C) 35 years
(D) 38 years

81. What will Aaron Spencer talk about today?

(A) His job
(B) His patients
(C) His latest book
(D) His country

82. What will happen after this speech?

(A) The speaker will meet Aaron's father.
(B) Aaron Spencer will move to Ohio.
(C) The listeners will disappear.
(D) Aaron Spencer will show up.

GO ON TO THE NEXT PAGE

83. Who will the speaker most likely be?

    (A) An African
    (B) A tour guide
    (C) A Californian
    (D) A flight attendant

84. Where will the listeners start their safari?

    (A) Mombasa
    (B) Lake Turkana
    (C) Ethiopia
    (D) Los Angeles

85. How far would the people travel towards the Ethiopian border by small plane?

    (A) 320 km
    (B) 400 km
    (C) 650 km
    (D) 970 km

86. What kind of business will Berlitz Education work for?

    (A) A private school
    (B) A school management service
    (C) An elementary school
    (D) A training service

87. How many Berlitz schools are in the area?

    (A) 14
    (B) 15
    (C) 40
    (D) 50

88. What does the speaker recommend the parents to do?

    (A) They will receive the finest education.
    (B) Their children will enter Berlitz school.
    (C) They will bring the best out of students.
    (D) They will develop their necessary skills.

89. What is the main purpose of the announcement?

    (A) To honor a speaker's achievement
    (B) To manage the recording company
    (C) To congratulate a singer
    (D) To revive the music industry

90. Why does the speaker say, "that's 10 awards"?

    (A) To express his amazement
    (B) To promote Jason Woodley's new song
    (C) To make a correction
    (D) To present an award

91. What did Jason Woodley ask the speaker to do?

    (A) To sing along the chorus
    (B) To produce his new album
    (C) To help him open a record shop
    (D) To manage his record company

92. According to the speaker, what happened last April?

    (A) Many employees worked harder.
    (B) Two companies were combined.
    (C) The markets were changed.
    (D) Tough competition disappeared.

93. What does the speaker imply when she says, "except for one"?

    (A) She is talking about the low-energy microwave oven.
    (B) The company experienced the worst year.
    (C) She is advertising the latest product.
    (D) Not all targets were accomplished.

94. What will the company do next year?

    (A) Acquire another competitor
    (B) Raise the market share
    (C) Release its new product
    (D) Increase sales by 10%

List

Serving	Dessert
Ten people	Chocolate
Twenty people	Cookies
Thirty people	Cones
Fifty people	Ice cream pie

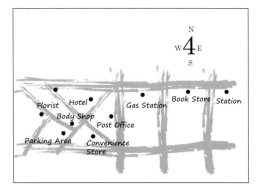

95. What is on sale in the farm product department?

(A) Bananas
(B) Oranges
(C) Apples
(D) Carrots

96. What can listeners get at the customer satisfaction center?

(A) A receipt
(B) A coupon
(C) A recipe
(D) A shopping bag

97. Look at the graphic. How many people will the free dessert be served?

(A) 10 people
(B) 20 people
(C) 30 people
(D) 50 people

98. What does the speaker ask the listeners to do?

(A) Report the results
(B) Follow his instructions
(C) Instruct visitors to use Fresh Pond metro station
(D) Look for the parking space for yourselves

99. Look at the graphic. Which of the following will the visitors pass through?

(A) Florist
(B) Post office
(C) Convenience store
(D) Hotel

100. What will the listeners do to enter the office?

(A) Press the intercom button
(B) Run the convenience store
(C) Contact the station
(D) Search for the office on a map

This is the end of the Listening test. Turn to Part 5 in your text book.

GO ON TO THE NEXT PAGE

READING TEST

In the Reading test, you will read a variety of texts and answer several different types of reading comprehension questions. The entire Reading test will last 75 minutes. There are three parts, and directions are given for each part. You are encouraged to answer as many questions as possible within the time allowed.

You must mark your answers on the separate answer sheet. Do not write your answers in your test book.

PART 5

Directions: A word or phrase is missing in each of the sentences below. Four answer choices are given below each sentence. Select the best answer to complete the sentence. Then mark the letter (A), (B), (C), or (D) on your answer sheet.

---

101. It is important that all drivers should observe the traffic -------.

(A) regular
(B) regularly
(C) regularize
(D) regulations

102. ------- of them knew how to deal with unsatisfied guests in a convincing way.

(A) Not
(B) No
(C) Never
(D) None

103. When the victims of the car accident decided to set up camp, they had walked ------- 30 miles.

(A) toward
(B) near
(C) approximately
(D) exact

104. I ------- value feedback, so please feel free to send an e-mail with any comments, suggestions, or complaints that you may have.

(A) too
(B) so
(C) very
(D) highly

105. Ms. Julia Moreland graduated from college last year, ------- to the increase of the unemployment rate.

(A) contribute
(B) contributed
(C) contributing
(D) to contribute

106. ------- recommend the firms allocate more dollars for consumer security and to treat online privacy like a strategic marketing initiative, rather than a compliance burden.

(A) Analysis
(B) Analyze
(C) Analyzing
(D) Analysts

107. People of taste are often believed to prefer fresh-brewed coffee ------- instant coffee.

(A) to
(B) in
(C) on
(D) at

108. The government of India claims that it will be technologically and economically ------- to produce cars by 2010.

(A) accessible
(B) available
(C) conceivable
(D) feasible

109. The rents charged by nonprofit housing organizations ------- among each different rental housing development built by the nonprofit organization.
(A) increase
(B) differ
(C) vary
(D) alter

110. Lately, more and more bosses are offering ------- to their employees so they become more devoted to working for them.
(A) guidelines
(B) titles
(C) alternatives
(D) incentives

111. ------- environmentalists' fear that the noise will harm animals, the Oceanographic Laboratory let marine biologists keep testing a sonar system for detecting deep-sea whales.
(A) Although
(B) Whereas
(C) In order to
(D) Despite

112. ------- a consumer has decided on a brand of paper for his or her printer, he or she may find it easier just to buy the same brand repeatedly, rather than to shop for a different brand on the next purchase.
(A) Because
(B) Unless
(C) Though
(D) Once

113. The district tax office suspects that Cover Girl Cosmetics is issuing phony checks to ------- its expenses and reduce the tax it owes.
(A) raise
(B) inflate
(C) decrease
(D) collect

114. If I had not double-checked my answers before I turned the exam paper in, I ------- 10 points.
(A) lost
(B) will lose
(C) would lose
(D) would have lost

115. A patent is legal ownership over a design that prevents a rival from ------- that design for a set period of time.
(A) use
(B) used
(C) using
(D) to use

116. Trump has finally come to recognize that Taiwan leader Chai Yingwon's push for independence benefits ------- China nor the United States.
(A) both
(B) either
(C) not
(D) neither

117. Ms. Lisa Beach gave a lecture on how professional asset managers ------- their portfolios such as bonds, stocks and cash.
(A) divide
(B) clarify
(C) allocate
(D) designate

118. Broadside Engineering has the most modern and ------- production facilities.
(A) update
(B) updates
(C) updated
(D) updating

119. Mr. Ryan Cassidy ------- completed his first three months as an intern at Northern Software Co.
(A) success
(B) succeed
(C) successful
(D) successfully

120. The State Trade Commission alleged that the defendant's claims that the consumer had won the lottery were false and ------- the rule of California State and the Telemarketing Sales Rule.
(A) disobeyed
(B) infringed
(C) violated
(D) disregard

GO ON TO THE NEXT PAGE

121. Ms. Courtney Mendez left her e-mail address so that Mr. Jake Allenberg, the airline staff member, could notify ------- when her baggage was found.
   (A) him
   (B) her
   (C) it
   (D) them

122. Before ------- a report, you may want to check the report for errors that might cause the report to be rejected by our supervisor.
   (A) file
   (B) files
   (C) filed
   (D) filing

123. Ever since the investor made his decision, the priority of the program has been on deployment, ------- on understanding whether the system works.
   (A) nor
   (B) not
   (C) no
   (D) none

124. Most successful ideas are hard to spot because they almost never look like big ------- in advance.
   (A) beginners
   (B) mediators
   (C) winners
   (D) donors

125. This 200-room hotel is equipped with five restaurants, ten meeting rooms, a discotheque, a swimming pool ------- facilities.
   (A) and other
   (B) such as
   (C) or also
   (D) so that

126. Customized products are being introduced so as to satisfy consumers of different ages and lifestyles because the international market is becoming more ------- .
   (A) exceptional
   (B) competitive
   (C) tentative
   (D) cooperative

127. Numerous brands of disposable diapers were sold in America prior to the entry of Haggis into the market, ------- means Haggis was not the first disposable diaper.
   (A) who
   (B) whom
   (C) whose
   (D) which

128. The new civil law forbids the use or selling of customers' personal information ------- a written agreement.
   (A) about
   (B) without
   (C) on
   (D) between

129. In this rapidly changing world, maybe many people are unemployed because technological progress has made their skills -------.
   (A) extinct
   (B) obsolete
   (C) discarded
   (D) contemporary

130. Start with a physical check up at the medical clinic and follow the fitness program designed for you by our ------- trainers.
   (A) experience
   (B) experienced
   (C) experiencing
   (D) experiences

PART 6

Directions: Read the texts that follow. A word, phrase, or sentence is missing in parts of each text. Four answer choices for each question are given below the text. Select the best answer to complete the text. Then mark the letter (A), (B), (C), or (D) on your answer sheet.

Questions 131-134 refer to the following letter.

Dear Mr. Ralph Martin,

Your shipment of veneer board arrived on July 1 as expected. The size, quality, and quantity all meet the ------- outlined in our original order. -------, the price per unit was listed
                                              131.   **132.**
at $34.5 for a total cost of $34,500. That's over 15 percent higher than the price we agreed upon, which was $30 per piece, according to our records.

In the light of this, we find the invoiced amount unacceptable, and have directed our accounting department not to ------- your payment at this time.
                                                        133.

Please contact us within five working days with an explanation and a corrected invoice. We will be unable to continue our business relationship with your firm until this matter has been resolved to our satisfaction. ------- .
                                              134.

Lynn Pierce

131. (A) specify
     (B) specific
     (C) specifically
     (D) specifications

132. (A) Consequently
     (B) However
     (C) Furthermore
     (D) Therefore

133. (A) incur
     (B) maintain
     (C) process
     (D) withdraw

134. (A) It will pay attention to decreasing income taxes.
     (B) Additional charges will be applied.
     (C) We sincerely thank our business relationship.
     (D) We look forward to hearing from you.

GO ON TO THE NEXT PAGE

BLUE-Navi 2016 GPS Navigator

Cover price: $800.00

You save: -$160.00

$640.00(sale price)

Just imagine that you have a personal ------- in your car who guides you with a friendly
135.
voice and visual signals when you don't know where you are.

That's exactly which you get with the BLUE-Navi 2016 GPS navigator. No need to sort

through large folding paper maps or ------- the time to print out Internet directions any
136.
more. With a built-in map database of the entire nation, you don't need to download

mapping information from your PC. Simply turn it on, and select a destination using the

latest full-color touch screen technology. ------- .
137.

Developed with our distinguished BLUE-Navi 2016 GPS Navigator technology, and road-

tested by millions of drivers, the BLUE-Navi 2016 GPS Navigator makes your driving

easier and more enjoyable. Revolutionarily lightweight and truly portable, BLUE-Navi 2016

GPS Navigator goes ------- you go from your personal car, van or RV to your business
138.
vehicle. Turn it on, start your engine and go!

---

135. (A) assist
(B) assistant
(C) assistance
(D) assisting

136. (A) spend
(B) spent
(C) spending
(D) spends

137. (A) If so, you're on your way within
seconds.
(B) Start your engine and you will go
anywhere.
(C) Otherwise, it makes your driving
easier.
(D) Unless you turn it on, print out
Internet directions.

138. (A) whomever
(B) whichever
(C) whatever
(D) wherever

Questions 139-142 refer to the following e-mail.

Dear Mr. Lonnie Wardlow,

I am writing this letter ------- Booker Talkington. Ms. Talkington is an excellent employee
139.
who ------- for me for the last 10 years.
140.

She is hard working and diligent. ------- . As an on-site engineer, she has received nothing
141.
but the highest praise from all of our customers whom she has visited. While I am not

eager to see her leave our company, I urge you to ------- consider her for the position of
142.
Senior Engineer at your company.

Please contact me if you have any questions regarding Ms. Talkington.

Yours truly,

Gavin Pennock

General Engineering Inc.

139. (A) in charge of
(B) with regards to
(C) as a result of
(D) in accordance with

140. (A) works
(B) is working
(C) has worked
(D) worked

141. (A) But she has praised her colleagues.
(B) And she is willing to leave our
company.
(C) So she has contacted all of our
customers.
(D) She also performs all of her duties as
well as any of my other employees.

142. (A) strongly
(B) strong
(C) stronger
(D) strongest

GO ON TO THE NEXT PAGE

Questions 143-146 refer to the following press release.

Changes in Corporate Management

At its board of directors meeting today, Machine Finder Ltd. decided on revisions in

corporate management that will take ------- late next month.
                                        143.

Perry Young, managing director, will resign on the day of the general shareholders'

meeting, which is scheduled ------- late April. He will then ------- the post of statutory
                              144.   **145.**
auditor.

Elisha Sally will be elected as a director at the same general shareholders' meeting.

------- . She will also serve as executive officer of New Holland Mechanicals. For further
146.
information, please contact the Public and Investors Relations Department.

Phone: 070-341-2695

E-mail: pird@mfltd.com

---

143. (A) outcome
     (B) impact
     (C) impression
     (D) effect

144. (A) for
     (B) in
     (C) over
     (D) with

145. (A) adopt
     (B) presume
     (C) establish
     (D) assume

146. (A) She was dismissed on the day of the
         general shareholders' meeting.
     (B) She will arrange the general
         shareholders' meeting in late April.
     (C) She will be promoted to managing
         director at the subsequent board
         meeting on the same day.
     (D) She wanted to decide on revisions in
         corporate management.

PART 7

Directions: In this part you will read a selection of texts, such as magazine and newspaper articles, e-mails, and instant messages. Each text or set of texts is followed by several questions. Select the best answer for each question and mark the letter (A), (B), (C), or (D) on your answer sheet.

Questions 147-148 refer to the following information.

Gio's Mexican Restaurant

town main street

Tel : 080-788-7322

"More for less!"

Dine-in and Pick up Hours:

Monday–Thursday	11:00 A.M.–11:00P.M.
Friday & Saturday	11:00A.M.–Midnight
Sunday & Holiday	4:30 P.M.–10:00P.M.

Delivery Hours:

Monday–Thursday	4:30 P.M.–10:00P.M.
Friday & Saturday	11:30 A.M.–Midnight
Sunday & Holiday	4:30P.M.–10:00P.M.

10% off pick-up orders over $25.00

147. How can customers receive a discount?

(A) By eating in the restaurant
(B) By ordering food for delivery
(C) By picking up orders worth more than $25.00
(D) By presenting a special coupon

148. When can food be delivered?

(A) On Monday at 11:00A.M.
(B) On Thursday at 3:00P.M.
(C) On Saturday at 1:00A.M.
(D) On Sunday at 6:00P.M.

GO ON TO THE NEXT PAGE

Questions 149-150 refer to the following text message chain.

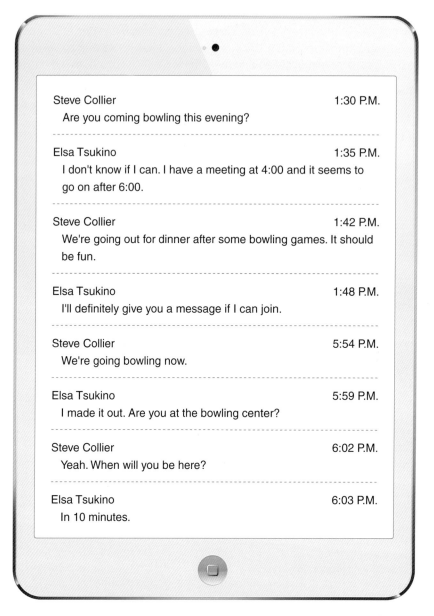

Steve Collier	1:30 P.M.
Are you coming bowling this evening?	
Elsa Tsukino	1:35 P.M.
I don't know if I can. I have a meeting at 4:00 and it seems to go on after 6:00.	
Steve Collier	1:42 P.M.
We're going out for dinner after some bowling games. It should be fun.	
Elsa Tsukino	1:48 P.M.
I'll definitely give you a message if I can join.	
Steve Collier	5:54 P.M.
We're going bowling now.	
Elsa Tsukino	5:59 P.M.
I made it out. Are you at the bowling center?	
Steve Collier	6:02 P.M.
Yeah. When will you be here?	
Elsa Tsukino	6:03 P.M.
In 10 minutes.	

149. Why did Mr. Collier send the text message?

(A) To invite a colleague to a gathering
(B) To schedule a meeting
(C) To request assistance with some work
(D) To recommend a restaurant

150. At 5:59 P.M., what does Ms. Tsukino mean when she writes, "I made it out"?

(A) She has filled out a form.
(B) She has drawn up an invoice.
(C) She was able to understand a message.
(D) She has left a meeting.

Questions 151-153 refer to the following announcement.

Animal Images in Traditional South African Art
A display of traditional drawing and sketch that reflects the customs and rituals throughout South Africa over the last five centuries.

City Hall Museum
500 Tripose Avenue
Peter Schreier West Galley
October 3 – December 12

Exhibition sponsored by South Africa Arts Council

Opening Reception, "Highlights of animal images in South African Art", a presentation by the professor, Mohamed Hazar, a art historian and visiting professor, "Evory University" Friday, October 3 at 7:30 P.M. Light refreshments will be served.

151. What is being announced?

(A) A job opening
(B) A new museum
(C) A research project
(D) An art show

152. What will most likely happen on December 3?

(A) An exhibition will close down.
(B) A scholar will visit Evory University.
(C) A reception will be held.
(D) A group of educators will tour East Africa.

153. What is indicated about Mohamed Hazar?

(A) He manages a gallery.
(B) He teaches at a university.
(C) He is a member of the South Africa Arts Council.
(D) He paints and sculpts images found in anture.

GO ON TO THE NEXT PAGE

The Vintage Reporter
Business briefs

August 10, Boston — Fred Hanstenmeier, CEO of FIT Footware, announced the company plans yesterday that the company adds shops in Miami, New York, Los Angeles, and Washington D.C within a year.

Mr. Hanstenmeier acknowledged that an earlier attempt at expansion had not been successful because the company moved too quickly. He admitted the company "had underestimated the challenge posed by expansion" Now that FIT Footware, whose headquarters are located in Boston, has strong and clear marketing strategies in place, Mr. Hanstenmeier claimed the expansion will be easier.

FIT Footware, whose target market is children and teenagers, was founded by entrepreneur Annelise Hanstenmeier, who promoted a unique way of fitting children's shoes. The stores use scanners within a smiley face to measure children's feet. The company will add a limited number of adult's shoes early next year. The company executives will be watching closely to see how well those shoes will sell. Overall this year the company expect the record sales at its five stores, all located in New York, due to advertisement campaign that was started recently.

154. What is suggested about FIT Footgear?

(A) Its merchandise is currently limited to young people's sizes.
(B) It recently closed some of its stores.
(C) It will start selling children's clothing.
(D) It moved its main office to Philadelphia.

155. Where is FIT Footgear currently located?

(A) In Baltimore
(B) In Boston
(C) In NewYork
(D) In Washington D.C

Questions 156-157 refer to the following invoice.

OBI Electronics Wahehouse

500 May Highway, Denver, Colorado, 407-700-9799

Delivery Invoice
Date: March 3
Invoice No:45003
Purchased by : Ed Brown
Delivery Address : Rose Garden 540, Phoenix, AZ 374

Electra Chrome Computer Desk / Workstation	$149.95
Comfortmax Swivel Chair	$99.95
PCI 21-inch Monitor	$249.99
PCI Computer (Model #: A150)	$ 999.99
Subtotal	$ 1499.88
Frequent Shopper Discount	$ 150.00
Tax	$ 80.99
Total	$ 1430.87

Thank you for shopping at OBI Warehouse.

156. What is suggested about Ed Brown?

(A) He often shops at OBI Electronics Warehouse.
(B) He works for a delivery company.
(C) He has a new mailing address.
(D) He will purchase a new computer next month.

157. What is the total amount paid on this invoice?

(A) $1,499.88
(B) $1,430.87
(C) $999.99
(D) $150.00

GO ON TO THE NEXT PAGE

Questions 158-160 refer to the following advertisement.

Located in a scenic country setting, the Oakwood Center (OC) is just a 30-minute drive from downtown, Hueville and 40 minutes from the city's airport. The OC is the perfect place for business travelers to stay and conduct their meetings. ---[1]--- For a small fee, guests can also enjoy our fitness center. ---[2]---

With a variety of small, medium and large conference rooms that can comfortably seat groups ranging from 20 to 300 people, the OC is an ideal venue for corporate events. ---[3]--- Our event planner will be happy to help you map out your next corporate event. ---[4]---

For reservations, please call the front desk at 561-777-5961, or e-mail us at reservation@ oc.com. To contact our event planner, please call 561-761-5961. Additional information about the OC, including directions to the facility, is available on our Web site, www.oc.com

158. What is indicated about the Oakwood Center?

(A) It is located in the center of the city.
(B) It can accommodate groups of various sizes.
(C) It provides catering service.
(D) It has a coffee shop on site.

159. What is available for an additional charge?

(A) Transportation from the airport
(B) A larger guess room
(C) Use of the exercise facility
(D) Internet access

160. In which of the positions marked [1], [2], [3], and [4] does the following sentence best belong?

"Our guest rooms include coffee makers, Internet access, and plenty of work space."

(A) [1]
(B) [2]
(C) [3]
(D) [4]

Notice

Bentam International Airport would like to inform passengers that wireless Internet access has recently been installed throughout all terminals. Our wireless service provides easy-to-use access so you can use the Internet and send or receive e-mail 24 hours a day. The service is complimentary. All you need to get connected to the Internet is a laptop computer.

If you do not have a laptop computer but would like to access the Internet, computer stations are located throughout Terminal B for your convenience and are marked by blue signs. This service is available at the nominal charge of one euro per ten minutes and is accessible 7 days a week from 5 A.M. until midnight.

If you require technical support or more information or if you are dissatisfied with the service, come to our 24 hours Help Desk, located at Gate 20 in Terminal A. We are happy to do all we can to better serve you.

161. What is the purpose of this notice?

(A) To request assistance
(B) To advertise merchandise
(C) To publicize service
(D) To provide directions

162. What does the notice state about the computer station?

(A) It is indicated in blue sign.
(B) It is available 24 hours a day.
(C) It is located in Terminal A.
(D) It is available free of charge.

163. What are users asked to do when they need a help?

(A) Call computer service center
(B) Go to Gate 20
(C) Send e-mail to Airport manager
(D) Contact computer manager

Questions 164-167 refer to the following online chat discussion.

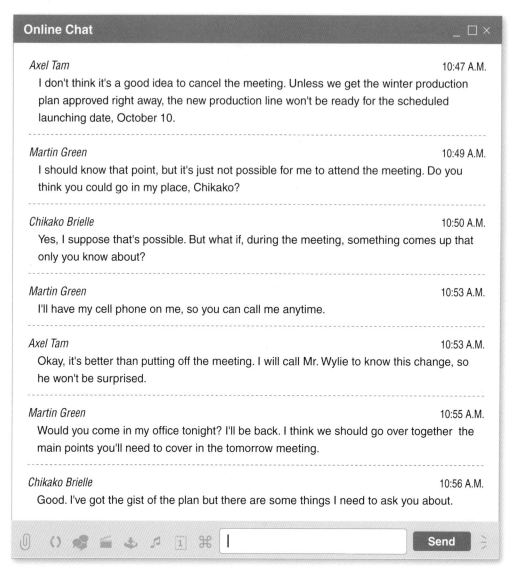

Online Chat   _ □ ×

Axel Tam   10:47 A.M.
I don't think it's a good idea to cancel the meeting. Unless we get the winter production plan approved right away, the new production line won't be ready for the scheduled launching date, October 10.

Martin Green   10:49 A.M.
I should know that point, but it's just not possible for me to attend the meeting. Do you think you could go in my place, Chikako?

Chikako Brielle   10:50 A.M.
Yes, I suppose that's possible. But what if, during the meeting, something comes up that only you know about?

Martin Green   10:53 A.M.
I'll have my cell phone on me, so you can call me anytime.

Axel Tam   10:53 A.M.
Okay, it's better than putting off the meeting. I will call Mr. Wylie to know this change, so he won't be surprised.

Martin Green   10:55 A.M.
Would you come in my office tonight? I'll be back. I think we should go over together the main points you'll need to cover in the tomorrow meeting.

Chikako Brielle   10:56 A.M.
Good. I've got the gist of the plan but there are some things I need to ask you about.

[Send]

164. Why is Mr. Green asking Ms. Tam to talk to Mr. Wylie?

(A) He doesn't want to go to the meeting.
(B) He prefers working in the factory.
(C) He has to take care of a serious problem.
(D) He doesn't have any suggestions.

165. What is supposed to happen on October 10?

(A) Production will begin.
(B) An important meeting is scheduled.
(C) Mr. Wylie will visit the factory.
(D) A meeting to discuss treat with new ideas will be held.

166. What does Mr. Green ask Ms. Brielle to do?

(A) Move the meeting place to the factory
(B) Replace him at the meeting
(C) Call him on his cell phone
(D) Get materials ready for the meeting

167. At 10:56 A.M., what does Ms. Brielle mean when she says, "I've got the gist of the plan"?

(A) She knows all the details of the plan.
(B) She has all the documents related to the plan.
(C) She knows some key points of the plan.
(D) She is not familar with the plan.

Brescia Dielectrics

The undersigned employee hereby agrees to and acknowledges the following:
That I may, during the employment, be exposed to information confidential to Brescia Dielectrics (the company). This may include (but not limited to) technical information (including methods, process, formula, and techniques) and business information (including a list of clients, pricing data and financial data)

I agree not to disclose such information to others including future employer at any time during and after the termination of the employment.

At termination of the employment, I will surrender to company all documents including blueprints, reports, manuals, correspondences and all the materials related to company business. I further agree not to retain copies and notes.

I have received a copy of the agreement
  Signed: Ernesto Tagliaferri
  Title: Senior Engineer
  Date: Oct. 12

---

168. What is the purpose of the document?

(A) To list the main responsibilities for a job
(B) To describe employee benefits
(C) To specify dates of employment
(D) To detail the terms of an agreement

169. What is NOT specified as confidential?

(A) Information about pricing
(B) Information about employees
(C) Formulas
(D) Technical procedures

170. What is Mr. Tagliaferri required to do when he leaves his job at Brescia Dielectrics?

(A) Return company papers
(B) Submit a summary of his work
(C) Take an inventory of company property
(D) Destroy technical documents

171. The word "retain" in paragraph 3, line 3 is closest in meaning to

(A) make
(B) keep
(C) remain
(D) employ

GO ON TO THE NEXT PAGE

To: P&A Executive Group
From: Business operations committee
Date: July 21
Re: Business strategies report

---[1]---. P&A has a stellar reputation for manufacturing high-quality construction machinery, thank to our many years of experience in this industry. ---[2]---. As you all know, manufacturing prices have risen by 9 percent over the last two years. ---[3]---. We have considered various options to better cover the costs. ---[4]---. Many people have suggested increasing the price of our products, but raising prices was seen as likely to discourage customers.

Please keep in mind that our business strategies are effective. Our television and radio advertisements are widely aired and customers respond well to them. We recommend our funding for the advertisements continue at the same level. However, we recommend an increase in funding for the development of our new and innovative products to meet our needs in this market. We can adjust pricing without discouraging our potential customers. It will help us to recover our lost revenue.

172. What is stated about P&A corporation?

(A) They are well regarded in their field.
(B) They manufactured road-repair machinery.
(C) They are international company.
(D) They have invested in research equipment.

173. Why does P&A corporation have a problem?

(A) Their advertisements are not popular.
(B) Few of their business strategies have been effective.
(C) The quality of their products has decreased.
(D) Production has become more expensive.

174. What does the committee recommend that P&A corporation do?

(A) Increase prices
(B) Decrease production
(C) Merge with another company
(D) Invest in new product development

175. In which of the positions marked [1], [2], [3], and [4] does the following sentence best belong?

"However, we are now at a difficult crossroad."

(A) [1]
(B) [2]
(C) [3]
(D) [4]

GO ON TO THE NEXT PAGE

GOOD FOR YOU
Health Food Company

We launch the new product, Vitamin C Power.

Most people don't know the fact that disease-fighting elements can be found in Vitamin C. Recent research shows that Vitamin C includes anti-oxidants important in defending against heart trouble and several types of cancer. You have to eat at least five oranges a day to get enough anti-oxidants in your body. Who wants to eat all those oranges in one day? Not you. That's why you'll love our new product, "Vitamin C Power". It gives you all the goodness of five oranges in a simple pill or liquid form. Take it anytime after breakfast, lunch or dinner, and feel good about yourself. Don't be taken in by imitation Vitamin C supplements that cost $2 or more EACH. You pay less than $1 each for Vitamin C Power – one box has 50 pills or convenient liquid caps for only $49.5, plus tax.
The easiest way to keep disease at bay – Vitamin C Power every day!

This coupon can be used to get Vitamin C Power.

The research is not conducted by the Health Ministry.
This product does not claim to treat or cure any disease.

Five Oranges a Day or One little Pill?

Which would you choose to prevent cancer and heart disease?
To help you decide, we're offering a free sample of Vitamin C Power. You can receive 25 of our Vitamin C Power pills just by writing your name and address on the back of this coupon and mailing it.
Send in the coupon today!

Postage free if mailed within the United States.
Please allow four weeks for delivery.

Offer valid until 12/31/17

176. Who manufactures Vitamin C Power?

(A) The Health Ministry
(B) A research cooperative
(C) Good For You
(D) Better Health

177. In the advertisement, the words "taken in" line 7 is closest in meaning to

(A) brought
(B) deceived
(C) encouraged
(D) allowed

178. What is NOT true about Vitamin C Power?

(A) It must be taken before every meal.
(B) It contains anti-oxidants.
(C) A sample is available till December 31.
(D) It comes in two forms.

179. How can people get Vitamin C Power pills?

(A) By getting the prescription from a doctor
(B) By sending the coupon after writing in their name and address
(C) By filling out a questionnaire about the medicine
(D) By visiting a health food store and showing the coupon

180. How many pills can people get if they use the coupon?

(A) A pill
(B) Two pills
(C) Half a box
(D) A box

GO ON TO THE NEXT PAGE

To	Andrew Cummings
From	Page Wagner, Dept. of Maritime Industries
Subject	Re: Your research

Dear Mr. Andrew Cummings,

I've attached a list of a few of the cruise ship incidents you inquired about for your research. I hope that it is helpful. I also hope you aren't writing an 'anti-cruising' piece for your travel magazine. On the whole, cruise ship journeys are among the safest types of vacations.

For more specific information about these incidents and accidents, get in touch with the cruise lines in question or the port authorities in the respective locations.

Best of luck with your article.

Page Wagner
Port of Yaquina

MAJOR INCIDENTS INVOLVING INTERNATIONAL CRUISE SHIPS

Cruise Line	Month/Date/Year	Incident/Location
Novervian	02/13/03	Capsized in heavy storms North Atlantic
Holiday Lines	12/01/07	Foundered on sand bar San Diego, California
Royal Netherlands	04/12/09	Major fire required evacuation (Ship eventually sank) Riau, Indonesia
Novervian	11/23/11	Collision with pleasure craft (Forced evacuation) Tahiti, French Polynesia

MINOR INCIDENTS DURING THE LAST FIVE YEARS

Cruise Line	Month/Date/Year	Incident/Location
Royal Holland	03/07/10	Health code violation in kitchen Port Au Prince, Haiti
Nostella	09/23/11	Fuel leakage in harbor Anchorage, Alaska
Holiday Lines	12/31/13	Robberies in port San Diego, California
Novervian	02/09/14	Food poisoning outbreak South Pacific

181. Who can provide more information on the November 23, 2011 incident?

(A) Page Wagner
(B) Magna Carta Cruise Lines
(C) Port of Yaquina authority
(D) Tahitian harbor officials

182. Why were passengers evacuated from the Novervian cruise in 2011?

(A) Due to a collision
(B) Due to a fire
(C) Due to health code violations
(D) Due to fuel leakage

183. Where does Page Wagner likely work?

(A) In Anchorage
(B) In the South Pacific
(C) In Yaquina
(D) In Tahiti

184. What is true about the fuel leakage of the Nostella ship?

(A) It is not so serious.
(B) It is frequent.
(C) It is dangerous.
(D) It is requiring evacuation.

185. Why does Andrew Cummings probably want the cruise ship information?

(A) He's going on a cruise soon.
(B) He's writing a magazine article.
(C) He thinks cruises are the most popular tour item.
(D) He works for a travel agency.

GO ON TO THE NEXT PAGE

Questions 186-190 refer to the following advertisement, online shopping cart and e-mail.

Personalized Presents Co.

Giving a watch or a piece of jewelry to a family member, your spouse or someone who you love has long been best one of the ways to show affection. But do you know that there is a simple way to make it even more special? Personalized Presents Co. makes your gifts special with some engraved messages for the individual who receive it. What you have to do is simply to choose the item you would like to give, and draft your message in the box below. You can choose regular shipping which will take 3 to 5 working days, or next-day delivery for a small additional fee. All of our shipping methods come with a tracking number to make sure that your gifts will be delivered safely.

* Please make sure that you enter the message exactly which you would like us to engrave on your gifts as you want it. As you can fully understand, we cannot accept returns because of spelling mistakes or other errors on the part of the customer. If there is an error by the engraving staff, please contact us and a replacement with correct message will be sent as soon as possible.

http://www.personalizedpresents.net/shoppingcart

Personalized Presents Co.

Order Reference 892542	Customer : Chris Weidman		
Item	Quantity	Price	Engraving message
Silver watch	5	$1000	Harry Corona Billy Ramos Terry Swanson
18K-Gold watch	1	$400	Ricky Yates
24K-Gold watch	1	$400	Karen Vinson
Platinum watch	2	$2000	Jack Halpern
Order Total			$3,800.00
Sales tax (10%)			$380.00
Total Amount Due			$4,180.00

To : Orders <ordersupport@personlaizedpresents.net>
From : Chris Weidman <chrisno1@zmail.com>
Date : May 12th, 2017
Subject : Problem with order #892542

To whom it may concern,
I received my order of nine engraved watches from you yesterday.
All of them look great except for only one. I ordered two platinum
watches and asked that two different names be engraved on each
of them: Jack and Halpern, respectively. Unfortunately, both of the
watches have only one name "Jack" engraved. These watches
were ordered for the ushers in my wedding ceremony and this very
important ceremony will be held in just two weeks. Would you be
able to send me a new platinum watch with correct name as soon as
possible so that my wedding will go on smoothly? I will return one of
the two "Jack" to you right now.

I look forward to your reply.

Chris Weidman

186. What are Personalized Presents'
customers recommended to do?

(A) Choose next day delivery
(B) Be careful when writing down what
they want engraved
(C) Visit a store to try on the watch
(D) Order more than one watch to get a
discount

187. In the advertisement, the word "draft" in
paragraph 1, line 5, is closest in meaning
to

(A) plan
(B) describe
(C) draw
(D) prepare

188. What is most likely true about order
#892542?

(A) It included an extra watch.
(B) It was the largest order the store
received.
(C) It arrived late.
(D) It was ordered in May.

189. According to Mr. Weidman, in what item
did Personalized Presents make an
error?

(A) Silver watch
(B) 18K-Gold watch
(C) 24K-Gold watch
(D) Platinum watch

190. What does Mr. Weidman hope to get
from the shop?

(A) A sincere apology
(B) A prompt reply and a replacement
(C) A discount on another watch
(D) A full refund on one of the watches

GO ON TO THE NEXT PAGE

Francis Home Furniture poised to expand into the Chinese market

After a year of record-setting profits, Francis Home Furniture has announced yesterday that it will be opening a new location in Hong Kong. The CEO of Francis Home Furniture, Wendell Steele, says, "It is a very natural move for us. Our market research indicates that Western brands are highly regarded in the Chinese market and are perceived as providing good quality, convenience and customer service. This research result should give us a key advantage." Steele alluded to the possibility for the company opening a new factory in China to support their retail store if the expansion in Hong Kong is successful. Francis Home Furniture has built a good reputation for itself by providing quality home furnishings since its beginning in 1994. It provides products which are marketed as wood furnishings and include a range of offerings for the home, including dining, bedroom, living room, home office, home entertainment, and children furniture. This family owned and operated business has over twenty locations across the country in addition to an established online presence.

To	Kelly Lawson
From	Gordon Austin
Date	April 24th
Subject	On your promotion and about our office-wide party

Hello, Kelly

As you have heard you are being promoted to manager and are to lead the marketing department at our new location in China. I'd like to offer my sincere congratulations to you. And I think that you have been working very hard to earn the position and you deserve it well. As we have some matters to discuss before you leave, please stop by my office at some point tomorrow.

I also want to let you know that we have settled on a date and location for our office-wide party celebrating the expansion of our company. We will be holding it at the event hall across the road from our head office, the same one where we held our last Christmas party, which you also attended. As for the date and time, it will be at 7 P.M. next Saturday. And if you have some questions about your transition and the party, would you get in touch with Marty Crawford? He has recently arrived from vacation trip and will be managing the transition between locations, and he will also be handling the celebration party. His e-mail address is mc@ francishomefurniture.com.

To	Marty Crawford
From	Kelly Lawson
Date	April 24
Subject	Location transition

Hello, Marty

I am writing to inform you that I will be able to attend the celebration party next Saturday, and I will be bringing my boyfriend.

I also need to mention that I have been accidentally locked out from company's computer security system as my ID & password to login doesn't work. I believe this may be related to the fact that I am changing locations. I need to access the computer system as there are some matters I need to finalize before I leave. I have asked some of our company they all referred me to you since you are in charge of the transition. I hope that this problem will be solved as soon as possible.

Regards,

Kelly Lawson

191. What is NOT indicated about Francis Home Furniture?

(A) It is operating well financially.
(B) It does business online.
(C) It will be expanding into China.
(D) It specializes in industrial supplies.

192. What is stated about the Chinese market?

(A) It is difficult to break into.
(B) It values Western products.
(C) It has been experiencing a downturn.
(D) It is growing rapidly.

193. What does Mr. Austin mention about Mr. Crawford?

(A) He is highly recommended.
(B) He is in charge of IT.
(C) He is the head of research and development.
(D) He is managing the reorganization.

194. What is suggested about Ms. Lawson?

(A) She is new member of the company.
(B) She is in the marketing division.
(C) She is in charge of events.
(D) She is unable to attend the party.

195. What will Ms. Lawson do next Saturday?

(A) Receive her home furniture
(B) Attend an event at a place she knows
(C) Teach a training class
(D) Revise her marketing proposal

GO ON TO THE NEXT PAGE

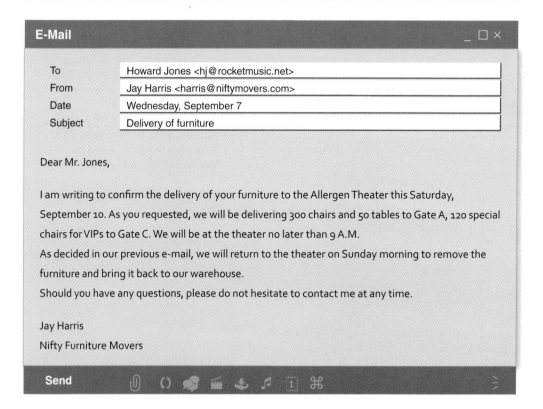

Attention Everyone: Arrangements for the "World Music Festival"

As you all know, this Saturday we will be holding our first ever "World Music Festival."
The concert is scheduled to start at 8 P.M. and finish around 11 P.M. And the concert will
be held at the Allergen Theater, just ten minutes walk from our office.
Rehearsals for the concert are scheduled at 10 A.M. on Saturday. At the same time, we
will be setting up the venue to make sure that everything is ready on time. Chairs and
tables will be delivered to the theater by 9 A.M.
Please make sure that you all are at the theater by 9:45 A.M. to begin arranging chairs
and tables for the concert. A VIP from the local arts council of our city will be attending
with his wife, so let us do our best to make our good impression on them.
Larry Rasmussen has greatly contributed to this music festival, and he and his spouse
will be special guests. Staffs in charge of their seating area need to prepare so that they
will enjoy the special evening.

E-Mail _ □ ×

To	Howard Jones <hj@rocketmusic.net>
From	Jay Harris <harris@niftymovers.com>
Date	Wednesday, September 7
Subject	Delivery of furniture

Dear Mr. Jones,

I am writing to confirm the delivery of your furniture to the Allergen Theater this Saturday,
September 10. As you requested, we will be delivering 300 chairs and 50 tables to Gate A, 120 special
chairs for VIPs to Gate C. We will be at the theater no later than 9 A.M.
As decided in our previous e-mail, we will return to the theater on Sunday morning to remove the
furniture and bring it back to our warehouse.
Should you have any questions, please do not hesitate to contact me at any time.

Jay Harris
Nifty Furniture Movers

Send

The Allergen Theater, home of many memorable theater and music productions, hosted the first ever World Music Festival on last Saturday. The music festival provided performances by a number of musicians from all corners of the globe, and featured both traditional and modern music.

After closing all the performances, local arts council representative Larry Rasmussen said, "Everyone in the audience had a wonderful experience. I'm sure that this music event will attract many more talented performers and artists to our city in the near future."

One of the highlights of the festival was a special performance by world-renowned violinist Seamus O'Brian, who delighted the audience with his own brand of traditional Irish music. This was the first and only one performance that Mr. O'Brian has performed outside of his own country in the recent ten years. In addition, to increase the audience's happiness, he performed with a very special group of musicians made up of seven members from seven different countries. Ms. Springer, a crew from Channel 4, which is one of the leading music broadcasting companies on cable TV channel, broadcasted the entire concert live, and the event was a huge success, judging from the faces of the audience. "This experience has been one of the most wonderful evenings of my life," said Mr. Rasmussen from his seat at the end of the festival, before leaving the hall from the exit near where he and his wife sat.

Mr. Rasmussen, who worked to make this very special music festival a success, said "This event has set a high standard for the future of the music-show."

196. What are the staff members instructed to do?
(A) Bring musical instruments to the venue
(B) Help to set up the chairs and tables
(C) Clean the theater
(D) Sell tickets for the concert

197. Where will Mr. Harris likely deliver the supplies to?
(A) To Mr. Jones' office
(B) To the warehouse of Nifty Furniture Movers
(C) To gates of the theater
(D) To the arts council

198. What is indicated about the World Music Festival?
(A) It has been running for many years.
(B) It was held during the day.
(C) It was a indoor music concert.
(D) It was involved with multi-cultural musicians.

199. What is true about Mr. O'Brian?
(A) He has not performed in another country for a decade.
(B) He is not very well known outside of his own country.
(C) He plays the piano.
(D) He always plays solo.

200. Who is in charge of broadcasting the concert?
(A) Mr. Rasmussen
(B) Mr. O'Brian
(C) Mr. Harris
(D) Ms. Springer

Stop! This is the end of the test. If you finish before time is called, you may go back to Parts 5, 6, and 7 and check your work.

新토익 시험 진행 안내

❶ 시험 시간 : 120분(2시간)

오전 시험	오후 시험	시간	비고
9:20	2:20		입실
9:30 ~ 9:45	2:30 ~ 2:45	15분	답안지 작성에 관한 Orientation
9:45 ~ 9:50	2:45 ~ 2:50	5분	수험자 휴식시간
9:50 ~ 10:05	2:50 ~ 3:05	15분	신분증 확인 (감독 교사)
10:05 ~ 10:10	3:05 ~ 3:10	5분	문제지 배부 및 파본 확인
10:10 ~ 10:55	3:10 ~ 3:55	45분	듣기 평가(L/C)
10:55 ~ 12:10	3:55 ~ 5:10	75분	독해 평가(R/C) * 2차 신분확인

　　※ L/C 진행 후 휴식 시간 없이 바로 R/C 진행

❷ 준비물

　» 신분증 : 규정 신분증만 가능 (주민등록증, 운전면허증, 기간 만료 전의 여권, 공무원증 등)
　» 필기구 : 연필, 지우개 (볼펜이나 사인펜은 사용 금지)

❸ 시험 응시 준수 사항

　» 시험 시작 10분 전 입실 (오전 9:50, 오후 2:50 이후에는 입실 불가)
　» 종료 30분 전과 10분 전에 시험 종료 공지함
　» 휴대전화의 전원은 미리 꺼둘 것

❹ OMR 답안지 표기 요령

　» 반드시 지정된 필기구로 표기
　※ 성명, 주민등록번호 등을 틀리게 표기하였을 경우 채점 및 성적 확인이 불가능하므로 주의하시기 바랍니다.

OMR 답안지 표기 Sample				
O	Ⓐ	Ⓑ	●	Ⓓ
X	Ⓐ	Ⓥ	Ⓒ	Ⓓ
X	Ⓐ	Ⓑ	Ⓒ	⊠
X	Ⓐ	Ⓑ	Ⓒ	Ⓓ
X	Ⓐ	Ⓑ	Ⓒ	Ⓓ

토익 EDGE 실전
1000제
LR SET 3

지금부터 Actual Test를 진행합니다.
실제 시험과 동일한 방식으로 진행됨을 말씀드리며,
방송 음성은 QR코드로 청취하실 수 있습니다.

준비 되셨으면 바로 시작하세요.!

LISTENING TEST

In the Listening test, you will be asked to demonstrate how well you understand spoken English. The entire Listening test will last approximately 45 minutes. There are four parts, and directions are given for each part. You must mark your answers on the separate answer sheet. Do not write your answers in your test book.

PART 1

Directions: For each question in this part, you will hear four statements about a picture in your test book. When you hear the statements, you must select the one statement that best describes what you see in the picture. Then find the number of the question on your answer sheet and mark your answer. The statements will not be printed in your test book and will be spoken only one time.

Statment (A), "Some people are paddling through the water," is the best description of the picture, so you should select answer (A) and mark it on your answer sheet.

1.

2.

GO ON TO THE NEXT PAGE

3.

4.

5.

6.

GO ON TO THE NEXT PAGE

Directions: You will hear a question or statement and three responses spoken in English. They will not be printed in your test book and will be spoken only one time. Select the best response to the question or statement and mark the letter (A), (B), or (C) on your answer sheet.

7. Mark your answer on your answer sheet.

8. Mark your answer on your answer sheet.

9. Mark your answer on your answer sheet.

10. Mark your answer on your answer sheet.

11. Mark your answer on your answer sheet.

12. Mark your answer on your answer sheet.

13. Mark your answer on your answer sheet.

14. Mark your answer on your answer sheet.

15. Mark your answer on your answer sheet.

16. Mark your answer on your answer sheet.

17. Mark your answer on your answer sheet.

18. Mark your answer on your answer sheet.

19. Mark your answer on your answer sheet.

20. Mark your answer on your answer sheet.

21. Mark your answer on your answer sheet.

22. Mark your answer on your answer sheet.

23. Mark your answer on your answer sheet.

24. Mark your answer on your answer sheet.

25. Mark your answer on your answer sheet.

26. Mark your answer on your answer sheet.

27. Mark your answer on your answer sheet.

28. Mark your answer on your answer sheet.

29. Mark your answer on your answer sheet.

30. Mark your answer on your answer sheet.

31. Mark your answer on your answer sheet.

Directions: You will hear some conversations between two or more people. You will be asked to answer three questions about what the speakers say in each conversation. Select the best response to each question and mark the letter (A), (B), (C), or (D) on your answer sheet. The conversations will not be printed in your test book and will be spoken only one time.

32. How often does the conference take place?
(A) Once a week
(B) Once a month
(C) Once a quarter
(D) Once a year

33. Why does the man say, "It's not fair"?
(A) To express a surprising
(B) To inform the regular meeting
(C) To notify a bad situation
(D) To indicate the injustice

34. Who will the speakers most likely be?
(A) Caterers
(B) Rangers
(C) Office workers
(D) Cleaning up crew

35. Where will this conversation most likely take place?
(A) At an amusement park
(B) At a passenger terminal
(C) At an airport
(D) At a bus stop

36. Why does the woman want to switch the order of the line?
(A) She can go to a party later.
(B) He looks so tired.
(C) He waited too long.
(D) There are people to come to.

37. How longer will the woman be waiting in line?
(A) For about 10 minutes
(B) For about 20 minutes
(C) For about 30 minutes
(D) For about one hour

38. Why does the man call the woman?
(A) To subscribe to May issue
(B) To know that he wants her article
(C) To have the contract signed
(D) To edit the article quickly

39. According to the man, what issue will the woman's article be published?
(A) May issue
(B) June issue
(C) July issue
(D) August issue

40. Which method does the woman prefer to deal with the contract?
(A) Having it delivered by person
(B) Receiving it by the e-mail
(C) Acquiring it by the mail
(D) Signing it where they meet

41. Why are the speakers buying a gift for Eddie?
(A) He's just been through an operation.
(B) He was a close friend of the woman.
(C) He is leaving the company soon.
(D) He was replaced from a temporary to a full timer.

42. What does the man ask the woman to do?
(A) Offer him a full time job
(B) Pay a call to him
(C) Make a present to Eddie
(D) Introduce a worker to him

43. What does the woman suggest the man to do?
(A) Divide his work and do it together
(B) Employ a full time worker instead
(C) Appoint a worker on probation
(D) Contact the headhunter office

GO ON TO THE NEXT PAGE

44. What are the speakers complaining about?

(A) The quality of the popcorn
(B) The price of a movie ticket
(C) The cost of downloading the video file
(D) The size of the screen in the theater

45. Why does the man like to see the movie in the theater?

(A) To save the money and time
(B) To prefer the large screen
(C) To release the new video files
(D) To download a game item

46. Why does the man say, "Isn't it a wise decision"?

(A) To express his dissatisfaction
(B) To complain about the movie
(C) To consent for his action
(D) To ask the compensation from the theater

47. What did Dylan say about Tyler?

(A) Tyler was dismissed from his position.
(B) Tyler was promoted.
(C) Tyler went home after his shift.
(D) Tyler wanted to work with his coworkers.

48. Who told Clayton that Tyler didn't want to work with the people in the company?

(A) Dylan
(B) Julia
(C) Silvia
(D) Milton

49. Why did Silvia want to speak with Tyler?

(A) To check if he really is Tyler Wakefield
(B) To recognize what happened to Clayton
(C) To confirm whether the news about him is true
(D) To require him to switch work shifts with her

50. What is the conversation mainly about?

(A) Schedules for the holiday period
(B) An equipment delivery
(C) A business trip
(D) Hiring new employee

51. Why does the man say, "That is a relief"?

(A) To represent his disappointment for the education
(B) To highlight his excitement of the early arrival
(C) To express his delight at the process of a training
(D) To indicate his wait for the holidays

52. What does the man say about the education during the holidays?

(A) It will result in few participants.
(B) Many employees will complain about it.
(C) We will have difficulty in organizing the schedule.
(D) We are suffering from the lack of equipment.

53. What is the conversation mainly about?

(A) A next examination
(B) A new branch office
(C) A promotional campaign
(D) An upcoming survey

54. What does the woman mean when she says, "I've been thinking about that"?

(A) She is looking forward to the branch opening.
(B) She has no idea about the branch opening.
(C) She knows she should do something.
(D) She must confirm a date.

55. What will the woman do next?

(A) Collect the employees for a conference
(B) Hire the new staff
(C) Examine the foreign market
(D) Ask the company president for her opinion

56. What will happen after the one month?

(A) A plan to form a better client base

(B) A transfer of the company headquarters

(C) A exchange of office furniture

(D) An advance into a new market

57. What did Mr. Guillen say about the current workplace?

(A) It is a leading construction company.

(B) It is not in good structural condition.

(C) It has a very large space.

(D) It has been too busy throughout the year.

58. According to the woman, why is it difficult to access to the office?

(A) Because there is no more bus service

(B) Because there is a negative impact on the commuters

(C) Because there is no change in the transportation system

(D) Because it brought them the extra cost

---

59. What problem did the man report?

(A) Some of the brochures have too many typing error.

(B) The photo on page 15 is missed.

(C) The delivery is a week late.

(D) Each brochure is lacking pages.

60. What will the man do next?

(A) Search a different printing company to reprint the pamphlets

(B) Confirm that the draft of the pamphlets was correct

(C) Contact the printing company and say the problem

(D) Send her complaint to the printing company

61. What do the women indicate about the printing company?

(A) It apologized for the typing error and mends it.

(B) It is slow to respond to e-mail.

(C) It has not shipped the pamphlets.

(D) It is reliable.

Discount Coupon

3% off from 1 to 5
5% off from 6 to 10
7% off from 11 to 20
10% off from 21 to 30

Until 30th June

62. Why is the man visiting the store?

(A) To buy some light bulbs

(B) To obtain a refund

(C) To ask for information about lighting

(D) To make an exchange

63. Where does the woman ask the man to go?

(A) To the cash register

(B) To the information desk

(C) To the rear of the store

(D) To her office

64. Look at the graphic. How many items did the man most likely purchase?

(A) 4

(B) 7

(C) 18

(D) 23

GO ON TO THE NEXT PAGE

PRODUCT MODEL	UNIT PRICE
ABA001 (with four drawers)	*$499*
ACC005 (with three drawers)	*$599*
BDG002 (with four drawers)	*$699*
BFA007 (with three drawers)	*$799*

Basic Package	Premium Package
90 mins, all you can drink (food extra) $10/person	120 mins, all you can drink + all you can eat pizza and pasta $30/person
Deluxe Package	**Party Package**
90 mins, all you can drink + all you can eat pasta $20/person	120 mins, all you can drink + all you can eat pizza and pasta + birthday cake $50/person

65. What department does the man work at?

(A) At the personnel department
(B) At the advertising department
(C) At the accounting department
(D) At the marketing department

66. What problem does the woman report?

(A) Its desk is expensive.
(B) Furniture is unavailable.
(C) A delivery is delayed.
(D) A price is too high.

67. Look at the graphic. What model will the woman buy?

(A) ABA001
(B) ACC005
(C) BDG002
(D) BFA007

68. What is the conversation mainly about?

(A) The delicious foods
(B) A bargain sale
(C) A new restaurant
(D) The president's birthday party

69. Who will prepare the birthday cake?

(A) Dorian
(B) Jordan
(C) Randy
(D) Tracy

70. Look at the graphic. What package will the speakers likely choose?

(A) Basic Package
(B) Deluxe Package
(C) Premium Package
(D) Party Package

PART 4

Directions: You will hear some talks given by a single speaker. You will be asked to answer three questions about what the speakers say in each talk. Select the best response to each question and mark the letter (A), (B), (C), or (D) on your answer sheet. The talks will not be printed in your test book and will be spoken only one time.

71. Where will this announcement take place?

(A) In a department
(B) On a farm
(C) In a restaurant
(D) In a grocery store

72. Which of the following is NOT discounted at Duluth Mega Mart?

(A) Corns
(B) Wheats
(C) Bread
(D) Eggs

73. How long will the special on pork and meat last?

(A) 30 minutes
(B) One hour
(C) All day long
(D) Throughout a week

74. What is Friday evening's weather forecast for the state?

(A) Clear sky over the entire state
(B) Light rain over the entire state
(C) Heavy showers over the southern part
(D) Some rain in parts of the state

75. About what time should skies start to clear up on Saturday?

(A) Approximately 6:00 A.M.
(B) Approximately 10:00 A.M.
(C) Approximately 3:00 P.M.
(D) Approximately 9:00 P.M.

76. What event will occur on Saturday evening?

(A) The rain will be weak.
(B) The earth's shadow will cover the moon.
(C) Rainbow will appear in the sky.
(D) Shooting stars will be visible.

77. On what day of the week was this recorded message left?

(A) Tuesday
(B) Wednesday
(C) Thursday
(D) Friday

78. According to the speaker, how long will the examination take?

(A) For 2 hours
(B) For 3 hours
(C) For 10 hours
(D) For 12 hours

79. What does Ms. Silvia O'Neal ask the listener to do?

(A) Call the physical examination Center
(B) Mail the regular check-up results
(C) Be a little early
(D) Avoid eating after 10 P.M.

80. What is the main purpose of this speech?

(A) To follow this presentation
(B) To inform the participants of the acquisition
(C) To join Diamond Corporation
(D) To acquire Mill & Mills Financial

81. Who will Ms. Stevie Taylor most likely be?

(A) The CEO of Mill & Mills Financial
(B) A sales representative
(C) A conference planner
(D) The boss of Diamond Corporation

82. What does the speaker think about Mill & Mills Financial strategy?

(A) It is exciting at Diamond Corporation.
(B) It accelerates its implementation.
(C) It corresponds with Diamond Corporation's business.
(D) It enters into Diamond Corporation.

GO ON TO THE NEXT PAGE

83. What is the main purpose of this advertisement?

   (A) To offer address searching services at reasonable rates
   (B) To announce the new service of the ManCom Service
   (C) To recommend people to join class action notice programs
   (D) To inform the opening of mancom.net

84. Which of the following is NOT a service the ManCom Service provides?

   (A) Customized class action notice delivery
   (B) All kinds of information subscribers need
   (C) On-line consultation
   (D) Morning newspaper delivery

85. What does ManCom Service do to post financial notices?

   (A) They forward personal letters to clients.
   (B) They publish the notices in a magazine.
   (C) They maintain their own homepage.
   (D) They contact clients.

86. Where will this announcement most likely take place?

   (A) At a train station
   (B) At a bus terminal
   (C) At an airport
   (D) At a shopping mall

87. What is the purpose of this announcement?

   (A) To thank the Topeka community
   (B) To notify the changes
   (C) To inform the bankruptcy
   (D) To discuss the route modifications

88. According to the speaker, what will happen this spring?

   (A) Topeka & Richland Transit Company will utilize its shuttle services.
   (B) The Topeka Campus Connector Shuttle will be discontinued.
   (C) Topeka & Richland Transit Company will examine the clients' response.
   (D) The conductor, Jake Walker will improve shuttle service for the Topeka community.

89. Who is Devon Addington?

   (A) A travel agent
   (B) A tenant
   (C) A home owner
   (D) A real estate agent

90. According to the speaker, what does Lowell want?

   (A) A reasonable rent
   (B) A convenient traffic
   (C) A sunny living space
   (D) A large office

91. What does the speaker imply when she says, "The best thing about this house is the price"?

   (A) She will buy the house for herself.
   (B) She thinks the house will be sold soon.
   (C) She thinks the house is expensive.
   (D) She thinks the house is popular.

92. What is the topic of the speech?

   (A) Dr. Cliford's university is well-funded.
   (B) Natural mineral resources are decreasing.
   (C) Dr. Cliford appreciates the support of her team.
   (D) Dr. Cliford achieved his goal.

93. What does the speaker imply when she says "All of us have achieved what we hope to get in our lifetime"?

   (A) They would like to be able to do as much as Dr. Cliford.
   (B) They believes they has done as much as Dr. Cliford has.
   (C) They would like to explain further about Dr. Cliford's hopes.
   (D) They would do even more for the field that they have.

94. What will the speaker do next?

   (A) Start a new research team
   (B) Receive her award
   (C) Introduce her coworkers
   (D) Leave for the university

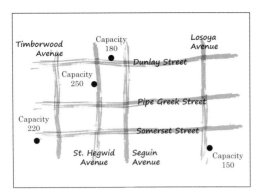

Couple's Day	Couples get a 30% discount for "Hangover"
Mega Mondays	Free large drink with adult ticket purchase for "Valley of the Best"
Discount Day	All tickets 50% off during business hours (except "Tropic Thunder")
Family Fridays	Buy one adult ticket for "Locked and Loaded", and get one child ticket free.

Test 01
Test 02
Test 03
Test 04
Test 05

95. According to the speaker, what will be closed tomorrow?

(A) A vehicle factory
(B) A film theater
(C) A local road
(D) A parking lot

96. According to the speaker, what will happen tomorrow morning?

(A) The road will be under construction.
(B) A film will be being taken.
(C) The car racing will be holding.
(D) A street parade will be going.

97. Look at the graphic. Where is the public parking lot located?

(A) On Somerset Street
(B) On Dunlay Street
(C) On St. Hegwid Avenue
(D) On Losoya Avenue

98. What is being advertised?

(A) The program of a movie
(B) The order of performance
(C) The price of a ticket
(D) The discount policy of a theater

99. What kind of movies are discounted on Sundays?

(A) Romance
(B) Drama
(C) Children's animation
(D) Horror

100. Look at the graphic. Which movie is providing the audience with a complimentary beverage?

(A) Hangover
(B) Valley of the Best
(C) Tropic Thunder
(D) Locked and Loaded

This is the end of the Listening test. Turn to Part 5 in your text book.

GO ON TO THE NEXT PAGE

READING TEST

In the Reading test, you will read a variety of texts and answer several different types of reading comprehension questions. The entire Reading test will last 75 minutes. There are three parts, and directions are given for each part. You are encouraged to answer as many questions as possible within the time allowed.

You must mark your answers on the separate answer sheet. Do not write your answers in your test book.

PART 5

Directions: A word or phrase is missing in each of the sentences below. Four answer choices are given below each sentence. Select the best answer to complete the sentence. Then mark the letter (A), (B), (C), or (D) on your answer sheet.

101. The rule of labor guarantees that current wages of all workers should be preserved ------- working hours are decreased by 20 hours per month.

(A) however
(B) although
(C) despite
(D) nevertheless

102. Chef Kent Wang is running a Chinese restaurant ------- a lot of gourmets frequent for its outstanding food.

(A) who
(B) which
(C) what
(D) that

103. Because environmentalists fear dangerous ------- consequences, they try to keep the environment untouched.

(A) unbiased
(B) unattended
(C) unloaded
(D) unintended

104. Taiwan has a very different culture compared with ------- provinces because it's an island far away from the inland.

(A) other
(B) another
(C) one
(D) others

105. Public relations is ------- important to the long-term success of a company that the presidents should expect to spend no less than half of their time on PR.

(A) as
(B) too
(C) so
(D) very

106. The weather can be changed ------- in a short time, and large temperature shifts are common in this spring.

(A) occasionally
(B) drastically
(C) amply
(D) significantly

107. Ms. Jackson said she decided ------- a seat in Parliament with her father's full support.

(A) seek
(B) seeking
(C) sought
(D) to seek

108. Local carmakers are lowering automobile prices according to the government's excise tax cut ------- at boosting the sluggish economy.

(A) aim
(B) aimed
(C) aiming
(D) to aim

109. Some car importers have taken advantage of the tax reduction to raise the price tags on their vehicles ------- triggering the anger of consumers.
(A) among
(B) throughout
(C) by
(D) without

110. ------- you do not have a fax machine in your room, please request the list of services to the front desk, to which you will be automatically connected.
(A) Unless
(B) Whereas
(C) Once
(D) If

111. Silicon Alley formed in New York lies ------- to a large-scale commercial area, so it offers great potential for the media industrial development.
(A) relevant
(B) relative
(C) adjacent
(D) adhesive

112. IONIC Computers has extensive experience ------- closely held enterprises in many different industries.
(A) represent
(B) represented
(C) representing
(D) represents

113. Park's Health Food shop will open on April 25, ------ which time its homemade dishes will be sold.
(A) to
(B) in
(C) on
(D) at

114. Please remember to ------- your flight reservation 48 hours before your scheduled departure.
(A) restore
(B) reconcile
(C) recommit
(D) reconfirm

115. For the ------- of its textile division, Forever 21 Apparel Industries has recently recruited more than ten new designers.
(A) extension
(B) separation
(C) expansion
(D) reduction

116. The cosmetics company which hit the Chinese market last year has been ------- the possibility of making inroads into the Japanese market.
(A) exploring
(B) postponing
(C) withdrawing
(D) abandoning

117. Because Ms. Melissa found the item defective, she sent it back and asked for another one -------.
(A) to deliver
(B) to be delivered
(C) delivering
(D) delivers

118. By the 2000s, companies were distributing personal computers ------- their operations rather than concentrating their data processing in one large mainframe machine.
(A) along
(B) for
(C) throughout
(D) into

119. Some important things that you should do when ------- for an interview is to dress appropriately, relax and be comfortable.
(A) prepare
(B) preparing
(C) prepared
(D) prepares

120. If you would like to receive more information ------- temporary employment openings, please enter the following information.
(A) notwithstanding
(B) regarding
(C) excluding
(D) excepting

GO ON TO THE NEXT PAGE

121. The conference was called by IIBC Chairman Derick Rossi's request and the participants were welcomed to the host museum by ------- director.
(A) its
(B) his
(C) her
(D) their

122. Sugar seems to be blamed for nearly every modern health problem, ------- in some foods sugar is an essential part of the structure and recipe.
(A) which
(B) and
(C) or
(D) but

123. Mr. Kenny Stanton has ------- high values and was extremely happy to finally be associated with a fair federation.
(A) reliably
(B) officially
(C) incredibly
(D) freshly

124. Whereas most Westerners usually place an exceptionally high ------- on time, viewing time as an asset, many Asians place more worth on relationships.
(A) attraction
(B) priority
(C) anticipation
(D) comprehension

125. The cost of mobile phone calls ------- at a steady rate over the three decades since the initiation of phone service.
(A) decrease
(B) decreased
(C) have decreased
(D) has decreased

126. The wise presidents know that choosing both ------- and adaptive thinkers is the best way to get projects completed and problems solved.
(A) punctual
(B) opposite
(C) innovative
(D) viable

127. In an attempt to create a more efficient working -------, several executives of this conglomerate are looking into the flexible working hour system.
(A) opportunity
(B) attention
(C) environment
(D) policy

128. Mr. Nick Stewart is a very talented artist ------- works are being displayed in an art gallery on Abbey Street.
(A) who
(B) whom
(C) whose
(D) which

129. The company farewell party had started, but little did ------- at the party held at the company lounge know that it was their president who was retiring.
(A) anyone
(B) someone
(C) everyone
(D) none

130. It is essential that the information requested on this application ------- out.
(A) fill
(B) fills
(C) is filled
(D) be filled

PART 6

Directions: Read the texts that follow. A word, phrase, or sentence is missing in parts of each text. Four answer choices for each question are given below the text. Select the best answer to complete the text. Then mark the letter (A), (B), (C), or (D) on your answer sheet.

Questions 131-134 refer to the following letter.

Dear our readers:

We at Conde Nast Traveler would like to thank you very much for subscribing to our periodical. Our records show that your subscription will ------- soon. So if you would like to
131.
renew, now is your chance. At this time, we are proud to announce special savings on our already discounted 1-year subscription. If you act ------- 15 days of receipt of this letter, you
132.
can get a 1-year subscription for the low price of 24 dollars per year. That's a full 20% off the newsstand price. To take advantage of this one-time offer, simply fill out the enclosed order ------- today. ------- .
133.   **134.**

131. (A) renew
     (B) expire
     (C) extend
     (D) update

132. (A) within
     (B) on
     (C) over
     (D) at

133. (A) bill
     (B) receipt
     (C) form
     (D) claim

134. (A) Any stamp is necessary if mailed between our own states.
     (B) You will get a one-year subscription for the lowest price.
     (C) We are proud to terminate your contract soon.
     (D) Postage is not required if mailed within the Continental United States.

GO ON TO THE NEXT PAGE

Questions 135-138 refer to the following notice.

When you check in at the airport, you will need to present the above confirmation number

along with your government-issued photo identification. ------- . ------- , at a growing number
135. **136.**

of airports, customers need to have a boarding pass with their government-issued ID to

proceed through the security checkpoint.

Customers should remember that Southeast Airways' seating policy is to allow passengers

to choose their seats upon ------- the aircraft, based upon their order of check-in. Those
137.

passengers wishing to sit in groups are advised to arrive at the airport well ------- .
138.

---

135. (A) Samples of improper identification
are an overdue social security card.
(B) Examples of acceptable identification
are a valid driver's license, passport,
or state-issued ID.
(C) Most Travelers hope to take window
seats to see the sky.
(D) All passengers should have their
boarding pass for security reasons.

136. (A) Instead
(B) As a result
(C) In addition
(D) By the way

137. (A) landing
(B) taking off
(C) getting off
(D) entering

138. (A) by turns
(B) at the same time
(C) afterwards
(D) in advance

Questions 139-142 refer to the following article.

According to a data from 2005, people use almost 15 billion kilograms of plastic each

year, and only about 2% of it is recycled! ------- , recycled artificial goods can be turned
                                          139.
into many useful goods ranging from food containers to modern furniture. And since most

plastics are made from petroleum, recycling them conserves this valuable resource.

In many states, plastic containers and bottles can be returned to stores, some of -------
                                                                               140.
also accept plastic bags for re-use. Recycling programs vary to ------- from region. ------- .
                                                               141.   **142.**
The most commonly recycled plastics are those in soft drink bottles, milk and water jugs,

and cooking oil bottles.

139. (A) In case
     (B) In general
     (C) In fact
     (D) For example

140. (A) which
     (B) who
     (C) whom
     (D) that

141. (A) and
     (B) but
     (C) or
     (D) so

142. (A) So, re-use programs can be changed
         according to the policy of state.
     (B) However, certain kinds of artificial
         goods may be taken in some regions.
     (C) The most frequently reused artificial
         goods are those in beverage bottles,
         juice and alcohol jugs and body
         lotion bottles.
     (D) And particular types of plastic may
         not be accepted in certain areas.

GO ON TO THE NEXT PAGE

I recently received a response from Pacific Shipping Company on the missing shipment of parts, which was supposed to arrive in August. Mr. Gomez, a manager of the Paris office, explained that a dock strike in Belgium delayed a great deal of freight last month. He said that he was ------- to trace the shipment, since it had to be.
143.

Mr. Gomez also claimed that his company was in no way responsible for costs incurred by the delay, since the contract between two companies specifically states that neither company shall be liable for shipping problems or delays which are beyond their -------.
144.

I would like you to review our contract and ------- whether Mr. Gomez's claim is in fact true.
145.

I would also like you to offer an opinion on whether any other recourse is available to us, because the shipment has been paid for in advance. ------- .
146.

143. (A) deciding
     (B) attempting
     (C) planning
     (D) managing

144. (A) recognition
     (B) description
     (C) repair
     (D) control

145. (A) confirm
     (B) doubt
     (C) wonder
     (D) revise

146. (A) Still, we are willing to go over our agreement.
     (B) Also, we would like you to express your opinion.
     (C) But, we have yet to receive it.
     (D) However, no one is responsible for its shipping problem.

PART 7

Directions: In this part you will read a selection of texts, such as magazine and newspaper articles, e-mails, and instant messages. Each text or set of texts is followed by several questions. Select the best answer for each question and mark the letter (A), (B), (C), or (D) on your answer sheet.

Questions 147-148 refer to the following advertisement

When you need a set of wheels, let Mobile Vehicle steer you in the right direction for car rentals. You can search for a rental car quickly and easily – just type in your destination, pick-up and drop-off dates. And we'll find you the best money – saving deal. Whether you're looking for a family mini-van, sexy convertible or sleek luxury vehicle, let Mobile Vehicle help you find your next car rental.

147. What kind of business is Mobile Vehicle in ?

(A) Car rental
(B) Car sale
(C) Car repair
(D) Limousine service

148. How a customer you find the suitable rental car which he wants ?

(A) Going to the shop
(B) Contacting the owner
(C) Calling the shop
(D) Using Computer

GO ON TO THE NEXT PAGE

Whether your idea of a perfect getaway is a golf vacation in the Pacific Resort, or an all inclusive vacation in Hawaii, or a Disney vacation package for the family, we will help you find the best vacations for your needs. Check for daily cheap vacation deals that can save you hundreds of dollars. With so many options and places to see, let us do the work and take care of the details!

149. What kind of business is advertised in the advertisement?

(A) Laundry
(B) Packaging
(C) Banking
(D) Tourism

150. What place is mentioned as a exemplary place for a golf vacation?

(A) Pacific Resort
(B) Hawaii
(C) Disney
(D) Guam

Questions 151-152 refer to the following text message chain.

Text Message	_ ☐ ×
Dwight Pascal 14:00 P.M.	I'm in a taxi, half way from the airport. I may be late because of the traffic jam.
Dwight Pascal 14:01 P.M.	So, is it possible to push back my presentation by 15 minutes?
Irene Kalla 14:06 P.M.	I'll try as far as I can do. Is there anything else you need?
Dwight Pascal 14:07 P.M.	I just wanted to share some more information with my audience. Can you make photocopies?
Irene Kalla 14:08 P.M.	It depends on the volume. How many pages?
Dwight Pascal 14:10 P.M.	Just one page and I'll e-mail it to you right away. May I ask you of color copies?
Irene Kalla 14:12 P.M.	No problem. Now, when you reach the main entrance at the Togo Convention Center, please let me know. I'll come down and meet you there.
Dwight Pascal 14:15 P.M.	Sure. Thanks for your help.

151. What is suggested about Mr. Pascal?
   (A) He has just arrived at the airport.
   (B) He has never been to the area.
   (C) He plans to make a presentation.
   (D) He works at the Togo Convention Center.

152. At 14:06 P.M., what does Ms. Kalla mean when she writes, "I'll try as far as I can do."?
   (A) She would like to confirm the presentation time.
   (B) She is sure that Mr. Pascal can find the meeting place.
   (C) She would like to help delay the scheduled time.
   (D) She tries to offer faster transportation to Mr. Pascal.

GO ON TO THE NEXT PAGE

Test 01

Test 02

Test 03

Test 04

Test 05

135

Questions 153-154 refer to the following message.

We flew out of New York and arrived in Minneapolis around 1:30 in the afternoon. We checked our luggage so we had plenty of room to bring home our purchases. After collecting our bags, we caught the complimentary shuttle to our hotel. There was a large convention at the hotel while we were there but it didn't bother us much. The hotel was great and the beds were awesome. The hotel has a complimentary shuttle to the Mall of Apricot.

153. Between which places does the hotel operate the free shuttle?

(A) Airport and hotel
(B) Airport and home
(C) Airport and New York
(D) Airport and downtown

154. What is true of the big meeting in the hotel ?

(A) The clients were not troubled
(B) The clients were irritated
(C) The clients were astonished
(D) The clients maintained their kindness

Questions 155-157 refer to the following advertisement.

Set in the heart of downtown San Francisco's "South of Market", Rio Hotel stands out with the offbeat, yet sophisticated spirit of the city. Nearby the SF Museum of Modern Art, a five-block walk from Union Square, and a block away from The Metreon. The lobby at the Rio Hotel is an octagonal, three-story space with tinted solar glass and flowing curtains. The hotel is also home to the Rio Cafe and Luck Restaurant, a bi-level eatery and wine bar serving French-inspired California cuisine. The hotel offers the use of cardiovascular fitness and weight rooms as well as an atrium pool, steam room and whirlpool. The modern Deluxe rooms feature framed black and white photos of San Francisco. All rooms come with cable TV, VCRs, pay-per-view movies, WebTV, CD players, and two phones.

155. Where is the Rio Hotel located ?
(A) In downtown San Francisco
(B) Near the river
(C) In the middle of market
(D) Near the city hall

156. Which place is mentioned as a nearby place to the hotel ?
(A) Union Square
(B) The Metreon
(C) The Stadium
(D) SF Museum of Modern Art

157. Which is NOT offered in the hotel room ?
(A) Cable TV
(B) Pay-per-view movies
(C) CD players
(D) An atrium pool

GO ON TO THE NEXT PAGE

Questions 158-160 refer to the advertisement.

---[1]---. Tony Group, Inc. headquartered in Los Angeles, is one of the world's largest commercial real estate services firm in terms of 2015 revenue. ---[2]---. With over 9,000 employees, the Company serves real estate owners, investors and occupiers through more than 300 offices worldwide. ---[3]---. Tony Group offers strategic advice and execution for property sales and leasing; corporate services; property, facilities and project management; mortgage banking; appraisal and valuation; development services; investment management; and research and consulting. ---[4]---. Tony Group is proud to be an equal opportunity employer.

158. What kind of business is Tony Group involved in?

(A) Business M&A
(B) Tourism
(C) Machinery
(D) Real estate

159. Which is indicated as the thing Tony Group is proud of?

(A) It employs employees regardless of sex, age, race and color.
(B) It follows the rules of the supervisory organization.
(C) It donates a lot of money to the poor.
(D) It builds libraries for the community.

160. In which of the positions marked [1], [2], [3], and [4] does the following sentence best belong?

"Please visit our Web site at www.TonyGroup.com."

(A) [1]
(B) [2]
(C) [3]
(D) [4]

Questions 161-164 refer to the following article.

Obesity can be caused by lots of things including genetics, lack of exercise, and nutrition. ---[1]---. I may have eaten some hamburgers from time to time back in the day. ---[2]---. Those spots were a hangout because it was cheap, fast, and as they say close to the school. But the rate of diabetes and heart disease among young people is growing, so this is serious. ---[3]---. State and local governments in California have started to ban certain foods in schools including soda, junk food, trans fats, and even bake sales. ---[4]---. Should they go ahead and ban the restaurants that serve this kind of stuff, too? Some CafeMoms feel parents are the ones who should teach their kids good eating habits, so they would make the right choices.

161. According the article, why is fast food popular?

(A) Its low price and easy access
(B) Its nutrition and easy access
(C) Its low price and nutrition
(D) Its advertisement and nutrition

162. What is the purpose of banning certain food in California?

(A) To prevent the increasing rate of diseases among young people
(B) To lower the price of food
(C) To increase the nutritional ingredients in food
(D) To stop the spread of infectious diseases

163. Who does the CafeMom feel should be in charge of the kid's health?

(A) Fast food restaurants
(B) Teachers
(C) Food manufacturers
(D) Parents

164. In which of the positions marked [1], [2], [3], and [4] does the following sentence best belong?

"But some researchers believe that fast food proximity to schools is a contributing factor."

(A) [1]
(B) [2]
(C) [3]
(D) [4]

GO ON TO THE NEXT PAGE

Questions 165-167 refer to the following article.

This program defines the means of ensuring this delicate balance that aligns human resource strategy with the overall business strategy. As human capital moves to assume a pivotal role in helping organizations achieve competitive advantage in the knowledge-based economy, the human resource function is increasingly being called upon to assume a more strategic orientation to drive success. This re-orientation of the HR function toward corporate and business strategy has multiple impacts upon the role of every class of manager in the organization.

165. What is indicated as an important thing to gain advantage in the economy?

(A) Balance between management and union
(B) Capital accumulation
(C) Strategy
(D) Human resource

166. The words "called upon" line 4 is closest in meaning to

(A) revealed
(B) sent
(C) persuaded
(D) requested

167. Who will be influenced by the re-orientation of the HR function ?

(A) Employees
(B) Managers
(C) Owners
(D) Debtors

Frequently Asked Questions

Q. Why didn't my credit card approve?

A. If AidFirm is not able to successfully claim your credit card, we will e-mail you about the fact that we were unable to claim your credit card and the reason for the rejection.

If you are curious about why your credit card didn't approve properly, please call your credit card company for more reasons. If you have any other accounting questions, please look at the accounting FAQs or contact AidFirm Customer Service.

Q. How do I re-submit a credit card that did not approve properly?

A. If you want to re-submit from a disapproval credit card, please log in to the Account Management department of our website. You should write all transactions which were a disapproval in re-submission form, and please re-submit if there are several failed charges.

* General Fact
If you had an e-mail content as this following: "This will inform you that your request reconsidered in AidFirm. We have been received and are waiting for permission from our Accounting Management division. Occasionally, we will manually evaluate a credit card before they settle your account. We will take care of your credit card charge as soon as possible, but if you have any questions about that while we are considering with your order, please call AidFirm Customer Service.

168. Where would this FAQs most likely to be found?

(A) In a newspaper
(B) On the cable company's website
(C) On the credit card company's website
(D) In a restaurant

169. How could a customer re-submit failed charges?

(A) Automatically on the web-site
(B) Contact the credit card company
(C) Contact Customer Service
(D) Log into the Account Management department

170. How often does the AidFirm review credit card charges before approval?

(A) Occasionally
(B) Every hour
(C) Manually
(D) Every month

171. Which of the following is NOT mentioned in the above announcement?

(A) You can know in Frequently Asked Questions why your credit card didn't approve.
(B) AidFirm advises customers that they should log in to the Account Management department of our website to re-submit from a disapproval credit card.
(C) After the review of your credit card by hand once in a while, you can use your account.
(D) Without the approval of our Accounting Management division, we will issue your credit card.

GO ON TO THE NEXT PAGE

Questions 172-175 refer to the following online chat discussion.

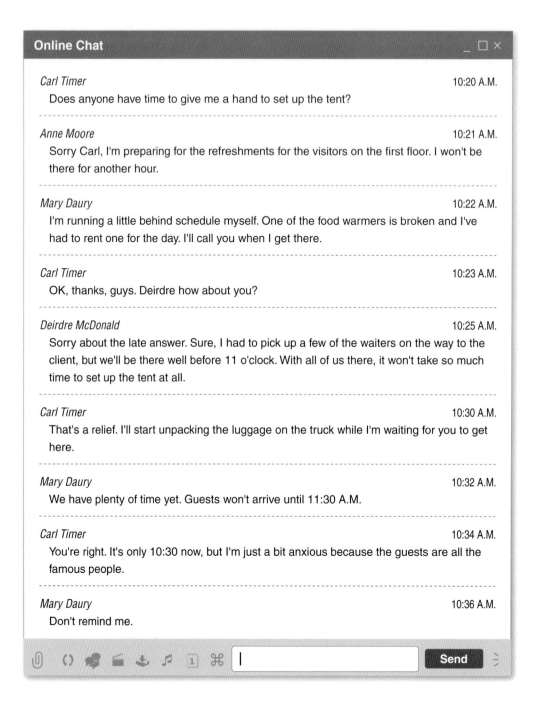

Online Chat   _ □ ×

Carl Timer   10:20 A.M.
  Does anyone have time to give me a hand to set up the tent?

Anne Moore   10:21 A.M.
  Sorry Carl, I'm preparing for the refreshments for the visitors on the first floor. I won't be
  there for another hour.

Mary Daury   10:22 A.M.
  I'm running a little behind schedule myself. One of the food warmers is broken and I've
  had to rent one for the day. I'll call you when I get there.

Carl Timer   10:23 A.M.
  OK, thanks, guys. Deirdre how about you?

Deirdre McDonald   10:25 A.M.
  Sorry about the late answer. Sure, I had to pick up a few of the waiters on the way to the
  client, but we'll be there well before 11 o'clock. With all of us there, it won't take so much
  time to set up the tent at all.

Carl Timer   10:30 A.M.
  That's a relief. I'll start unpacking the luggage on the truck while I'm waiting for you to get
  here.

Mary Daury   10:32 A.M.
  We have plenty of time yet. Guests won't arrive until 11:30 A.M.

Carl Timer   10:34 A.M.
  You're right. It's only 10:30 now, but I'm just a bit anxious because the guests are all the
  famous people.

Mary Daury   10:36 A.M.
  Don't remind me.

〗 () 🗨 🎬 ⬇ 🎵 [1] ⌘ | **Send** ≫

172. What kind of business do the writers most likely work for?

(A) An interior decorator
(B) A catering firm
(C) A financial institution
(D) A tour company

173. What does Mr. Timer write that he will do?

(A) Redesign a floor plan
(B) Contact a business associate
(C) Unload equipment from a vehicle
(D) Fill in a review form of service

174. What time will the visitors arrive?

(A) At 10:30 A.M.
(B) At 11:00 A.M.
(C) At 11:30 A.M.
(D) At 12:30 P.M.

175. At 10:36 A.M., what does Ms. Daury imply when she writes, "Don't remind me"?

(A) She knows what she has to do.
(B) Another staff member is responsible for the job.
(C) She is not required to attend an event.
(D) A previous job did not go smoothly.

GO ON TO THE NEXT PAGE

DISCOUNT PRESEASON TICKETS for the GOLDEN THEATER

For a limited time, preseason discount theater tickets are available for all orders received by May 31st. The season ticket will be offered at a rate of 20 percent off the published rate of $120.

Please send a check or money order to The Golden Theater, 700 South Tennessee Avenue, Etowah, Tennessee 37919, or contact us via our website at http://www.tennesseetheaters.com/, or e-mail at tickets@tennesseetheaters.com.

I am sorry, but no telephone orders can be accepted. The season tickets will be mailed to you with the 2016 Program Schedule, which should be published around August 1st.

The Golden Players is the official Resident Theater Company of Etowah, Tennessee. The Golden Players recently celebrated their eleventh anniversary performing quality dramas, comedies, and musicals at the Golden Theater downtown Etowah. The Golden Players was formed in March 1st 1993, and their first production was "Arsenic and Old Lace."

The Golden Players normally produces a minimum of 4 productions a year, all in the historic Golden Theater.

Subject	Re: Discount Preseason Tickets

Dear Sirs:

I am writing in response to the advertisement posted last week on the Etowah Community bulletin board. Please set aside two season tickets at the discount rate of $96 per ticket for the 2016 season of the Golden Theater.

I would also like to inquire about the possibility of obtaining a further 10 percent senior citizen discount, as I am enrolled as such with my membership in the Etowah Chamber of Commerce. As your theater is also a member of the chamber, please consult your policy on this matter if such an additional discount applies.

If such an additional discount applies, please notify me immediately, and I will send you my check for the tickets. Thank you very much.

Ms. Amy Okita
790 Whitemann Road
Etowah, TN 37920

176. What is the main purpose of the advertisement?

(A) To promote the discounted price
(B) To offer discounts on gold
(C) To advertise the Chamber of Commerce
(D) To announce the 2016 Program Schedule

177. When should the orders be sent to benefit from the discount?

(A) By March 1st
(B) By May 31st
(C) By July 1st
(D) By August 1st

178. What is NOT true about the Golden Players?

(A) 'Arsenic and Old Lace' was their first show.
(B) It always performs more than 5 times a year.
(C) It presents comedies and musicals.
(D) It is theatrical group in the state of Tennessee.

179. What would Ms. Amy Okita like to do?

(A) Reserve tickets and ask for a cheaper price
(B) Join the Chamber of Commerce
(C) Send the tickets to her children in Etowah
(D) Pay by credit card rather than mail a check

180. What is suggested about Ms. Amy Okita in her letter?

(A) That she will send her money when she gets the tickets
(B) That she is a member of the Golden Players
(C) That she needs extra tickets for the Chamber of Commerce
(D) That she is an elderly person

GO ON TO THE NEXT PAGE

Event for Tasty tea lovers

Held once a month, the drawing is on the first day of each month.
The prize is a box of loose-leaf tasty red or green tea.
Please put a √ in the box next to the type of tea you prefer on the entry.

Beneficiaries will be contacted by e-mail.

[ ]	Name, Last, First, Middle Initial with period
[ ]	Street Address
[ ]	City/Province
[ ]	Postal Code
[ ]	Prefer Green Tea
[ ]	Prefer Red Tea
[ ]	Your E-mail Address (make sure this is written correctly!)
[ ]	Special Comments

[Submit Event Entry to Tastytealovers.com]   [Reset]

From: Jameson Rider <jrider@hotmail.com>
To: support@tastytealovers.com
Date: June 19, 2016
Subject: Event Entry Form

Dear Tastytealevers.com:

I was recently visiting your website and I came across the event entry form. I have been to your shop many times and I know you are located about 25 minutes away from my home in Detroit, Michigan, across the border in Windsor, Canada. I have purchased a variety of tea from you in the past. It doesn't say anywhere on the page that this event is just for people in Canada. I tried to enter my U.S. address and the page asked me to re-enter all the address fields on the form. As a customer, I am a little surprised that your event wouldn't be open to those of us on the other side of the border. Because of your location and the fact that the population of Detroit is much larger than the population of Windsor, I venture to say that you have more US customers than Canadian customers. I hope you will reconsider your form or explain to me how I can enter the draw.

Sincerely,
Jameson Rider

181. What kind of event is offered?

(A) An event to create a new tea
(B) A new tea tasting event being held next month
(C) An event to get some tea every month
(D) An event to get discounted tea for a year

182. How will beneficiaries be contacted?

(A) By mail
(B) By online
(C) By phone
(D) By fax

183. How should someone participating input the type of prize they want?

(A) Write the words RED or GREEN in the "Special Comments" box
(B) Write the word, "YES" in either the "Prefer Red" or the "Prefer Green tea" box
(C) Write the word, "NO" in either the "Prefer Red" or the "Prefer Green tea" box
(D) Mark a √ in either the "Prefer Red" or "Prefer Green tea" box

184. What problem did Jameson Rider have with the event form?

(A) She couldn't get the form to reset after making a mistake.
(B) The form would not accept a U.S. address.
(C) The form rejected her corporate e-mail address.
(D) The form kept asking her for a middle name.

185. What point does Jameson Rider make about the shop's customers?

(A) Most people who are fans of the tea are not interested in events.
(B) Many customers are health-conscious and prefer the green tea to the black.
(C) Due to the location, there could be more American than Canadian customers.
(D) Most people find it inconvenient to apply for the event by Internet.

GO ON TO THE NEXT PAGE

BYLOS M7 32GB 4G plus accessories = $250

SELLER : Elecsforyou

Brand new! Bylos M7 32GB (midnight blue) 10" 4G tablet.
Includes charger, cables, case (yellow), in-ear headphones.
$250 for quick sale. Bargain price - worth double! Free shipping with secure
packaging. Don't delay!
Do not contact this seller with services or commercial interests.
Alert! Beware of scams (requesting money wire, cashier's checks).
Contact freesellhelp@freesell.org for help or more information.

E-Mail _ □ ×

To	freesellhelp@freesell.org
From	Dan Stanton <dans@outpost.com>
Date	July 16th 7:00 A.M.
Subject	I HAVE A DISPUTE. ITEM DOES NOT MATCH DESCRIPTION

Twelve days after completing the transaction for item #98537668 and despite the fact that the seller and I are living in the same city, a lime green tablet in a midnight blue case, finally arrived. It had been sent in a standard envelope, with no wrapping, which may have caused the about two-inch screen crack and three scratches along the sides.

And it has not some additional parts; charger and cable. What is worse, it looked more like a previously used item which has some faded or lose color. Over the past two months, I have sent 28 e-mails attempting to get missing additional parts and repairs for the crack and scratches. However Elecsforyou remains unresponsive until now, so I'd appreciate your advice on how I should cover this matter further.

Dwight Pascal

Send

From	dtpl@outpost.com
To	Olivia Newton <freesellhelp@freesell.org>
Date	July 16th 2:57 P.M.
Subject	RE: I HAVE A DISPUTE. ITEM DOES NOT MATCH DESCRIPTION

Dear Mr. Stanton,

Thank you for contacting Freesell. I can fully understand how upsetting it is when a purchase turns out not to be as described.

Under our Freesell Buyer Defender program, 50 days is the maximum time limit within which buyers can be submitted their complaints to us. Just last month, we also introduced a new option to file a case to the Conflict Mediating Board up to 70 days after a transaction. However, this process is simply another route for buyer-seller interaction so that a mutual settlement might be reached.

Alternatively, you could file a petition with statesumer.us, a national public site dealing with consumer protection. They will recommend solutions, and may be able to help you get your money back, but neither they nor Freesell can guarantee a positive or favorable result for you. I hope this information above is of some help to you.

Sincerely,
Olivia Newton, Freesell California Office

186. What does the seller mention about the item?

(A) It will be sent without delay.
(B) It comes in a blue box.
(C) It is the only one in existence.
(D) It has a value of $500.

187. Which of the following did Mr. Stanton NOT experience?

(A) An unworking tablet
(B) An item with damaged surfaces
(C) A poorly packaged delivery
(D) An absence of extra equipment

188. In the e-mail, the word "cover" in paragraph 2, line 4, is closest in meaning to

(A) pay for
(B) shield
(C) hide
(D) provide help with

189. What is indicated about Dan Stanton and Olivia Newton?

(A) They all own a tablet device.
(B) They are in the same location.
(C) They are all employed by Freesell.
(D) They each sent an e-mail in July.

190. What is true about Freesell?

(A) It makes tablets in only one color.
(B) It has a mediation service for buyers and sellers.
(C) It runs a national consumer support site.
(D) It sent nearly thirty e-mails to one of its customers.

GO ON TO THE NEXT PAGE

THROUGH THE LIGHT TO THE DARK
Busch Memorial Hall, N. Tremont Ave. Chicago, IL
May 18-20 9:00-17:00
(Awards Gala 20:00 May 20th)

Top Prize	$4,000
Runner-up	$2,500
Third Place	$1,750

Now in its seventh year, the Light To The Dark, one of competition of photographic works, has grown to the level of accepting submissions from across all the countries of the world. This competition aims to find out and promote up-and-coming artists from all over the world of contemporary photography industry.

By submitting their works, entrants can enjoy the benefit of being exposed to wide media coverage, receiving top-level judging feedback from high profile photographers, and making vital relationship with which could generate sales and copy right commissions for many years to come.

Competition Entry Fees : Single $17, Series $30
Deadline for entries and payment : March 11th
All background music provided by Arvid Jacoby Records (DIG)

Date   *May 19th*

Hi again, Alizadeh,

I hope you are enjoying the photography contest event and your first stay in our city. After our dinner meeting last night, I was approached by Arvid Jacoby, a leading executive in the music industry of our country. He said once that he was impressed by your whole series and in particular, the entry, "Always." He inquired about purchasing the license to the image of your work for the CD cover and MP3 online display for an upcoming release on his label, DIG. This could be your first sale!

He is scheduled to stay here until tomorrow and would like to have a word with you before he leaves. Here is his contact information: arvid@pictorias.com. If you need to speak to me, my mobile is (409) 299-7041. Good luck!

James Gunter (sales)

From: arvid@pictorias.com
To: Alizadeh Mitra <mitrabest@pinmail.com>
Date: May 19th 18:32
Subject: The copyright to "Always"

Dear Mr. Jacoby,

Thank you so much for asking to James Gunter of my work. Actually, one of my works "Always" seems to be a lucky image for me. It won first prize at my university graduation exhibition last summer – the Dakota College of Arts – the same as you did! I am very interested in your proposal and I think we can come to an arrangement of mutual consent. As you know, it is very important for me to build on my career portfolio at every opportunity, so I'd like to discuss if it is possible to put my name and credit as an artist on the album cover as part of the copyright transfer negotiations. I have to be present in the Hall tomorrow until evening, but if you have time, I would like to meet up in the area before the gala show. Please let me know if this is possible.

Sincerely,
Alizadeh Mitra

191. What is offered by the organization of competition?

(A) Free entry
(B) Employment in the media company
(C) Photography lessons
(D) Building networks chances

192. In the note, the word "once" in paragraph 1, in line 3, is closest in meaning to

(A) at the time
(B) in the past
(C) when
(D) only if

193. Which is true about Arvid Jacoby?

(A) He has his own fashion label.
(B) He studied with Alizadeh at Dakota College of Arts.
(C) He is creating music based on Alizadeh's work.
(D) He spoke to James about Alizadeh on May 18.

194. What is indicated about Alizadeh Mitra?

(A) She is visiting Chicago for the first time.
(B) She has never met James Gunter.
(C) She is about to graduate from university.
(D) She paid $17 to enter the competition.

195. What condition does Alizadeh Mitra suggest to Arvid Jacoby?

(A) She wants her name to be printed on a product.
(B) She wants to join him in his music business.
(C) She will demand a higher price when she wins the competition.
(D) She prefers to give him a temporary license to her work.

GO ON TO THE NEXT PAGE

Mulgrave Elementary School
West Vancouver, Vancouver

Position Title : Early Childhood Educator
Posted : July 22nd
Closing Date : August 7th
Salary : To be confirmed

As a result of our rapid growth, we are pleased to announce the launch of our new Early Childhood Program as of next March. Initially, we are planning to fill three openings from within our current workforce.

Responsibilities
- Planning, preparing and carrying out of program activities to meet the level of preschool children aged 4-5
- Supervising and caring for the safety and well-being of all children on the program during the school day and in the before-school / after-school of Mulgrave Kids Club

Requirements
- Early Childhood Education diploma
- At least 2 years' experience in the early learning field
- Ability to work both independently and as part of a team
- At least one year of consecutive employment at Mulgrave

Apply in writing to Margo Karajan, Principal.

* Currently open to internal candidates only. Be sure to inform your immediate supervisor when applying for an internally posted position.

Dear Ms. Karajan,

I'm writing to apply for the new position of Early Childhood Educator. I have a Master's degree in Early Years Development (0-5 years) and was previously employed for four years at a preschool education organization in Montreal where I collaborated with three other colleagues to develop a successful early learning curriculum for kids aged two to five. I am currently covering Grade 1 as a tentative replacement for Carrie Stiles while she is on maternity leave. I have also taken over both her Breakfast Club and Late Mulgrave Time, so I feel my background and experience could be a valuable additional resource to your new program.
I look forward to being able to discuss the position with you in detail.

Sincerely,
Mitchell Gibson

Dear Ms. Gibson,

Thank you for your response to the recent posting. We received a large number of applications from employees for this new program. We have looked at your resume with great interest and are very impressed with your experience and achievement in in Montreal as well as your linguistic ability in French, Spanish and German. I know well that you are with us until January when Carrie Stiles returns. At that point, you will have reached the required twelve months of continuous employment, which is one of the job requirements. I regret to say that the requirement must have been met by the time of application.

However, taking into consideration your extensive knowledge and experience, we would like to invite you to apply for the same position in December next year, when the second phase of hiring begins. We will be expecting at least two more openings then. I will be retiring at the end of this year, but my successor and all the staff at Mulgrave will look forward to seeing you next year.

Sincerely,
Marge Karajan

196. Where was this notice most likely posted?

(A) At a local job center
(B) At an elementary school
(C) In a regional newspaper
(D) On an employment web-site

197. What is true about Mulgrave Elementary School?

(A) It is going to start after-school activities.
(B) It needs one new member of staff.
(C) It will have a different head of school next year.
(D) It employs Carrie Stiles to teach second grade students.

198. What is indicated about Mitchell Gibson?

(A) She is a fluent speaker of Italian.
(B) She has lived in Sydney.
(C) She currently works in West Vancouver.
(D) She has recently a baby.

199. In the response, the word "met" in paragraph 1, line 8, is closest in meaning to

(A) visited
(B) seen
(C) satisfied
(D) beheld

200. What does Margo Karajan advise Mitchell Daury to do next year?

(A) Attain an extra diploma
(B) Get twelve more months of work experience
(C) Reapply for a job position later
(D) Take over Carrie Stiles' job

Stop! This is the end of the test. If you finish before time is called, you may go back to Parts 5, 6, and 7 and check your work.

新토익 시험 진행 안내

❶ 시험 시간 : 120분(2시간)

오전 시험	오후 시험	시간	비고
9:20	2:20		입실
9:30 ~ 9:45	2:30 ~ 2:45	15분	답안지 작성에 관한 Orientation
9:45 ~ 9:50	2:45 ~ 2:50	5분	수험자 휴식시간
9:50 ~ 10:05	2:50 ~ 3:05	15분	신분증 확인 (감독 교사)
10:05 ~ 10:10	3:05 ~ 3:10	5분	문제지 배부 및 파본 확인
10:10 ~ 10:55	3:10 ~ 3:55	45분	듣기 평가(L/C)
10:55 ~ 12:10	3:55 ~ 5:10	75분	독해 평가(R/C) * 2차 신분확인

※ L/C 진행 후 휴식 시간 없이 바로 R/C 진행

❷ 준비물

» 신분증 : 규정 신분증만 가능 (주민등록증, 운전면허증, 기간 만료 전의 여권, 공무원증 등)
» 필기구 : 연필, 지우개 (볼펜이나 사인펜은 사용 금지)

❸ 시험 응시 준수 사항

» 시험 시작 10분 전 입실 (오전 9:50, 오후 2:50 이후에는 입실 불가)
» 종료 30분 전과 10분 전에 시험 종료 공지함
» 휴대전화의 전원은 미리 꺼둘 것

❹ OMR 답안지 표기 요령

» 반드시 지정된 필기구로 표기
※ 성명, 주민등록번호 등을 틀리게 표기하였을 경우 채점 및 성적 확인이 불가능하므로 주의하시기 바랍니다.

OMR 답안지 표기 Sample				
O	Ⓐ	Ⓑ	●	Ⓓ
X	Ⓐ	Ⓥ	Ⓒ	Ⓓ
X	Ⓐ	Ⓑ	Ⓒ	⊗
X	Ⓐ	Ⓑ	Ⓒ	Ⓓ
X	Ⓐ	Ⓑ	Ⓒ	Ⓓ

토익 EDGE 실전
1000제
LR SET 4

지금부터 Actual Test를 진행합니다.
실제 시험과 동일한 방식으로 진행됨을 말씀드리며,
방송 음성은 QR코드로 청취하실 수 있습니다.

준비 되셨으면 바로 시작하세요.!

LISTENING TEST

In the Listening test, you will be asked to demonstrate how well you understand spoken English. The entire Listening test will last approximately 45 minutes. There are four parts, and directions are given for each part. You must mark your answers on the separate answer sheet. Do not write your answers in your test book.

PART 1

Directions: For each question in this part, you will hear four statements about a picture in your test book. When you hear the statements, you must select the one statement that best describes what you see in the picture. Then find the number of the question on your answer sheet and mark your answer. The statements will not be printed in your test book and will be spoken only one time.

Statment (A), "Some people are paddling through the water," is the best description of the picture, so you should select answer (A) and mark it on your answer sheet.

1.

2.

GO ON TO THE NEXT PAGE

3.

4.

5.

6.

GO ON TO THE NEXT PAGE

PART 2

Directions: You will hear a question or statement and three responses spoken in English. They will not be printed in your test book and will be spoken only one time. Select the best response to the question or statement and mark the letter (A), (B), or (C) on your answer sheet.

7. Mark your answer on your answer sheet.

8. Mark your answer on your answer sheet.

9. Mark your answer on your answer sheet.

10. Mark your answer on your answer sheet.

11. Mark your answer on your answer sheet.

12. Mark your answer on your answer sheet.

13. Mark your answer on your answer sheet.

14. Mark your answer on your answer sheet.

15. Mark your answer on your answer sheet.

16. Mark your answer on your answer sheet.

17. Mark your answer on your answer sheet.

18. Mark your answer on your answer sheet.

19. Mark your answer on your answer sheet.

20. Mark your answer on your answer sheet.

21. Mark your answer on your answer sheet.

22. Mark your answer on your answer sheet.

23. Mark your answer on your answer sheet.

24. Mark your answer on your answer sheet.

25. Mark your answer on your answer sheet.

26. Mark your answer on your answer sheet.

27. Mark your answer on your answer sheet.

28. Mark your answer on your answer sheet.

29. Mark your answer on your answer sheet.

30. Mark your answer on your answer sheet.

31. Mark your answer on your answer sheet.

PART 3

Directions: You will hear some conversations between two or more people. You will be asked to answer three questions about what the speakers say in each conversation. Select the best response to each question and mark the letter (A), (B), (C), or (D) on your answer sheet. The conversations will not be printed in your test book and will be spoken only one time.

32. What is the man looking for?

(A) Projector
(B) His document
(C) Conference room
(D) His briefcase

33. What will the man probably do next?

(A) Go to the conference room
(B) Search for the report
(C) Print out the document again
(D) Postpone the conference

34. What does the man ask the woman to do?

(A) Make an extra copy
(B) Prepare for some equipment
(C) Find the conference room
(D) Print out the document

35. Where will the speakers most likely be working?

(A) In a manufacturing company
(B) In a head hunting company
(C) In a moving company
(D) In a telephone company

36. What will the man do next?

(A) Pay more money
(B) Place a large order
(C) Call the buyer
(D) Work on the weekend

37. What did the woman suggest the man do to solve the problem?

(A) Repay the money to the customer
(B) Seek another country
(C) Reduce the labor wage
(D) Ask the customer for compensation

38. Why was the woman late for work?

(A) She was fired.
(B) She took the day off.
(C) She had a cold.
(D) She disliked working.

39. How many times was Ms. Leroy late?

(A) Once
(B) Twice
(C) Three times
(D) Four times

40. What does the man advise the woman to do?

(A) Communicate with an employee
(B) Repair the photocopy machine
(C) Complete her work early
(D) Go home and get some rest

41. Why does the woman call the man?

(A) To inquire about a Delmar & Lewis studio
(B) To ask about the price for the pictures
(C) To confirm whether he received some photos
(D) To check for her missing files

42. What will the woman's job most likely be?

(A) A delivery person
(B) A photographer
(C) An assistant
(D) A wedding planner

43. What did Shawn do for Quincy?

(A) Shawn fixed Delma's files.
(B) Shawn called Quincy last weekend.
(C) Shawn took Quincy's photos.
(D) Shawn settled a bill for Quincy.

GO ON TO THE NEXT PAGE

44. What will the speakers do next month?
    (A) Play golf
    (B) Leave the company
    (C) Meet suppliers of golf equipment
    (D) Give a business presentation

45. What does the woman mean when she says, "I always knew we could count on you"?
    (A) She believes Bryant is an expert tour guide.
    (B) She's confident of Bryant's capabilities.
    (C) She thinks Bryant knows Manila very well.
    (D) She thinks Bryant is good at making clubs.

46. What company do the speakers work for?
    (A) A hotel
    (B) A travel agency
    (C) A golf equipment manufacturer
    (D) An airline

_____

47. What is the main topic of the conversation?
    (A) The on-line class
    (B) The expenses of all divisions
    (C) The financial software
    (D) The training duration for the software

48. According to the man, what is most important about the software?
    (A) Exactness
    (B) Confidentiality
    (C) Convenience
    (D) Fastness

49. What does the man allow the woman to do?
    (A) She will forward an inventory list to him by email.
    (B) She will send his order through a courier service to him.
    (C) She will register for the training course instead of him.
    (D) She will introduce the software-training course to him.

50. Which of the following is NOT delivered to the exhibition hall?
    (A) The display cases
    (B) The sample products
    (C) The posters
    (D) The leaflets

51. What does the man mean when he says, "that's not a minute too soon"?
    (A) Tomorrow is the due date.
    (B) He is staying late.
    (C) The deadline is getting close.
    (D) He has much work left.

52. What will the man do next?
    (A) Do business with the planner
    (B) Order at another print shop
    (C) Consider tomorrow's exhibition
    (D) Check the lists

_____

53. What does the man want to do?
    (A) Prepare for a conference
    (B) Forward an order form
    (C) Talk about a sales plan
    (D) Write a marketing report

54. Where does the woman say she will go?
    (A) To a copy room
    (B) To a plant
    (C) To a customer's office
    (D) To a lobby

55. What does the woman mean when she says, "You've got it already"?
    (A) She puts the cases down.
    (B) She is satisfied with a performance.
    (C) She understands his situation.
    (D) She put the sales plan on his desk.

56. What is the main topic of the conversation?

(A) Buying office supplies
(B) Reducing the size of an office
(C) Recruiting a new assistant
(D) Moving to a new area

57. What do the women imply about the company?

(A) It will have a lack of conference space.
(B) It has been growing slowly.
(C) It will give employees more benefits.
(D) It will spend a lot of money on renovations.

58. What does the man mean, when he says, "You're not wrong"?

(A) He is not available.
(B) He comes back to the company.
(C) He knows who made mistake.
(D) He feels the same.

59. What is the main topic of the conversation?

(A) Renovated theater
(B) An old film
(C) A big sports match
(D) Free movie tickets

60. What can be inferred about the women?

(A) They will invest money on a movie.
(B) They will be out of the downtown.
(C) They will be changing their jobs.
(D) They have the same interest.

61. What will the man do next?

(A) Call a box office
(B) Ask a refund
(C) Contact his colleague
(D) Buy tickets

UTILITIES

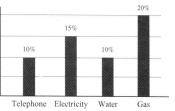

62. What is the conversation mainly about?

(A) Employees in the accounting department
(B) Reducing expenses
(C) Environmental problems
(D) Increasing the company budget

63. Look at the graphic. According to Brianna, what could be lowered?

(A) Telephone
(B) Electricity
(C) Water
(D) Gas

64. What will the man ask Brianna to do?

(A) Give a presentation at the meeting
(B) Hold a meeting
(C) Promote to one of the board members
(D) Retire in honor

GO ON TO THE NEXT PAGE

Program

Subject	Time
Compliance	09:30 ~ 10:00
Corporate Ethics	10:00 ~ 10:30
Work Efficiency	10:30 ~ 11:00
Innovations	11:00 ~ 11:30

Room A	Room B
Shelby Banker : "Basic Networking Skills"	Haywood Fassett : "Sales skill for Beginners"
Isaias Marrow : "Online Marketing"	Preston Ordway : "Effective Communication Skills in the Workplace"
Snacks and refreshments	Walker Essex : "Advertising Trends"
Kelly Dustin : "How to Advertise on TV"	Dinner Party (until 8 P.M.)

65. What problem does the man report?

(A) The convention place will be changed.
(B) Some equipment is out of order.
(C) A presenter will not be available.
(D) The subject has not yet been decided.

66. Look at the graphic. What will the final topic be?

(A) Compliance
(B) Corporate ethics
(C) Work efficiency
(D) Innovations

67. What will the woman do next?

(A) Replace Ms. Roosevelt with a new speaker
(B) Look for another place
(C) Help to prepare for a convention
(D) Contact the participants of the conference

68. Where will the conversation most likely take place?

(A) At a market
(B) At a parking lot
(C) At a conference
(D) At a company picnic

69. Look at the graphic. Whose session is the woman planning to go to first?

(A) Shelby Banker's
(B) Haywood Fassett's
(C) Preston Ordway's
(D) Walker Essex'

70. What does the woman recommend for the man to do?

(A) Skip Walker's speech
(B) Eat before the event is over
(C) Get refreshments from Room A
(D) Meet a presenter at the party after Kelly's talk

PART 4

Directions: You will hear some talks given by a single speaker. You will be asked to answer three questions about what the speakers say in each talk. Select the best response to each question and mark the letter (A), (B), (C), or (D) on your answer sheet. The talks will not be printed in your test book and will be spoken only one time.

71. What time will the passengers board the ship?

    (A) At 6:00 A.M.
    (B) At 8:00 A.M.
    (C) At 9:00 A.M.
    (D) At 10:00 A.M.

72. How long should a passport be valid after the date of return?

    (A) For one month
    (B) For two months
    (C) For three months
    (D) For six months

73. What country doesn't charge travelers who don't have valid passports?

    (A) Haiti
    (B) Puerto Rico
    (C) Dominican Republic
    (D) Panama

74. What is this advertisement about?

    (A) A head hunting service
    (B) An education service
    (C) An advertisement service
    (D) A promotion service

75. How long has Ace Manpower Service been in this business?

    (A) It just started.
    (B) For about two years
    (C) For about twelve years
    (D) For about twenty years

76. What happened to Ace Manpower Service recently?

    (A) Find itself buried in work
    (B) Dismiss its employees
    (C) Develop its business throughout the state
    (D) Train new workers

77. According to the speaker, where does the train pass?

    (A) Around the Travelers Information Center
    (B) Around the suburbs of Curitiba
    (C) Around downtown Curitiba
    (D) To the Curitiba city hall

78. How long does the trip last?

    (A) Half an hour
    (B) An hour
    (C) An hour and half an hour
    (D) Two hours

79. How can tickets for the urban circulation railway be obtained?

    (A) Through a lottery
    (B) Through the Internet
    (C) By waiting in line
    (D) By making reservations

80. Who will most likely be interested in the convention?

    (A) A manager
    (B) A buyer
    (C) A technician
    (D) A sales man

81. According to the speaker, what does option 9 inform of the listeners?

    (A) How to register
    (B) The time of coffee break
    (C) The hotel prices
    (D) The script for extension

82. Where is the speaker now?

    (A) In a hotel room
    (B) In a restaurant
    (C) In a staff meeting room
    (D) At the information desk

GO ON TO THE NEXT PAGE

83. What is this announcement mainly about?
   (A) The benefits of the hotels in the Canada
   (B) The steps to take when you lose luggage
   (C) The location of the lost and found
   (D) The insurance policy for missing baggage

84. What should passengers do first when they lose their baggage?
   (A) Make a claim for lost luggage
   (B) Call the airport
   (C) Go to the Lost and Found
   (D) Ask the airline for the location

85. What should the passengers offer to the Lost and Found?
   (A) The weight of their luggage
   (B) The receptionist's name and address
   (C) The name and the number of their accommodation
   (D) The cost of the delivery

86. What is true about Cindy's Yoga Video?
   (A) It is reasonable, but non-refundable.
   (B) It is intended for adults only.
   (C) It requires other equipment to increase effect.
   (D) It is very useful to improve people's figures.

87. How can the listeners pay their money?
   (A) By check
   (B) By cash
   (C) By credit card
   (D) By wire

88. What should the listeners do when they are not satisfied with the Cindy's Yoga Video?
   (A) Ask for an exchange to the company
   (B) Return the product with a fee of $14.00
   (C) Just call off the order within 14 days
   (D) Forward the bill immediately

89. What does Ms. Nancy Farley mention about today's workshop?
   (A) It offers the chance of job search to the listeners.
   (B) It enables the banks to increase their profits.
   (C) It informs the participants how to protect their money.
   (D) It advises the businessman to merge the competitors.

90. Why does the speaker say, "there will be a good thing"?
   (A) To introduce something useful
   (B) To mention a new service
   (C) To notify what she wanted
   (D) To hold a workshop

91. What will be included in Mr. Collins' folder?
   (A) The addressor's resume
   (B) Information on investing
   (C) A workshop survey sheet
   (D) A bank account application form

92. Who is the intended audience for the talk?
   (A) Restaurant owners
   (B) Corporate employees
   (C) Vending machine sellers
   (D) Coffee baristas

93. What does the speaker imply when he says, "there's a catch"?
   (A) He wonders whether people are listening.
   (B) He thinks the company overpaid for a device.
   (C) He wants to solve a problem.
   (D) He likes the new machine.

94. What does the speaker ask the listeners to do?
   (A) Call a new supplier for the coffee pods
   (B) Replace a machine with new one
   (C) Go outside for their drinking coffees
   (D) Pay a contribution for drinks

Menu

Kid's Meal	Dessert
Crispy Coconut Shrimp	Grapefruit Sherbet
St. Louis Pork Ribs	Fruit Parfait
Chicken Strips	Strawberry Ice Cream
Pastrami Spring Rolls	Coffee Jelly

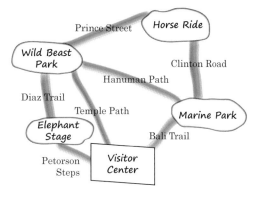

95. Who will Parker Reed most likely be?

(A) A cook
(B) A driver
(C) A waiter
(D) A owner

96. Look at the graphic. What dessert does the recommended kid's meal come with?

(A) Grapefruit Sherbet
(B) Fruit Parfait
(C) Strawberry Ice Cream
(D) Coffee Jelly

97. What will the speaker do next?

(A) Take orders
(B) Watch the menu
(C) Wait for the kids
(D) Bring the dessert in

98. Who is the announcement intended for?

(A) Employees
(B) Guides
(C) Tourists
(D) Hunters

99. Look at the graphic. Where will the listeners be unable to go today?

(A) The Visitor Center
(B) The Marine Park
(C) The Wild Beast Park
(D) The Elephant Stage

100. What does the speaker encourage the listeners to do?

(A) Borrow an umbrella
(B) Obtain a map
(C) Wear sunglasses
(D) Bring their own lunch

This is the end of the Listening test. Turn to Part 5 in your text book.

READING TEST

In the Reading test, you will read a variety of texts and answer several different types of reading comprehension questions. The entire Reading test will last 75 minutes. There are three parts, and directions are given for each part. You are encouraged to answer as many questions as possible within the time allowed.

You must mark your answers on the separate answer sheet. Do not write your answers in your test book.

PART 5

Directions: A word or phrase is missing in each of the sentences below. Four answer choices are given below each sentence. Select the best answer to complete the sentence. Then mark the letter (A), (B), (C), or (D) on your answer sheet.

---

101. Our spacious guest rooms ------- with wireless Internet service provide a comfortable haven for you.

(A) equip
(B) equipped
(C) equipping
(D) to equip

102. As Fullerton Bay Hotel ------- the beautiful landscape of downtown Singapore, it is the perfect venue for any casual event.

(A) disregards
(B) overlooks
(C) encounters
(D) sustains

103. Our resourceful and multilingual floor managers stationed on each floor will be helpful, ------- you arrange your business or personal meetings.

(A) on
(B) during
(C) when
(D) meantime

104. It's unique because it can be built ------- all kinds of printing devices.

(A) to
(B) as
(C) onto
(D) into

105. Despite the ------- with the awfully designed package, the actual software is pretty good.

(A) statistics
(B) coverage
(C) flaw
(D) variety

106. For females in their 70s, the death rate was below 30.5% but climbed to 67.5% for ------- in their 80s.

(A) her
(B) them
(C) that
(D) those

107. Clake Quay Cafe offers nightly piano, saxophone, and clarinet performances from 7 P.M. ------- 2:00 A.M. and live concerts of talented underground artists.

(A) through
(B) about
(C) by
(D) toward

108. An assistant of -------, Ms. Bree Jackson, brought this feedback site to my attention.

(A) my
(B) mine
(C) me
(D) myself

109. All facilities are ------- serviced by expressly trained staff to make sure that you have a relaxing and healthy experience.
(A) remotely
(B) collaboratively
(C) impeccably
(D) comparatively

110. Ms. Lilly's presentation is scheduled to begin ------- approximately 10:00 A.M.
(A) at
(B) on
(C) in
(D) for

111. Please show your voucher to pick up your goods one or two hours ------- departure at the Duty Free counter in the airport.
(A) after
(B) before
(C) on
(D) amid

112. ------- you want to take a leisurely stroll or a rigorous power walk, Golden Bell Tours provides a course to suit your needs.
(A) When
(B) If
(C) Whether
(D) Because

113. With its rich array of colors, warm decoration, and classic ambiance, Forever Wedding Hall will convey ------- to every guest.
(A) grace
(B) simplicity
(C) luxury
(D) elegance

114. Upon the completion of reservation, your data will be transmitted to our reservation manager and stored in a database -------.
(A) immensely
(B) exclusively
(C) personally
(D) simultaneously

115. Many posters and leaflets were distributed ------- throughout the region in hopes of finding the perfect applicants.
(A) wide
(B) widely
(C) wideness
(D) widen

116. Before you order at Chinese restaurants, make sure that they do not use MSG, which scientists say causes headaches and other ------- effects.
(A) uniform
(B) adverse
(C) subsequent
(D) remarkable

117. You may check your reservation status and cancel your reservations ------- logging in and going to the Confirm Menu on the left.
(A) as
(B) by
(C) for
(D) through

118. Unimark Design Group has consistently impressed me with its ------- and originality.
(A) creativity
(B) authenticity
(C) sincerity
(D) compromise

119. These terms and conditions will become effective ------- a member receives his membership identification number.
(A) provided that
(B) whereas
(C) unless
(D) until

120. Trojan inner Circle is not in ------- of any loss of benefits due to reservations made without using membership card.
(A) support
(B) charge
(C) observance
(D) anticipation

GO ON TO THE NEXT PAGE

121. For international workers, these will be sent to your department for you to collect ------- arrival.

(A) as soon as
(B) upon
(C) concurrently
(D) with

122. Reference has been made to ------- the expenses when complaints are proven.

(A) discount
(B) raise
(C) accept
(D) reimburse

123. ------- our worldwide reputation has been built steadily over these 30 years, we will continue to expand our standards of excellence.

(A) Unless
(B) Although
(C) When
(D) Before

124. ------- ongoing problems with its structure, the office building will be investigated by structural engineers.

(A) In charge of
(B) As a result of
(C) In addition to
(D) In anticipation for

125. The guesthouse is ------- entirely reserved for the weekend, but some rooms are on hold for regular guests at $250 a night.

(A) well
(B) soon
(C) already
(D) ever

126. So as to revise the billing error, you can request a renewed invoice ------- send us the original shipping documents.

(A) additionally
(B) and also
(C) or else
(D) insomuch as

127. Our total safety and security system makes commitment to your safety and protects your office from burglars ------- the night and vacation time.

(A) for
(B) in
(C) to
(D) during

128. Since its opening in 2010, we have made every effort to provide our distinguished guests with state-of-the-art, -------, and impeccable services and facilities.

(A) conditional
(B) essential
(C) convenient
(D) periodic

129. Without your help, we could not have figured out ------- caused such an enormous deficit.

(A) that
(B) who
(C) which
(D) what

130. ------- your banquet will be held, we will bring all the dignity and elegance of great cuisine and complete service to you.

(A) Which
(B) What
(C) When
(D) Wherever

PART 6

Directions: Read the texts that follow. A word, phrase, or sentence is missing in parts of each text. Four answer choices for each question are given below the text. Select the best answer to complete the text. Then mark the letter (A), (B), (C), or (D) on your answer sheet.

Questions 131-134 refer to the following advertisement.

JOB OPENING

RECEPTIONIST

The ------- candidate would be professional, friendly, a quick learner, and enthusiastic
    131.
about the fitness industry. Good communication skills are absolutely necessary. Previous

gym experience is not a requirement but is a definite -------.
                 132.

Responsibilities include making guests feel welcomed, answering phones, processing

payments and assisting co-workers as -------. As well as being outgoing and friendly, the
               133.
best candidate will also have experience in data entry. ------- .
                      134.

131. (A) residential
    (B) industrious
    (C) considerate
    (D) ideal

132. (A) reward
    (B) asset
    (C) worth
    (D) benefit

133. (A) need
    (B) needs
    (C) needed
    (D) needing

134. (A) If you want to be part of the exciting world of fitness, please send a cover letter and resume to us.
    (B) Even if you have any questions, don't try to call me.
    (C) Give me a call, whether you have arranged the meeting or not.
    (D) Make sure the position is best to you.

GO ON TO THE NEXT PAGE ➤

Questions 135-138 refer to the following letter.

Dear Ms. Linda Plowman:

I regret to inform you that Verizon Wireless Co. no longer requires your services as a sales representative at our Basing Ridge, New Jersey location. Your termination is ------- **135.** immediately. Our disappointment in your work is not only due to your poor sales record. ------- **136.** . You frequently arrive late to work and often take lunches much longer than one hour allowed.

------- **137.** that termination could be avoided, we invested in additional training for you. We also gave you a warning three weeks ago that your sales numbers and work habits would have to improve or you would risk termination. I ------- **138.** your final check.

Sincerely,

Eric Watterson

General Manager, Verizon Wireless Co.

135. (A) effective
(B) increasing
(C) accidental
(D) reluctant

136. (A) Your termination should have been avoided.
(B) We warn you not to arrive late to work.
(C) We want your sales numbers to improve dramatically.
(D) You have also failed to demonstrate interest in the job.

137. (A) Hope
(B) Hoped
(C) Hoping
(D) To hope

138. (A) enclosed
(B) have enclosed
(C) will enclose
(D) will have enclosed

To: Maintenance Personnel

From: Lynn Dixon

Subject: Monthly Cleaning

Date: July 15, 2016

The maintenance personnel is advised to conduct the monthly cleaning and -------
139.
equipment check on July 22 instead of July 30. ------- . Conducting the inspection will
140.
be the top executives of the company including the board of directors and some major

investors.

Everyone is expected to comply with every directive coming from my office ------- better
141.
prepare for the event. ------- have branches in different parts of the world including
142.
Singapore, Australia, and the United States.

139. (A) previous
(B) comprehensive
(C) intensive
(D) regular

140. (A) Human resources department asks
every employee to clean their desks.
(B) The top executives of the company
exclude all directors and investors.
(C) This is to accommodate the change
in schedule of the company-wide
inspection for the month of July.
(D) It is good to comply with every order
upon request.

141. (A) in order to
(B) as well as
(C) so that
(D) for the purpose of

142. (A) We
(B) You
(C) They
(D) These

GO ON TO THE NEXT PAGE

Test 01
Test 02
Test 03
Test 04
Test 05

Questions 143-146 refer to the following article.

Retail Giant W-Mart announced last month its first earnings drop in five years, ------- can

143.

be attributed to its withdrawal from England and weak America sales at a time of rising

fuel prices. The America-based chain also said that its third quarter net profit ------- by

144.

24% to $1.88 billion, after it booked a charge of $767 million for the sale of its England

stores to Euro Store Inc. But at 68 cents a share, the company's earnings not including the

proceeds from the sale were well within what Wall Street forecasters were expecting for

the three months to July 30.

The company's revenues rose 12.4% from the same quarter of 2015 to $83.45 billion.

------- . However, the company's president Sean Phillip raises that the company will be able

145.

to post higher sales figures in the next quarter ------- the America economy is expected to

146.

grow in the second half of the year.

143. (A) who
(B) whom
(C) whose
(D) which

144. (A) released
(B) abandoned
(C) dropped
(D) dumped

145. (A) The company's president Sean
Phillip announced last week its first
earnings drop in ten years.
(B) That was below the consensus
forecast made by Almighty
Consulting of $85.35 billion.
(C) Retail Giant W-Mart wonders whether
the company will post higher sales
figures in the coming quarters or not.
(D) All forecasters of Almighty Consulting
were expecting the increase of the
sales figures.

146. (A) as
(B) before
(C) until
(D) unless

PART 7

Directions: In this part you will read a selection of texts, such as magazine and newspaper articles, e-mails, and instant messages. Each text or set of texts is followed by several questions. Select the best answer for each question and mark the letter (A), (B), (C), or (D) on your answer sheet.

Questions 147-148 refer to the following text messages.

Luke Camara	4:12 P.M.
Did you hear that Mr. Suzuki is coming back from his business trip to Nagoya office earlier than the schedule?	
Sam Thelen	4:14 P.M.
No, I didn't. When is he back?	
Luke Camara	4:15 P.M.
Tomorrow. Apparently, as the clients signed immediately there is no more job he has to do.	
Sam Thelen	4:16 P.M.
How about that!	
Luke Camara	4:17 P.M.
Yeah! I know. I'm so happy for his coming soon. We really need him to help with our latest ad campaign.	
Sam Thelen	4:25 P.M.
Are you going to meet him at the airport tomorrow morning at 8:00?	
Luke Camara	4:30 P.M.
No. I think it's better for him to take a taxi, as it is too early in the morning.	
Sam Thelen	4:31 P.M.
Oh! You are right. Anyway, let me know if there is any change.	

147. What is mentioned about Mr. Suzuki?

(A) He will return from a trip ahead of schedule.
(B) He works in the Nagoya office.
(C) He is a company president.
(D) He has requested a pickup at the airport.

148. At 4:16 P.M., why does Mr. Thelen write, "How about that"?

(A) He would like to hear an opinion.
(B) He is pleasantly surprised.
(C) He is making a suggestion.
(D) He will demonstrate a tool.

GO ON TO THE NEXT PAGE →

Questions 149-150 refer to the following message.

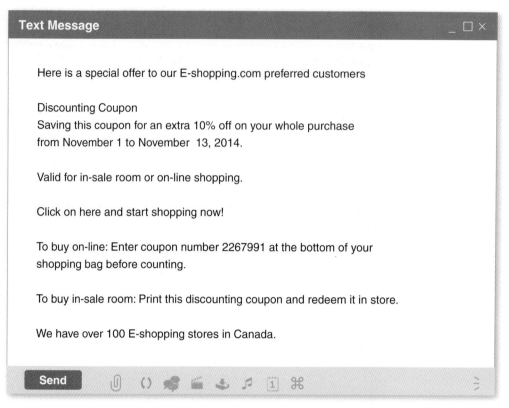

Here is a special offer to our E-shopping.com preferred customers

Discounting Coupon
Saving this coupon for an extra 10% off on your whole purchase
from November 1 to November 13, 2014.

Valid for in-sale room or on-line shopping.

Click on here and start shopping now!

To buy on-line: Enter coupon number 2267991 at the bottom of your
shopping bag before counting.

To buy in-sale room: Print this discounting coupon and redeem it in store.

We have over 100 E-shopping stores in Canada.

149. What advantage can customers get by
using this coupon?
(A) They can use all the E-shopping
stores in Canada.
(B) They can save 10% more on their
purchase.
(C) They can get a full refund for any
products .
(D) They can shop both online and in-
sale room.

150. According to the advertisement, what do
customers need to do to shop online?
(A) Fill out a form
(B) Show their ID cards
(C) Call a E-shopping store
(D) Enter a coupon code

Secondhand Car Work-list

You can calculate the cost of each vehicle which is your considering from use a copy of empty work-list. However, you have to make sure the fees are reasonable before agree to payment with them and require the dealer explains about additional costs.
Dealers and financial institutions have to reveal the entire interest rate information and the total amount to be paid.

Vehicle Manufacturer: _____   Model: _____

Boday Style: _____   Year: _____

Market price $ _____
  +State and/or Provincial taxes $ _____
  +License taxes $ _____
  +Additional costs $ _____
  =Total purchase fee $ _____
  -Trade-in allowance $ _____
  =Total amount paid $ _____
  -Earnest money $ _____
  =Amount to be raise funds $ _____
  +interest $ _____

_____ months at _____ percent
annual percentage rate(APR)

=Total amount to be paid $ _____
(_____ monthly payments of $ _____ in each)

151. What is this work-list for?
(A) Calculating interest for a loan
(B) Informing employees of a company's expenditure
(C) Calculating the cost for buying a secondhand car
(D) Estimating repairing fees for a secondhand car

152. Which of the following will NOT be included in this work-list?
(A) Vehicle model
(B) Interest rate
(C) Dealer commission
(D) Total amount to be paid

GO ON TO THE NEXT PAGE

May 12, 2014
To all staffs :

This is a kind of our attention and it comes to us. Our attention which is the sharing of software has become a common practice in our office. While this may look like to many to be a trivial and common-place event, in fact it is the kind of activity that puts our firm at danger. First, it is the legal issue that we probably possibility to face with illegal copying of software products which is already registered. So this area has several lawsuits and often take place in the past few years, and the settlement amounts have not been trivial, to say the least.

More important to routine business operation is the growth problem such as data security and integrity. Such as the overwhelming insurgence of computer viruses, spywars, worms, Trojans and many different types of terrible devices which travel via software recently, the software's transmission that perhaps unaware harboring like threat is a potentially dangerous act.

We have to ask that this practice stop quickly. If further abuses continue and are found, some form of penalty has to be allocated. Your cooperation is sincerely requested in this effort.

The management.

153. What is the purpose of this letter?
(A) To encourage the sharing of electronic media among employees
(B) To make the average employee more aware of common practices
(C) To request that employee refrain from passing software to coworkers
(D) To threaten the increasing use of computer penalties on the market

154. Which of these was NOT related with a risk in data sharing?
(A) The increase in computer-transmitted viruses
(B) The possibility of receiving financial penalty
(C) The risk of damage to data
(D) The threat to good relations with the customers involved

Questions 155-157 refer to the following article.

Australia Oyster Industry Closed by Red Tide

Almost of Oyster farms have been closing in Australia due to the fact that there were the worst algae bloom in the area since the early 1980s. ---[1]---. For the third time in two years, the large and dense spots of red algae have presented in coastal waters from Perth to Adelaide. ---[2]---. Red tide algae should be included neurotoxins which can be poisonous to fish and other oceanic life. ---[3]---. These kinds of toxins can be spreaded to animals that have been eating those creatures including humans and living on the land, it can cause very serious intestinal and neurological disorders. ---[4]---.

While the algae found in the southeast tend not to be as toxic as those found further north, the Ministry of Maritime Affairs and Fisheries has mandated the shutdown of all oyster farms wherever the red tide has presented, and sent scientists to monitor toxin levels up and down the coast.

The red tide phenomenon takes place naturally, a lot of scientists believe that this kind of phenomenon occurring frequently due to the fact that nutrients running into the sea from industrial areas all along the Australia coastline. A 2001 Ministry of Maritime Affairs and Fisheries report examining the problem of nutrient over-enrichment in coastal waters concluded that human activity played a main role in increasing oceanic algae levels, including species of algae known to contaminate seafood. The oyster farms are expected to maintain closed indefinitely.

155. What is correct about the algae bloom in Australia?

(A) It started in eastern waters.
(B) It is not harmful to oyster.
(C) It also occurred the previous year.
(D) It occurs every two years, on average.

156. What is the Ministry of Maritime Affairs and Fisheries said to be doing?

(A) Spreading a chemical to kill the red tide algae
(B) Measuring red tide toxin levels found in the ocean
(C) Looking for ways to lower the levels of toxin in red tide algae
(D) Working to identify the species of algae responsible for red tide

157. In which of the positions marked [1], [2], [3], and [4] does the following sentence best belong?

"This is a natural phenomenon which is called red tide."

(A) [1]
(B) [2]
(C) [3]
(D) [4]

GO ON TO THE NEXT PAGE

Questions 158-160 refer to the following list.

List of Selected Private Schools

All Asia Comprehensive database
Characters more than 15,000 schools across Asia.
- Includes Army, Naval Service, Military, Christian, Residential & Day Boarding Schools.
- Database covers School Name, address, City, Headmaster Name (50%), Email(15%), Phone.
- Ideal for ad agencies, telemarketing companies, finance companies, banks, corporate, direct marketing agencies and others marketers.

Region	Data Count
North Asian Schools (Han-Kuk, JP, Shinjuku, Pergy and K & Y)	4,900
South Asian Schools (Gong-Lo, Melton, AL, Wahingon)	3,700
Western Region Schools (Mashuri, Tokyo, Gang-Nam, HG, Reing)	3,200
Eastern Region Schools (East Beling, Airlong, Asina etc.)	3,300

Price : Rs. 850/-for the full database. Shipping / VPP charges Rs.20 additional.
(VPP orders are delivered from the Asian Postal Service and allow you to pay in cash upon receiving the CD.)
Note : Database in not sold respectively region wise. You have to purchase the full database, which comes in Excel format and is delivered on a CD.
To order by VPP (Cash on delivery) :
Offer your company name, address, and reach person. We will send the CD by VPP. Delivery anywhere in Asia. You need to pay Rs. 850/- + 20. i.e. Rs. 870/-to the postman at the time of delivery. Order NOW!
We also have more databases as the following below:
CEOs, Newest Investors, Latest Mobile Bosses, Schools, Salaried Managements and many more. If more detailed information, please emil us.

158. What type of firm is this list from?

(A) An educational resource development company
(B) A mailing list supplier and handler
(C) A data-analysis firm
(D) An advertising agency

159. What is the price if shipment is made to Han-Kuk?

(A) Rs. 4,900
(B) Rs. 850
(C) Rs. 870
(D) Rs. 3,200

160. Which one is NOT included in the database data?

(A) The name of the principal of the school
(B) The email address of the school
(C) The finance company of the school
(D) The school's phone number

THE BUILDING DISTRICT
RECYCLE HERE FOR THE YEAR

REMOVE SCHEDULE

11 A.M. - 3 P.M. ON THE FOLLOWING DATES
JUNE 20   AUGUST 15   OCTOBER 16   DECEMBER 14

Item	Price	Explanation
Tires	$2	Remove rims, please. Less than 19 inches.
Furnitures	$16	More than 20kg, Pay $11
Big scale Machines	$6	Microwave, Washers, Oven, and so on.
Electronic Goods	$6	Computer body, monitors, DVD and video players, stereos, and so on (no mobile phones).
Fax Machines, Printers, Copiers	$11	
TV	$16	Up to 18-inch screen size
	$21	21-inch and more

Dispose of your items at Building District, 124 Wilson St, Virginia, VG 12085. For detail information contact (451)545-5032 or visit www. buildingdistrict.com.

Volunteers needed on collection days!

---

161. When would it be possible to recycle goods at The Building District?

(A) On June 21 at noon
(B) On August 15 at 1 P.M.
(C) On October 16 at 4 P.M.
(D) On December 14 at 9 A.M.

162. Which of the following electronics would not include for recycling?

(A) Stereos
(B) DVD players
(C) Cell phones
(D) Computer towers

163. How much will The Building District pay for a microwave?

(A) $6
(B) $11
(C) $16
(D) $21

164. What is a limitation on recycling tires at The Building District?

(A) They must have no punctures.
(B) They must be 19 inches or smaller
(C) They must be delivered before noon.
(D) They must weigh no more than 25 pounds each.

GO ON TO THE NEXT PAGE

Questions 165-167 refer to the following announcement.

Long-term Institution Breakfast

The Long-term Institution will be held 10th annual fundraising community breakfast at 7:40 a.m, July. 27 at the Grand Hall Hotel. The kind of coffee and conversation will commence at 7:10 a.m As the education, business, political, and parent communities start the new semester in school, Jack Doson who is in charge of a superintendent of educational affairs, will announce his state of the district address.

Julia Kim and Mack Tailor announced a record-breaking six supporters who donated $3,500 respectively. These supporters include Beny Group, Hin Town, Kant association, City-Life Bank, Maton hospital, and GPV telecommunication.

Tickets for the breakfast are $30 a person and are available from Cindy Chang at the Long-term Institution office at (313) 254-9854.

---

165. What is true about the Long-term Institution Community Breakfast?

(A) It costs $30 to attend.
(B) It is in its 13th year.
(C) It will have live music.
(D) It is a benefit for a school.

166. Who will make a speech at the event?

(A) Mack Tailor
(B) Cindy Chang
(C) Julia Kim
(D) Jack Doson

167. Why is Beny Group mentioned?

(A) It is hosting the event.
(B) It was the event's first sponsor.
(C) It paid all the expenses for the event.
(D) It made a large financial contribution.

Julie Kwon 10:13 A.M.	You know what? Leed's & Partners inquired about our application software. I need your opinion before I meet with them.
Akim Hasanov 10:14 A.M.	Oh, it's one of the largest law firms in the country, right?
Julie Kwon 10:15 A.M.	Yeah. They're telling us that they want a better client management software which of Miyo Technologies they're using now.
Ping Liu 10:17 A.M.	Miyo Technologies, one of our competitions? I know quite a lot about their programs. One of their programs' drawbacks is usage. Theirs are a little hard to use.
Julie Kwon 10:18 A.M.	Oh, good! Ping, can you make notes on their drawbacks in details and e-mail them to me?
Ping Liu 10:19 A.M.	No problem! I'll get on it right now.
Akim Hasanov 10:20 A.M.	Maybe, I should make a presentation material for explaining our merits to our potential clients. As you all know, I'm good at graphics.
Julie Kwon 10:21 A.M.	Thank you, that must be a great help.
Ping Liu 10:22 A.M.	Akim, I'll send you the detailed information on the rival's program as well.
Julie Kwon 10:23 A.M.	Thanks, I think we are all set.

168. What type of business does the potential client own?

(A) An accounting firm
(B) A software developer
(C) A graphic design firm
(D) A law office

169. What is mentioned about Miyo Technologies?

(A) It is focused on producing hardware.
(B) Its sales are far greater that the writers'.
(C) It failed to reach an agreement with Leed's &Partners.
(D) It is the writers' rival company.

170. What will Ms. Liu most likely do next?

(A) Contact her client
(B) Help prepare a document
(C) Give a demonstration
(D) Send her work sample via e-mail

171. At 10:23 A.M., what does Ms. Kwon mean when she writes, "I think we are all set"?

(A) She will set tables.
(B) She does not expect suggestions by the others.
(C) She will help marketing research.
(D) She is satisfied with the outcome of the discussion.

GO ON TO THE NEXT PAGE

Test 01 Test 02 Test 03 Test 04 Test 05

Questions 172-175 refer to the following introduction.

ANNOUNCEMENT
SUGGESTED PURCHASERS OF REAL PROPERTY COMPANY

According to Real Property Committee regulations, the person concerned with real property should understand peculiar and valuable role that real property middlemen and their companies play in real property market. The peculiar and valuable role has been defined over the years by law and custom. The contents are simply show up you about that role:

1) Middlemen and their agents may be hired in order to represent party for a real property business.
2) According to the usage, unless a buyer has a contract with a middleman that the middleman and the middleman's agent will show the buyer's interest items, the middleman's agents will show the list to the seller.
3) The person, the middleman and the middleman's agent represent is normally called the "client", and the other party is normally called the "customer".
4) The middleman and the middleman's agents ought to reveal, and also have honesty and sincerity. Simultaneously, middlemen and their agents have to treat all parties in a transaction fairly.

The Multicom Firm is the listing middleman in the business field. They represent instead of the seller and will be paid an allowance by the seller.

THE RELINQUISHMENT OF LEGAL CLAIM

---[1]---. The Multicom Firm and owners do not mark a guarantee about accuracy, and all buyers are supposed to expect on their financial goal. ---[2]---.
The financial statements which are already prepared are subject to mistakes, abbreviations and changes, which are or may be unknown to The Multicom Firm.
---[3]---. And also, if you have any questions after reading the reference, please ask the middleman or seek advisory committee. ---[4]---.

172. What will the person represented by the broker and the broker's agent be called?

(A) The Multicom Firm
(B) Customer
(C) Real Property Committee
(D) Client

173. How does The Multicom Firm get paid?

(A) By the seller
(B) By the disclaimer
(C) By allowance
(D) By the agent

174. What is NOT mentioned in this notice?

(A) The middleman and the middleman's agents owe the client duties of loyalty.
(B) The agency will gather all the clients and customers.
(C) The role has been defined as both custom and law.
(D) All purchasers should rely on their financial goals.

175. In which of the positions marked [1], [2], [3], and [4] does the following sentence best belong?

"This notice is for your reference materials."

(A) [1]
(B) [2]
(C) [3]
(D) [4]

GO ON TO THE NEXT PAGE

Questions 176-180 refer to the following two e-mails.

To: Customer Service <bookcs@books.com>
From: Michael Hector <mchlhctr@nifty.com>
Re: Lost book

To Whom it May Concern:

I am writing to inquire about The Mechanic's Handbook 4th edition I ordered through
your company. The order number is 34756. I ordered the book last month and still
have not received the book. I visited your website and confirmed that my shipping
information was correct, and that my credit card has been charged for the book; the
website also indicates that the book was shipped using your "Groundhog" service
the day after I ordered it. Considering that "Groundhog" shipments typically take two
weeks to arrive, I should have received my goods a week ago. However, my post
office informed me they have neither received nor delivered the book. Can you please
let me know what is going on as soon as possible?

Michael Hector

To	Michael Hector <mchlhctr@nifty.com>
From	Online New and Used Books <bookcs@books.com>
Subject	Re: Lost book

Dear Mr. Michael Hector,

Thank you for contacting us. Customer satisfaction is our first priority so I am
very sorry to hear that you have not received your merchandise. I looked up your
order number and discovered that the book had not been sent out as our website
information had indicated. I have rectified this mistake and sent the book to you
via express mail. It should arrive within two business days. With the book I have
also enclosed a coupon for half off your next order.

Again, I apologize for the inconvenience. If you have any more questions or need
further assistance, please contact me at 505-576-3800, or e-mail me at bookcs@
books.com.

Your business and concerns are deeply appreciated.

Sincerely,
Online Used and New Books
Lisa Forest, Customer Affairs

176. Why did Mr. Michael Hector send his e-mail?

(A) To request an update on new books
(B) To receive a technical manual
(C) To track down a missing item
(D) To cancel an order for merchandise

177. What is suggested about the order?

(A) The same product was charged for twice.
(B) The item was delivered to the wrong address.
(C) The book has been out of print.
(D) The payment for the order was accepted.

178. What error did the website contain?

(A) The order number was wrong.
(B) It indicated that the item had been shipped.
(C) Mr. Hector's address was incomplete.
(D) The price list has not been updated yet.

179. How did the company attempt to compensate the customer?

(A) They sent him a free book.
(B) They gave him the book for half price.
(C) They removed the charge from his credit card.
(D) They gave him a discount voucher.

180. Which of the following will be inferred?

(A) Mr. Hector placed his order 3 weeks ago.
(B) All of the orders are made by express mail.
(C) The book was sent out a month ago.
(D) The cost of delivery was included in the book's price.

GO ON TO THE NEXT PAGE

Questions 181-185 refer to the following order form and e-mail.

PURCHASE ORDER #322−C12   DATE: 6/4/16

Customer Name	Strongman Ltd.
Street Address	190 Woodward
City, State, Postal Code	Pelhan, AL, 35124
Telephone	(205) 988-3350
E-mail	strongman@strongmanltd.org
Customer ID Code	ZE441-DC22

Quantity	Item Number	Description	Price per Unit	Total
40	B24	12'x2'x4' wooden beams	$8.00	$320.00
16	S46	4'x6' plywood sheets	$12.50	$200.00
20	B16	12'x1'x6' wooden boards	$9.50	$190.00
1 box	N144	1000 flat-head carpentry nails	$11.00	$11.00
2 bottles	G6	24 oz. wood glue	$8.50	$17.00

Subtotal: $738.00

| From | Raymond Murphy <raymondbest@msn.com> |
| To | Strongman Ltd. <strongman@strongmanltd.org> |

Dear Strongman Ltd.:

Thank you for your business with us. We have received your Purchase Order Number 322-C12, dated 6-4-16. However, we regret to inform you that this order cannot be filled in its entirety at this time due to the following reason:
Item #G6 (True-Bond Adhesive) is temporarily out of stock.

To better serve you, we can substitute a comparable product (#G11, Woodlock Carpenter's Glue) and reduce the price to match that of item #G6. We will neither substitute items nor send backordered items later without our customer's direct consent, so you must reply to this e-mail and tell us how you wish to proceed. Otherwise, your partial order will be shipped on 6-9-06 and you will be contacted by a representative when we receive our next delivery of item #G6.

Best Regards,
Raymond Murphy

181. What does the most portion of the order consist of?

(A) Appliances
(B) Adhesive
(C) Lumber
(D) Tools

182. What is the purpose of the e-mail?

(A) To introduce a newly-arrived product
(B) To cancel an order from a supplier
(C) To announce a change in the price of goods
(D) To explain that an item is not available at the moment

183. What does Mr. Raymond Murphy say about the order?

(A) Item #G6 has been discontinued.
(B) A comparable adhesive is available.
(C) The order form was not filled out correctly.
(D) Each item will be delivered separately.

184. In the e-mail, the word "match" in paragraph 2, line 2 is closest in meaning to.

(A) meet
(B) combine
(C) fix
(D) charge

185. How can a customer get a backordered item?

(A) By checking a box on the purchase order
(B) By contacting Raymond Murphy online
(C) By accepting a substitute item
(D) By providing an alternative shipping address

GO ON TO THE NEXT PAGE

CABINS WITH YOU

Come Spend a Lovely Summer in the Kansas Countryside!
Our beautiful, quaint cabins nestled among the brooks and small country roads of southern Hays county offer the perfect balance of summer getaway and modern conveniences. Each of our packages includes:

* A one-bedroom cottage with luxurious furnishings and modern appliances
* Our premium breakfast service (experience a traditional American breakfast!)
* Free rounding in Winston's Golf Course, just 5 minutes by car
* A complimentary bottle of either white or red wine

Cottages are available Easter through the end of September. Weekly rates start from roughly $300. Recommended to reserve in advance, by phone at (785) 628-4387 or online at www.cabinwithyou.org.

Reservation Form

Check in : 06/01/2017
Time : 03:00 PM
Check out : 06/14/2017
(Check out time is 11:00 A.M., please use the comment form to arrange a later check out. An additional fee will be charged per hour.)

Please indicate your preferred complimentary wine:
√ Red (Goodman's Premium Merlot)
___ White (Greenwood Sauvignon Blanc)

Please write any comments or special requests below:

Hello,
I found your cabins through an Internet web surfing, and they all look absolutely beautiful and unique. My wife and I would like to arrange a stay of two weeks in June, but I have several requests to you.
First, my wife suffers from a heavy illness and has difficulty in walking. She usually uses a cane to walk, but on bad days she needs to use a wheelchair. I would like to reserve a cabin at the bottom of the hill to make it easier for her to come in and out.
Secondly, as my wife is not so well moving, it can take us longer time to get ready to check out in the morning. Therefore we would like to check out one hour late, at 12:00 A.M. Please let us know how much the extra fee is.
Finally, I will need to answer some e-mails from my office during my stay, so I would like to know if Wi-Fi is available in the cottage.

Sincerely,
James Portman

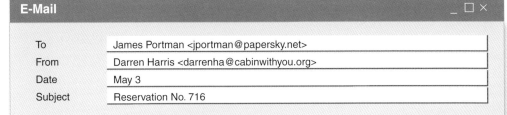

E-Mail   _ □ ×

To	James Portman <jportman@papersky.net>
From	Darren Harris <darrenha@cabinwithyou.org>
Date	May 3
Subject	Reservation No. 716

Dear Mr. Portman,

Thank you very much for your reservation. We look forward to serving you and your wife in June. All
our cabins are equipped with high speed wireless Internet, available at no charge.

I understand you wife's conditions, and so I have assigned Cabin No.03 for you. This cabin has two
kinds of path in the entrance; stairs for walking and ramp for wheelchair. This cabin also has a large
bathroom suitable for wheelchair users.

Usually there is a fee of $20 per hour for late check out, but in this case, showing my wish for your
wife's recovery, I have decided to waive the extra fee.

Please take sufficient the time you need for preparing check out in the morning.

Once again, we look forward to seeing you in June.

Regards,

Darren Harris

Send

---

186. In the notice, the word "roughly" in line
10, is closest in meaning to

  (A) nearly
  (B) approximately
  (C) highly
  (D) relatively

187. What is true about Cabins With You?

  (A) Guests can reserve a cabin online.
  (B) Dinner is included in the booking fee.
  (C) Guests may not choose the bottle of
     wine.
  (D) All of the cottages are difficult to
     access.

188. What is Mr. Portman's main concern?

  (A) His wife may be too ill to travel in
     June.
  (B) He may miss an important email from
     his company.
  (C) The cottage may be too small.
  (D) It will be difficult for his wife to walk
     up the hill.

189. Which of the following usually incurs an
additional fee?

  (A) A traditional American breakfast
  (B) Checking out after 11:00 A.M.
  (C) Drinking white wine in the room
  (D) Rounding in the golf course

190. What is good about Cabin No.03?

  (A) It has good views from the top of the
     hill.
  (B) It has faster Internet than the other
     cottages.
  (C) It is suitable for people with
     disabilities.
  (D) It has a luxurious bathroom.

GO ON TO THE NEXT PAGE ➤

Questions 191-195 efer to the following article and two e-mails.

Fordham News Magazine

Eco-friendly Energy Companies Looking Toward Partnership
Date : August 15

Preston, one of the foremost manufacturers of solar-powered home and business lighting solutions, has announced that it is in negotiations with JingGao Co., a company based in Beijing, China, to establish a new partnership between the two companies. Preston, headquartered in Houston, Texas, told our correspondents that they're hoping to work more closely with battery manufacturers in order to achieve greater efficiency in producing their items, and a partnership with JingGao Co. would be a promising way to fulfill this need.

Pierre Berger, the president of Preston, emphasized the need to achieve new technological advancements in the alternative energy sector in order to accelerate creation of green collar jobs, and said that he expects a partnership with JingGao Co. would "drive innovation, lower manufacturing costs, and spur new growth" in the industry. He further stressed that if such an agreement to cooperate each other is made, Preston may expand its business area by establishing a new office in China. Mr. Berger said that regardless of future partnerships, it's important to expand to meet the customer's growing demand for green energy world wide.

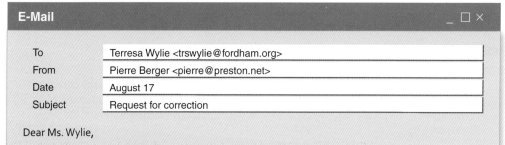

E-Mail

To	Terresa Wylie <trswylie@fordham.org>
From	Pierre Berger <pierre@preston.net>
Date	August 17
Subject	Request for correction

Dear Ms. Wylie,

Thank you very much for interviewing me last week. I also appreciated your article on Preston in the July issue of Fordham News, but there are a few inaccuracies in the article that I would like to correct. First of all, JingGao Co., with whom we are negotiating a partnership, is located in Shanghai, China, not Beijing.

More importantly, since we feel that our business would increase benefits from having an office in Asia, we are planning to open a public relations and sales center in Beijing regardless of making partnerships with companies in Asia. We wish to avoid potential confusion about our strategy. If you could carry these corrections above in an upcoming issue of Fordham News, I would very much appreciate it. If you have any questions about Preston you are welcome at any time to contact me directly at the number below.

Sincerely,

Pierre Berger, President

Preston

Send

To	Pierre Berger <pierre@preston.net>
From	Jacobson Wagner, Editor <editor@fordham.org>
Ce	Terresa Wylie <trswylie@fordham.org>
Date	August 18
Subject	RE: Request for correction

Dear Mr. Berger,

Hi, I'm Jacobson Wylie, the editor in chief of Fordham News. Terresa forwarded your e-mail to me, and I would like to thank you for your comments regarding the article.

Concerning the location, I contacted JingGao Co. directly, and they confirmed that their actual headquarters are in Shanghai, while the office in Beijing is only a branch.

I sincerely apologize for the mistakes in our article, particularly the misunderstanding regarding the strategic significance of new office in Asia. We'll include a correction on the inside cover of the coming issue that will be published in early October. Thank you again for your feedback.

191. What are Preston and JingGao Co. planning to do?

(A) They are planning to merge.
(B) They are planning to strategic cooperation.
(C) They are planning to compete over global market share.
(D) They are planning to cancel a collaborative project.

192. According to the article, what does Preston think is necessary?

(A) To invest in geothermal power
(B) To make solar products cheaper
(C) To advance eco-friendly technology
(D) To move its company overseas

193. What is Preston planning to do?

(A) Open a new sales center in Beijing
(B) Hire more people to work in the solar industry
(C) Begin manufacturing batteries as well as solar lighting
(D) Cooperate with more companies in Asia

194. What is NOT true about JingGao Co.?

(A) They signed a contract with Preston.
(B) They have offices in at least two cities.
(C) Their headquarter is located in Beijing.
(D) They provided information to Mr. Wagner.

195. What will happen in October?

(A) Another article about Preston will be published.
(B) A print correction will appear in the periodicals.
(C) The new Preston office will open in China.
(D) JingGao Co. will merge with Preston.

GO ON TO THE NEXT PAGE

The Sydney Primus Hotel Group

SYDNEY, AUSTRALIA (28 September) The Sydney Primus Hotel Group, one of global chains of luxury hotels, today announced the opening of first hotel in Sydney, Australia. The Sydney Primus Hotel Group will be the hotel chain's flagship for the country, and is the largest hotel built yet in the city. The hotel will be located within reach of Sydney Airport to attract business executives, and its five-star restaurants and opulent Australian architecture are sure to deeply impress travelers looking for a taste of luxury. The Grand Penthouse on the top floor will provide 360-degree views of the beautiful city, and is sure to attract celebrities and CEOs of multinational corporation alike. Bruce Friedman, the founder of this huge hotel chain, said, "I'm very proud of what we've been able to achieve until now. We were able to get this far because of our refusal to compromise on ordinary service, and we plan to continue to offer an wonderful experience to everyone who walks in and out through our doors. I'm looking forward to personally greeting our first guests during the opening night gala on October 6th. It's going to be an amazing night.

The opening show will be admission by invitation only, and will feature a performance by local traditional dance group Elisa, as well as a fireworks and laser show. The hotel will accept reservations through its web-site from October 7th.

Schedule

5:00 P.M. : Opening Ceremony, with a speech from CEO Bruce Friedman and ribbon cutting ceremony
6:00 P.M. : Traditional dance performance in West Courtyard
7:00 P.M. : Dinner featuring T-bone steak and lobster to be served in Banquet Hall A
7:30 P.M. : Sky Restaurant Bar opens, one free cocktail available per guest
9:00 P.M. : Fireworks and laser light show
1:00 A.M. : Sky Restaurant Bar will close

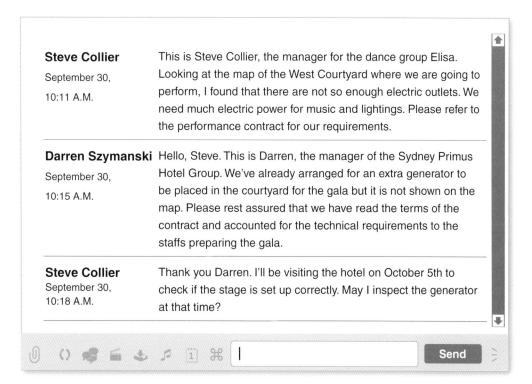

Steve Collier
September 30,
10:11 A.M.

This is Steve Collier, the manager for the dance group Elisa. Looking at the map of the West Courtyard where we are going to perform, I found that there are not so enough electric outlets. We need much electric power for music and lightings. Please refer to the performance contract for our requirements.

Darren Szymanski
September 30,
10:15 A.M.

Hello, Steve. This is Darren, the manager of the Sydney Primus Hotel Group. We've already arranged for an extra generator to be placed in the courtyard for the gala but it is not shown on the map. Please rest assured that we have read the terms of the contract and accounted for the technical requirements to the staffs preparing the gala.

Steve Collier
September 30,
10:18 A.M.

Thank you Darren. I'll be visiting the hotel on October 5th to check if the stage is set up correctly. May I inspect the generator at that time?

196. What will attract business executives to the hotel?

(A) The proximity to Sydney Airport
(B) The five-star restaurants
(C) The 360-degree views of the city from the hotel
(D) The beautiful architecture of the building

197. What does Mr. Friedman credit the success of his hotels to?

(A) Always providing outstanding service
(B) Building his hotels near airports
(C) Adapting to the local market and culture
(D) Celebrities and CEOs staying at the hotels

198. From what time can the guests at the gala purchase alcohol?

(A) 5:00 P.M.
(B) 7:30 P.M.
(C) 9:00 P.M.
(D) 1:00 A.M.

199. What is indicated about Elisa?

(A) They try to mix modern and traditional dance styles.
(B) They perform in exotic costumes.
(C) Their show requires a lot of electrical power.
(D) They have had problems at previous shows.

200. In the text message chain, the word "terms" in paragraph 2, line 4, is closest in meaning to

(A) periods
(B) relationships
(C) expressions
(D) conditions

Stop! This is the end of the test. If you finish before time is called, you may go back to Parts 5, 6, and 7 and check your work.

新토익 시험 진행 안내

❶ 시험 시간 : 120분(2시간)

오전 시험	오후 시험	시간	비고
9:20	2:20		입실
9:30 ~ 9:45	2:30 ~ 2:45	15분	답안지 작성에 관한 Orientation
9:45 ~ 9:50	2:45 ~ 2:50	5분	수험자 휴식시간
9:50 ~ 10:05	2:50 ~ 3:05	15분	신분증 확인 (감독 교사)
10:05 ~ 10:10	3:05 ~ 3:10	5분	문제지 배부 및 파본 확인
10:10 ~ 10:55	3:10 ~ 3:55	45분	듣기 평가(L/C)
10:55 ~ 12:10	3:55 ~ 5:10	75분	독해 평가(R/C) * 2차 신분확인

※ L/C 진행 후 휴식 시간 없이 바로 R/C 진행

❷ 준비물

» 신분증 : 규정 신분증만 가능 (주민등록증, 운전면허증, 기간 만료 전의 여권, 공무원증 등)
» 필기구 : 연필, 지우개 (볼펜이나 사인펜은 사용 금지)

❸ 시험 응시 준수 사항

» 시험 시작 10분 전 입실 (오전 9:50, 오후 2:50 이후에는 입실 불가)
» 종료 30분 전과 10분 전에 시험 종료 공지함
» 휴대전화의 전원은 미리 꺼둘 것

❹ OMR 답안지 표기 요령

» 반드시 지정된 필기구로 표기
※ 성명, 주민등록번호 등을 틀리게 표기하였을 경우 채점 및 성적 확인이 불가능하므로 주의하시기 바랍니다.

OMR 답안지 표기 Sample				
O	Ⓐ	Ⓑ	●	Ⓓ
X	Ⓐ	Ⓥ	Ⓒ	Ⓓ
X	Ⓐ	Ⓑ	Ⓒ	☒
X	Ⓐ	Ⓑ	Ⓒ	Ⓓ
X	Ⓐ	Ⓑ	Ⓒ	Ⓓ

토익 EDGE 실전
1000제
LR SET 5

지금부터 Actual Test를 진행합니다.
실제 시험과 동일한 방식으로 진행됨을 말씀드리며,
방송 음성은 QR코드로 청취하실 수 있습니다.

준비 되셨으면 바로 시작하세요.!

LISTENING TEST

In the Listening test, you will be asked to demonstrate how well you understand spoken English. The entire Listening test will last approximately 45 minutes. There are four parts, and directions are given for each part. You must mark your answers on the separate answer sheet. Do not write your answers in your test book.

PART 1

Directions: For each question in this part, you will hear four statements about a picture in your test book. When you hear the statements, you must select the one statement that best describes what you see in the picture. Then find the number of the question on your answer sheet and mark your answer. The statements will not be printed in your test book and will be spoken only one time.

Statment (A), "Some people are paddling through the water," is the best description of the picture, so you should select answer (A) and mark it on your answer sheet.

1.

2.

GO ON TO THE NEXT PAGE

3.

4.

5.

6.

GO ON TO THE NEXT PAGE

Directions: You will hear a question or statement and three responses spoken in English. They will not be printed in your test book and will be spoken only one time. Select the best response to the question or statement and mark the letter (A), (B), or (C) on your answer sheet.

7. Mark your answer on your answer sheet.

8. Mark your answer on your answer sheet.

9. Mark your answer on your answer sheet.

10. Mark your answer on your answer sheet.

11. Mark your answer on your answer sheet.

12. Mark your answer on your answer sheet.

13. Mark your answer on your answer sheet.

14. Mark your answer on your answer sheet.

15. Mark your answer on your answer sheet.

16. Mark your answer on your answer sheet.

17. Mark your answer on your answer sheet.

18. Mark your answer on your answer sheet.

19. Mark your answer on your answer sheet.

20. Mark your answer on your answer sheet.

21. Mark your answer on your answer sheet.

22. Mark your answer on your answer sheet.

23. Mark your answer on your answer sheet.

24. Mark your answer on your answer sheet.

25. Mark your answer on your answer sheet.

26. Mark your answer on your answer sheet.

27. Mark your answer on your answer sheet.

28. Mark your answer on your answer sheet.

29. Mark your answer on your answer sheet.

30. Mark your answer on your answer sheet.

31. Mark your answer on your answer sheet.

PART 3

Directions: You will hear some conversations between two or more people. You will be asked to answer three questions about what the speakers say in each conversation. Select the best response to each question and mark the letter (A), (B), (C), or (D) on your answer sheet. The conversations will not be printed in your test book and will be spoken only one time.

32. What is the main topic of the conversation?
(A) Updating the web-site
(B) Qualifications of the applicants
(C) Making a flight reservation
(D) Schedule to interview new employees

33. What will happen this Friday?
(A) Job interviews will be conducted.
(B) The company will make a new website.
(C) The man will fly to New Zealand.
(D) The woman will leave for a business trip.

34. What are some clients complaining about?
(A) Late delivery of the product
(B) Location of customer service center
(C) The website of the firm
(D) The quality of the firm's software

35. Why can't the woman go to eat lunch?
(A) She is not in the mood to have lunch.
(B) She had already eaten lunch.
(C) She had lots of work to do.
(D) She should relocate her desk.

36. What does the man suggest the woman to do?
(A) Submit her report
(B) Recommend something to buy
(C) Wait at her desk
(D) Have lunch later

37. What will the speakers do next?
(A) Go to the cafeteria with Lucas
(B) Have lunch with Bobbie at her desk
(C) Leave Lucas in the office
(D) Do research while having lunch

38. By when should the final copy of the proposal be submitted?
(A) By Monday
(B) By Wednesday
(C) By Thursday
(D) By Friday

39. What will the man forward the woman now?
(A) The cover letter of the proposal
(B) The draft of the proposal
(C) The final copy of the proposal
(D) The summary of the proposal

40. Why does the man say, "you can give us your feedback"?
(A) To work independently
(B) To delay the submission
(C) To correct a proposal
(D) To hasten the process of editing

41. What problem does the man mention?
(A) He needs to call Wendell.
(B) His mobile phone is worth the trouble.
(C) His mobile phone is out of charge.
(D) His mobile phone needs to be repaired.

42. Who was supposed to repair the outlet?
(A) Dion
(B) Wendell
(C) Victor
(D) Sherman

43. Why does the woman understand the man's situation?
(A) She owns more than one phone.
(B) She has experienced the same problem before.
(C) She often loses her phone.
(D) She likes helping fix defective outlets.

GO ON TO THE NEXT PAGE

44. Who sent the package?

    (A) Erin Reed
    (B) The head office
    (C) Mr. Tyson
    (D) A supplier from Detroit

45. According to the woman, where can the man find Mr. Tyson's secretary?

    (A) At the main office
    (B) In Detroit
    (C) In a conference room
    (D) In Boston

46. Why does the man need to find Erin Reed before 12:00 PM?

    (A) She's leaving for Detroit.
    (B) She's having lunch.
    (C) The delivery will leave immediately.
    (D) Mr. Tyson is going to Boston.

47. What was changed at the building lobby?

    (A) The doors were fixed.
    (B) Security cameras were installed.
    (C) The air-conditioning system was exchanged.
    (D) The steps were covered with a red carpet.

48. How does the woman think about the improvements?

    (A) She is not impressed with the new window.
    (B) She does not like air-conditioned lobbies.
    (C) She is worried about the color of the floor.
    (D) She does not like going to the lobby.

49. Why does the man prefer the new paint?

    (A) It makes up for the color of the window.
    (B) The security cameras will be harmonized with it.
    (C) He will look more handsome with those colors.
    (D) It's more restful compared to gold and red.

50. What will the woman do this afternoon?

    (A) Graduate from the university
    (B) Have an interview
    (C) Make a presentation
    (D) Hold a conference

51. What does the man think the woman to lack?

    (A) An experience as a salesperson
    (B) Positive references from her university
    (C) Excellent grades
    (D) The stock investment contest awards

52. What does the woman mean when she says, "I'm probably worried for no reason"?

    (A) She has rejected an offer.
    (B) She has prepared well.
    (C) She has changed her mind.
    (D) She has spent too much effort.

53. What has the man been doing?

    (A) Enjoying a dinner
    (B) Checking an online schedule
    (C) Confirming the weather forecast
    (D) Meeting with a guest

54. What does the man mean when he says, "It's difficult to think he will"?

    (A) He doubts that Mr. Martin will not approve a project.
    (B) He thinks that Mr. Martin will read his e-mail soon.
    (C) He does not expect Mr. Martin to attend the meeting.
    (D) He needs to go to another meeting room.

55. What will the woman offer Mr. Martin?

    (A) A expanded budget
    (B) A promotional campaign
    (C) A ticket to a concert
    (D) An extension of due date

56. Why is the woman calling?

    (A) To complain about the employee's service
    (B) To have her glass mended
    (C) To purchase goggles
    (D) To inquire about the catalog

57. What information does the man ask?

    (A) The woman's address
    (B) The item number
    (C) The color of goggles
    (D) The brand of catalogs

58. What does the man recommend the woman to do?

    (A) Order item with another color
    (B) Replace a different model
    (C) Buy what she wants online
    (D) Send her invoice

_____

59. According to the woman, what will the company do soon?

    (A) Consider moving to new office
    (B) Establish an overseas branch
    (C) Rent neighboring office
    (D) Organize a party

60. Who will Katie most likely be?

    (A) A company's president
    (B) A real estate agent
    (C) An owner of the building
    (D) A customer

61. What will the woman do next?

    (A) Make a phone call
    (B) Renew a price list
    (C) Leave on a business trip
    (D) Search for a new job

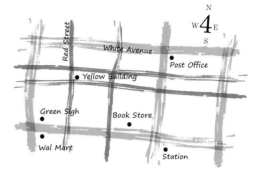

62. Why is the man calling?

    (A) To delay the meeting
    (B) To confirm the meeting time
    (C) To ask for the direction
    (D) To inform he will be late

63. Where is the woman's office?

    (A) At the Blue department
    (B) At the yellow building
    (C) On the white road
    (D) Near the green sign

64. Look at the graphic. Where is the man now?

    (A) At the north exit of station
    (B) Near the post office
    (C) Near the bookstore
    (D) In the front of Wal Mart

GO ON TO THE NEXT PAGE

ON SALE

BRAND NAME	DISCOUNTED PRICE
Bianca's	$40.00
Eleanor's	$48.00
Lolo's	$64.00
Vicky's	$80.00

Hotel	Capacity
Wild Cabin	30 people
Savoy Inn	50 people
Hilton Hotel	70 people
Pinetree Resorts	100 people

65. Where will the conversation most likely take place?
(A) At a beauty shop
(B) At a clothing shop
(C) At a cosmetic store
(D) At an electronic store

66. What does the man ask the woman to do?
(A) Show her receipt
(B) Choose the item
(C) Contact her manager
(D) Place the order

67. Look at the graphic. What is the correct price of the item?
(A) $40.00
(B) $48.00
(C) $64.00
(D) $80.00

68. Who is Mr. Freedman?
(A) A keynote addressor
(B) A professor
(C) A new employee
(D) A retiring executive

69. What does the woman ask the man to do?
(A) Hold a party
(B) Rent a space
(C) Organize a picnic
(D) Plan a tour

70. Look at the graphic. Where most likely will the woman choose?
(A) Wild Cabin
(B) Savoy Inn
(C) Hilton Hotel
(D) Pinetree Resorts

Directions: You will hear some talks given by a single speaker. You will be asked to answer three questions about what the speakers say in each talk. Select the best response to each question and mark the letter (A), (B), (C), or (D) on your answer sheet. The talks will not be printed in your test book and will be spoken only one time.

71. What is the main purpose of this news report?
(A) To hire new employees in Worley Parsons Construction
(B) To announce the construction of a large hotel
(C) To introduce hotels near Boston Logan International Airport
(D) To house a state-of-the-art exhibition center

72. How many employees will work in the room services?
(A) 20
(B) 30
(C) 100
(D) 200

73. Which of the following is planned to be included in the new hotel?
(A) A movie theater
(B) A gift shop
(C) An amusement facilities
(D) A swimming pool

74. What is the purpose for this event?
(A) To enhance mutual friendship
(B) To have an election campaign
(C) To have a fundraising campaign
(D) To establish a public school

75. How long will the bazaar take place?
(A) For 4 days
(B) For 5 days
(C) For 6 days
(D) For 7 days

76. Who will benefit from the funds raised?
(A) The Angels & Heaven Foundation
(B) The poor in the area
(C) The residents in Livonia County
(D) The civil officials

77. According to the speaker, why was the building of the museum of Sound and Light built at first?
(A) For an electronic shop
(B) For a hardware shop
(C) For a museum
(D) For a factory

78. What is on display now in this building?
(A) Telescopes
(B) Old phonographs
(C) Shoes from 1900
(D) Government documents

79. What does the speaker advise the visitors to do?
(A) Sit in the cafeteria
(B) Watch an old movie
(C) Go to the concert
(D) Visit another museum

80. What instrument does Samuel Bowler play?
(A) Piano
(B) Guitar
(C) Violin
(D) Trumpet

81. Who will the benefit from the concert be donated to?
(A) A hospital
(B) The city
(C) A school
(D) A farm

82. When will the concert begin?
(A) At 6:00 P.M.
(B) At 7:00 P.M.
(C) At 8:00 P.M.
(D) At 9:00 P.M.

GO ON TO THE NEXT PAGE

83. What kind of business will Ms. Bianca most likely do?

    (A) Commercial distribution
    (B) Advertising
    (C) Accounting
    (D) Communications

84. What is one of the speaker's chief concerns?

    (A) Cost
    (B) Fame
    (C) Accuracy
    (D) Period

85. What will the speaker do next?

    (A) Write a report for the boss
    (B) Reschedule the upcoming meeting
    (C) Discuss the matter with his coworkers
    (D) Call Ms. Bianca

---

86. What is a stated benefit of becoming a travel agent through Train Tour Teaching?

    (A) First class seating
    (B) A high wage
    (C) Travel discounts
    (D) Free hotel accommodations

87. How much does it cost to become a travel agent through Train Tour Teaching?

    (A) $3
    (B) $30
    (C) $300
    (D) $3,000

88. How do the listeners become certified?

    (A) They must send their identification card to Train Tour Teaching.
    (B) They are required to pass a test.
    (C) They must pay an authorized fee.
    (D) They are certified within two month.

89. What is the topic of the news report?

    (A) An increase in commodity prices
    (B) A delay in transporting parts
    (C) The introduction to a new executive
    (D) The demand for a new car model

90. What does the speaker imply when she says, "And it's already gone with the big success"?

    (A) The price has already gone up.
    (B) The colors should be varied.
    (C) A large sale has been achieved.
    (D) Merchandise will be out of stock soon.

91. What problem does the speaker mention with Galaxy?

    (A) There is a long waiting list to buy one.
    (B) The company is facing difficulty in keeping safe.
    (C) Its production line is temporarily closed.
    (D) Customers dislike its appearance.

---

92. Why is the speaker calling?

    (A) To prepare for a big sale
    (B) To confirm the schedule of a workshop
    (C) To report the result of a presentation
    (D) To leave his feedback

93. Why does the speaker say, "I missed the point"?

    (A) To inform his late arrival
    (B) To express that he didn't achieve a goal
    (C) To leave somewhere early
    (D) To discuss the topic of his speech

94. What does the speaker ask the listener to do tonight?

    (A) Make amendments to some slides
    (B) Purchase competitors' products
    (C) Review prices online
    (D) Check sales figures

Name	Skills
Ted Goldstein	Time Management
Janet Morrel	Analysis
Harry Cormier	Writing
Amy Veronica	Negotiation

Sellers and Items	Friday		Saturday	
	A.M.	P.M.	A.M.	P.M.
Plates and bowls	X	X	O	X
Clothing	O	O	O	O
Paintings and pictures	X	X	O	O
Handmade hats and shirts	O	O	X	X
Native American Jewelry	O	O	O	X

95. What is the purpose of the talk?

(A) To notify a retirement
(B) To collect the data of a meeting
(C) To pick a substitute
(D) To make a promise

96. What will Jessica Maywood do next Monday?

(A) Go abroad to work for
(B) Attend the presentation
(C) Deliver a speech
(D) Hold a conference

97. Look at the graphic. What is the recommended person good at?

(A) Time Management
(B) Analysis
(C) Writing
(D) Negotiation

98. What is being advertised?

(A) Cooking utensils
(B) Arts and crafts fair
(C) A movie
(D) A museum

99. Why are the visitors asked to attend both Friday and Saturday?

(A) The parking is free on both days.
(B) The hospital is organizing the event.
(C) Some shops will be open.
(D) Profits will be distributed to local communities.

100. Look at the graphic. When can the listeners purchase a kitchenware?

(A) Friday morning
(B) Friday afternoon
(C) Saturday morning
(D) Saturday afternoon

This is the end of the Listening test. Turn to Part 5 in your text book.

GO ON TO THE NEXT PAGE

In the Reading test, you will read a variety of texts and answer several different types of reading comprehension questions. The entire Reading test will last 75 minutes. There are three parts, and directions are given for each part. You are encouraged to answer as many questions as possible within the time allowed.

You must mark your answers on the separate answer sheet. Do not write your answers in your test book.

PART 5

Directions: A word or phrase is missing in each of the sentences below. Four answer choices are given below each sentence. Select the best answer to complete the sentence. Then mark the letter (A), (B), (C), or (D) on your answer sheet.

101. With the help of Top Floor Carpet, I can clean the carpet of my living room much more ------- than before.

   (A) easy
   (B) easily
   (C) easier
   (D) ease

102. Generally, most of people work for money and ------- benefits such as a sense of purpose and pride in their work.

   (A) absolute
   (B) material
   (C) intangible
   (D) monetary

103. When Air World Ltd. restructured its satellite division, Mr. Jeffrey had to ------- 100 engineers and program managers to simplify research and development.

   (A) reimburse
   (B) hire
   (C) dismiss
   (D) refer

104. All transaction records of the company are subject to ------- by outside auditors.

   (A) edit
   (B) amend
   (C) nominate
   (D) review

105. The reason for rapid growth of Clovis City is ------- it offers excellent tax incentives for new businesses.

   (A) that
   (B) what
   (C) which
   (D) who

106. Mr. Clinton enjoys all his college classes ------- says economics is very difficult.

   (A) and
   (B) but
   (C) or
   (D) so

107. The design team ------- for making valuable contributions to the company and to the field of industrial design since 1999.

   (A) recognized
   (B) has recognized
   (C) have been recognized
   (D) has been recognized

108. We are planning to hire at least five new engineers in order to enhance the work ------- of the project.

   (A) efficiency
   (B) procedure
   (C) condition
   (D) complexity

109. Most neighbors have finished putting up their Christmas lights, but we have not finished hanging ------- yet.

(A) us
(B) our
(C) ours
(D) ourselves

110. Decisions concerning the purpose and scope of this final project should be made ------ the time at which all members in the division have completed their work.

(A) rather than
(B) at least
(C) no later than
(D) as long as

111. A 2-week exchange privilege is just one of the ways the company ensures its customer's complete -------.

(A) satisfy
(B) satisfaction
(C) satisfactory
(D) satisfactorily

112. Mr. Fineda requested that the consultant ------- the impact of the financial transactions on the firm's working capital.

(A) analyze
(B) analyzed
(C) analyzes
(D) analyzing

113. The boss decided that it would be best not to hire more people in the next two years ------- the current economic downturn.

(A) because
(B) consequently
(C) nevertheless
(D) due to

114. Violent crimes declined by 30 percent because the number of police in the area -------.

(A) increased
(B) minimized
(C) remained
(D) stabilized

115. Building a system of ------- products provides no assurance of the security of that system.

(A) certify
(B) certified
(C) certifying
(D) certifies

116. Construction of the new hospital will be finished ------- the end of this month, but operations will not begin for another one month.

(A) until
(B) by
(C) to
(D) at

117. ------- improve the quality of our products, we should use better materials.

(A) So that
(B) For the purpose of
(C) As
(D) In order to

118. ------- Ms. Brett and Mr. Vince will be staying with us for an additional one week to prepare for the promotional campaign.

(A) Either
(B) Both
(C) Neither
(D) Not only

119. Even though the cost of transport and ------- was significantly lower than other companies, Plan A Company still failed to balance profit and loss.

(A) produce
(B) productive
(C) producer
(D) production

120. Some programmers prefer to work on their own because they concentrate well without distractions caused by -------.

(A) one
(B) another
(C) other
(D) others

GO ON TO THE NEXT PAGE

121. Ultimately, it would cost significantly less to buy a ------- out than to start our own operations in the industry.

(A) negotiator
(B) competitor
(C) novice
(D) subscriber

122. Puma's ------- new line of sports jackets and pants has won much praise from professional athletes.

(A) impress
(B) impression
(C) impressive
(D) impressively

123. Free copies of the travel brochure are ------- for distribution at the tourist information center.

(A) responsible
(B) viable
(C) accessible
(D) available

124. SteamAll Software manufactures products that meet customers' ------- as well as their changing requirements over time.

(A) probability
(B) exactness
(C) expectations
(D) reliability

125. Dedicated engineers with thorough knowledge of the latest technologies are our biggest -------.

(A) compensation
(B) prerequisite
(C) aim
(D) asset

126. While our company welcomes all applicants, we ------- encourage those with accounting experience.

(A) collaboratively
(B) particularly
(C) accordingly
(D) ideally

127. The Director of Finance and the Director of Sales & Marketing responded quite ------- to the question about budget increase.

(A) differ
(B) different
(C) difference
(D) differently

128. Mr. Luke had worked in the purchasing department for some years, ------- he moved to the marketing department.

(A) when
(B) after
(C) before
(D) as soon as

129. ------- Ms. Vicky was hired in the Finance Department, she has made contracts with many new customers.

(A) Because
(B) Since
(C) Once
(D) As

130. Chef Kent Wang is running a Chinese restaurant ------- a lot of gourmets frequent for its outstanding food.

(A) who
(B) which
(C) what
(D) where

PART 6

Directions: Read the texts that follow. A word, phrase, or sentence is missing in parts of each text. Four answer choices for each question are given below the text. Select the best answer to complete the text. Then mark the letter (A), (B), (C), or (D) on your answer sheet.

Questions 131-134 refer to the following advertisement.

------- . Florida is the sunniest, nicest state in the United States. If you'd like to know why
131.
we feel that way, we'd be happy to send you a free booklet telling you all about our state.

The ------- way to find out about the Sunshine State is to let us send you our A Guide
132.
to Florida Living for free. It will tell you all you need to know about Florida's climate and

recreational -------, about entertainment and lifestyle, about the homes available here and
133.
the communities in which they're located, about costs of living figures, taxes, and many

more interesting facts. We think that ------- you've read our free guide to Florida living, you'll
134.
agree with us that Florida is a great place to retire to.

131. (A) Most people will tell you that you
        need to retire to Florida.
     (B) Movers will receive the information
        about the cost of living.
     (C) There are many people who want to
        live in Florida.
     (D) We think that Florida may be a great
        place to retire to.

132. (A) easy
     (B) easier
     (C) easiest
     (D) easily

133. (A) rights
     (B) promotions
     (C) evidences
     (D) opportunities

134. (A) since
     (B) unless
     (C) once
     (D) although

GO ON TO THE NEXT PAGE

Erratic crops, unpredictable rainfall, unhealthy animals, and no holidays are leading to a sharp decrease in the number of privately-owned farms. Privately-owned farms could disappear soon because many people are selling their farms to work on corporately-run properties. ------- . While there are still more privately-run properties here in the
135.
Scottish lowlands, this may all change. Recent years have seen more farmers sell out to big companies ------- Higgs, Greencorp, and Yeastix. Farms that have been in families
136.
for generations are being traded in for small apartments and cottages. Greencorp, for example, has been ------- farmers full-time jobs in exchange for them selling their farms.
137.
"Not many people are really cut out to be full-time farmers anymore," says Rick Harp, president of Greencorp. Some people see the change as a loss of the town's cultural heritage, but ------- farmers are viewing it differently.
138.

135. (A) Privately-owned farms have managed to appear since many people sold their farms.
(B) Before there are still more corporately-run properties here in the Scottish lowlands, this may all change.
(C) Some farmers are viewing the town's cultural heritage differently.
(D) In the Ayr, Scotland, not far from Glasgow, corporately-run farms have been thriving.

136. (A) and
(B) but
(C) such as
(D) concerning

137. (A) agreeing
(B) declining
(C) offering
(D) refusing

138. (A) other
(B) others
(C) another
(D) one

To: Archid Global Partners

From: Emily Rosa, President, TTC Enterprises

First of all, I am very pleased to benefit from your company's advanced technology and

expertise in the field of remote satellite imagery. As you know, we plan to make significant

use of satellite photography in the future.

Our first goal, therefore, is to acquire more detailed knowledge of the field. To prepare for

some deep discussion regarding the direction we will pursue, we would like you to -------
139.

us with some background information.

Specifically, could you provide us with a list of books you recommend and authorities on

the subject with ------- we could consult? We would like to have the list by the end of this
140.

month; we hope that this will allow you enough time to respond to our -------.
141.

Please let us know if you need anything else before the end of the month. ------- .
142.

Best regards,

Lance Murphy

139. (A) expose
(B) teach
(C) supply
(D) deliver

140. (A) who
(B) whom
(C) whose
(D) whoever

141. (A) request
(B) offer
(C) submission
(D) claim

142. (A) We hope you will receive the list by
the end of this month.
(B) We look forward to working with you.
(C) We may need something else after
the end of the month.
(D) we want to consult the subject with
authorities.

GO ON TO THE NEXT PAGE

Questions 143-146 refer to the following notice.

In cooperation with the U.S. Consumer Product Safety Commission (CPSC) and the National Highway Traffic Safety Administration (NHTSA), Carseat Co. of Nevada, is recalling some three million seats. If the seat is used incorrectly, it can flip forward.

------- . There have been 200 reports in the United States of seats unexpectedly flipping,
   143.
resulting in 97 injuries. These reports include skull fractures, concussions, a broken leg,

and ------- scratches and bruises.
     144.

"Carseat is offering a free repairability to prevent the seat from flipping," said Carseat

President Peggy Brown. "It's an easy repair, and the seat is designed to protect you from

a very serious injury." Carseat will provide consumers with a free easy-to-install repair kit

that helps secure the seat. Consumers should not use the seat until it -------.
             145.

CPSC, NHTSA and Carseat remind people to follow all instructions when using the seat.

------- a free repair kit, call Carseat toll-free at (700) 478-0247 anytime.
  146.

---

143. (A) If the seat is used properly, it will result in 200 injuries.
    (B) The seat is designed to keep you in safe position.
    (C) Consumers tend to follow all instructions when buying the seat.
    (D) When this happens, people can suffer serious injuries.

144. (A) numerous
    (B) exact
    (C) subtle
    (D) significant

145. (A) has repaired
    (B) repaired
    (C) was repairing
    (D) has been repaired

146. (A) Receive
    (B) Receiving
    (C) Received
    (D) To receive

PART 7

Directions: In this part you will read a selection of texts, such as magazine and newspaper articles, e-mails, and instant messages. Each text or set of texts is followed by several questions. Select the best answer for each question and mark the letter (A), (B), (C), or (D) on your answer sheet.

Questions 147-148 refer to the following letter.

From: Stock Mall
Date: February 9, 2017
To: stockmall@hotmail.com
Subject: Order Cancelled

Dear Customer,

We would like to notice you that the last carpet you ordered was buy by a walk-in customer before we gained your order from Mall. We tried to contact with our suppliers on this product. But they responded that don't have this product in their stock. We apologize for the inconvenience and confusion on this happening. We had done a step of process on a full refund. You will receive a full refund confirmation from Mall as soon as possible. We regret that we were unable to complete the order. As I am certain this is an isolated incident, however, I look forward to continued with you in the future.
Please, contact us if you need some help.

Sincerely,
Stock Mall.com

147. What is the main purpose of this e-mail?
   (A) To request further information
   (B) To report the carpet status
   (C) To place an order
   (D) To make a reservation

148. How much of a refund will the customer receive?
   (A) A full refund
   (B) More than 20%
   (C) Less than 10%
   (D) A minimum of 80%

GO ON TO THE NEXT PAGE

The firm informed that James Dean will resign the position as Department of Human Resources Manager on 22 July 2016 to find out some interesting job. All staff thank to him for his contribution for the company's work over the past five years and wish him well in the future.

The firm is pleased to notify that Mac Tailor will participate the company as the new Human Resource Manager on 1 August 2016. Mac Tailor, 48, qualified as a Business management from the Northwestern University; he has been worked for 10 years in bank and is currently with the Core Group in LA where he leaves at the end of this year to join Neo Evan Agent.

Brianna Kim - company assistant
Neo Evan Agent
10th Floor, 5 Rocky road, Manchester C1A 6AL
Tel: (601) 243-3445
FAX: (601) 244-3445

149. What would be the best title for this announcement?

(A) Job offer
(B) HR director
(C) Personnel changes
(D) Northwestern University

150. How long has Mac Tailor been in the banking business?

(A) 46 years
(B) 10 years
(C) 3 years
(D) A half year

Online Chat   _ □ ×

Ranjit Tamboli 17:01	Hey, you still around or did you already leave for the station?
Alicia Krauss 17:03	Just on my way down to the lobby now, why?
Ranjit Tamboli 17:03	Thank goodness. I left our estimate sheets on the printer.
Alicia Krauss 17:04	Will head back and get them. Which one did you use?
Ranjit Tamboli 17:04	Blue color one, third along from the door.
Alicia Krauss 17:06	Good job! It is lucky for me to stay behind to close up.
Ranjit Tamboli 17:07	It'll be my turn to lock up the office tomorrow. See you on the platform. Appreciate it.

Send   📎 () 💬 📷 ⬇ ♫ ⓘ ⌘   ⌄⁄

151. What is suggested about Mr. Tamboli?

   (A) He is currently in his office.
   (B) He recently created some documents.
   (C) He is waiting in the lobby.
   (D) He forgot to mail the estimate sheets.

152. At 17:06, what does Ms. Krauss mean when she writes, "Good job"?

   (A) She evaluates high the work Mr. Tamboli did.
   (B) She attended the meeting in place of her colleague.
   (C) She has always been a laid-back person.
   (D) She thinks it was fortunate that Mr. Tamboli made a request.

GO ON TO THE NEXT PAGE

Does it right we have?

In recent, you applied us to send Finance Report journal subscription to a new address. To convince that Finance Report journal sends to reach you on a basis of regular and timely, please take a time to confirm your name and new address as it mention below.

Remember to check the postal code, and add an apartment number if you need. This chance is also a perfect time to extend your Finance Report subscription for a year or two years more. You will be protected from all increasing rate and ensured to flexible delivery. And you can consider a present of Finance Report to a friend, relative, or co-worker. Your thoughtfulness will be remembered for all year.

Old address:

Mac Kengi
478 Burer Street
Rosemary, RA 25012

Check new address: _____ Yes _____ No (fill in correction below)
Mac Kengi
5420 Long Tack, Apt. 6A
Bond, LD 54123

Correct new address:

Name: _____

Address: _____

City: _____ State: _____

Postal code: _____

Signature for:
_____1 year (12 issues, $34) _____ 2 years (24 issues, $66)

Send a gift subscription of Finance Report for:
_____ 1 year (12 issues, $34) _____ 2 years (24 issues, $66)

To:

Name: _____

Address: _____

City: _____ State: _____

Postal code: _____

153. What is the main reason this form was sent to Ms. Kengi?
- (A) Because she recently changed her address
- (B) Because she complained about irregular service
- (C) To remind her that her subscription is expiring soon
- (D) To remind her to send a past due payment for a subscription

154. What kind of benefit would Ms. Kengi gain from renewing her subscription now?
- (A) A free calendar
- (B) A second year at half price
- (C) A reduced rate for a gift subscription
- (D) A guarantee against future price increases

GO ON TO THE NEXT PAGE

Questions 155-157 refer to the following instruction.

A Disaster Supply Tool

Look at a disaster supply tool. Here is mentioned what it should include at least.

* Water supply. Make sure that at least one gallon per person per day for at least four days. The water should be locked, unbreakable containers and be replaced every five to seven months.
* A long-term battery CD player with extra batteries.
* An electric torch with extra batteries.
* A first-aid tool and a supply of any necessary prescription medicines.
* A supply of canned goods that are not perish or sealed foods and a manual can opener, bottle opener and stick knife.
* Baby food and formula if necessary.
* Bags, covers, cushions and warm clothing.
* Extra eyeglasses if you are necessary.
* Cash and credit cards.
* Extra keys for your home, car and safety-deposit box.
* Names and phone numbers of family physicians.
* Pet food if you are necessary.

You are able to maintain these items in a big duffel bag or suitcase, stored in a cool, dry place where they can be recovered immediately. The supply tool as a "mini-version" can be moved in your car trunk. In this case, you are away from house and something happens.

You have to keep copies in all your significant papers as concerned with your home supply tool. You are supposed to consider and keep including assurance policies, credit card detailed, valued phone numbers, medical histories, bank account, financial data etc. These types of documents should be easily accessible but secret enough so they can't easily be found by anyone else.

---

155. What kind of item was NOT suggested for inclusion in the tool?

(A) Emergency lighting supplies
(B) Money
(C) Personal information
(D) Reading material

156. What do these instructions recommend in the case of being away from house when disaster comes?

(A) Try to return home as quickly as possible
(B) Keep important documents out of the hands of strangers
(C) Keep a smaller version of the disaster tool in your car
(D) Make preparations for the care of your pets

157. Which item does the article mention as very significant documents?

(A) Bank account information
(B) Grocery store receipts
(C) Marriage license applications
(D) Letters from the family

Questions 158-160 refer to the following article.

Most Workers Do Not Want To Be Superior. ---[1]---. By Survey Managers who are worry about workers try to occupy your positions should be relaxed. ---[2]---. According to the recent survey, there are 70 percent of workers who do not want to be in charge. ---[3]---. The survey in BusinessLife consisted of experts of management and a manpower service firm that specializes in working with administrative professionals. ---[4]---. The current survey was progressed by an independent research company and included 800 men and women in the age of over 18 with professional environments.

Workers were asked:

1. "Would you like to take your superior's task?"
   Responses: No   70%
               Yes   25%
               Don't know   5%

2. "Do you think you could do a better performance than your superior?"
   Responses: No   65%
               Yes   30%
               Don't know   5%

"A kind of superior or manager can be a target by workplace humor," said Nick Jeremy, general manager of BusinessLife. "But become the superior can be demanding and many workers acknowledge that, even though they might not always agree with their manager's decisions."

158. What is BusinessLife?

(A) A research firm
(B) A government employment agency
(C) A provider of staffing services
(D) An organization of administrative professionals

159. What does Nick Jeremy say about most workers?

(A) They are happy with their supervisors.
(B) They do not think much about their bosses.
(C) They usually do not agree with their bosses.
(D) They understand that being a manager is not easy.

160. In which of the positions marked [1], [2], [3], and [4] does the following sentence best belong?

"In addition, 65 percent of respondents said that they maybe could not do a better job than their current superiors."

(A) [1]
(B) [2]
(C) [3]
(D) [4]

GO ON TO THE NEXT PAGE

Questions 161-163 refer to the following itinerary.

Wednesday, April 16

3:30 p.m. - Registration (South Hall lobby)

5:00 p.m. - Chairperson's reception
(Rosebird Room in South Hall)

6:30 p.m. - Film Viewing: "Outline a Business Plan
for Abroad Markets" (South Hall lobby)

Thursday, April 17

7:30 a.m. - Field registration and/or signature
(South Hall lobby)

7:30 a.m. - Continental Breakfast
(Rosebird Room in South Hall)

10:00 a.m. - Simultaneous sessions
(look conference catalog for session details)

11:35 a.m. - Take a rest

Noon - Luncheon (with Jonathan Miller - manager of North American
licensing for BioTech, Inc. and Shown Chang - director of Aisan
maketing for Zenxi Industries)
: Green Dining Hall

1:10 p.m. - Take a rest

1:35 p.m. - Simultaneous sessions
(look conference catalog for session details)

2:40 p.m. - Take a rest

3:00 p.m. - Simultaneous sessions
(look conference catalog for session details)

4:20 p.m. - Take a rest

6:00 p.m. - Dinner and Awards Ceremony hosted by Dr. John
Dauning (Green Dining Hall)

7:00 p.m. - Personal exchange (Alumni House)

Friday, April 18

8:00 a.m. - Breakfast and Present Speech: "Building
Business Relation Across Boundaries" by Ms.
Joan Klaudy (College Club)

9:30 a.m. - Panel Presentation: "A New Way in
International Economic Cooperation"
(Watson Library)

Noon - Closing ceremony (South Hall lobby)

161. What will meeting attendees do on Wednesday evening?

(A) Register
(B) Watch a film
(C) Attend a mixer
(D) Listen to a speech

162. What is the purpose on this meeting?

(A) The role of media in society
(B) Doing business internationally
(C) Using technology in manufacturing
(D) The impact of higher education on industry

163. Where is this meeting most likely being held?

(A) At a hotel
(B) In an office building
(C) On a university campus
(D) At a convention center

GO ON TO THE NEXT PAGE

Questions 164-167 refer to the following online chat discussion.

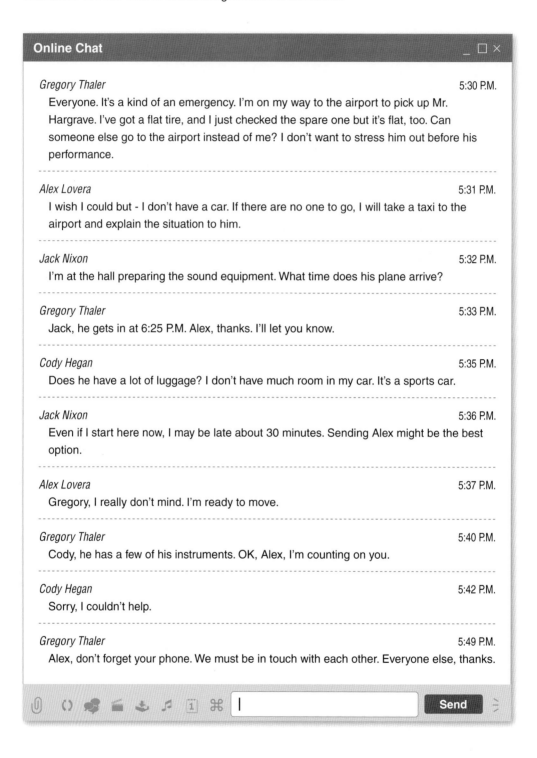

Online Chat   _ □ ×

Gregory Thaler   5:30 P.M.
   Everyone. It's a kind of an emergency. I'm on my way to the airport to pick up Mr.
   Hargrave. I've got a flat tire, and I just checked the spare one but it's flat, too. Can
   someone else go to the airport instead of me? I don't want to stress him out before his
   performance.

Alex Lovera   5:31 P.M.
   I wish I could but - I don't have a car. If there are no one to go, I will take a taxi to the
   airport and explain the situation to him.

Jack Nixon   5:32 P.M.
   I'm at the hall preparing the sound equipment. What time does his plane arrive?

Gregory Thaler   5:33 P.M.
   Jack, he gets in at 6:25 P.M. Alex, thanks. I'll let you know.

Cody Hegan   5:35 P.M.
   Does he have a lot of luggage? I don't have much room in my car. It's a sports car.

Jack Nixon   5:36 P.M.
   Even if I start here now, I may be late about 30 minutes. Sending Alex might be the best
   option.

Alex Lovera   5:37 P.M.
   Gregory, I really don't mind. I'm ready to move.

Gregory Thaler   5:40 P.M.
   Cody, he has a few of his instruments. OK, Alex, I'm counting on you.

Cody Hegan   5:42 P.M.
   Sorry, I couldn't help.

Gregory Thaler   5:49 P.M.
   Alex, don't forget your phone. We must be in touch with each other. Everyone else, thanks.

   [Send]

164. Why did Mr. Thaler start the chat?

    (A) To correct an error
    (B) To provide an update
    (C) To ask assistance
    (D) To praise a colleague

165. Who most likely is Mr. Hargrave?

    (A) An important contributor
    (B) A product reviewer
    (C) A returning colleague
    (D) A visiting musician

166. At 5:33 P.M., what does Mr. Thaler imply when he writes, "I'll let you know"?

    (A) An arrival time may change.
    (B) He will answer a question when he has more time.
    (C) He will wait to see if there is a better offer.
    (D) There is some beneficial information to share.

167. Who will most likely meet Mr. Hargrave at the airport?

    (A) Alex Lovera
    (B) Jack Nixon
    (C) Gregory Thaler
    (D) Cody Hegan

GO ON TO THE NEXT PAGE

The Labor Department said that there was an increase of 2.4 percent in its Employment Cost Index for the third quarter compared to the three months of second quarter of this year. The slowdown came fully from some increase in benefit costs, which increased 3.6 percent in the third quarter compared with a 4.8 percent rapidly increased in the second quarter. Salaries and wages, stymied the past several years by a fragile economy condition and lackluster job employment growth, increased 1.2 percent in the third quarter, the same rise as the second quarter of this year. Over the past 6 months, salaries rose by 5.0 percent, down from a 5.4 percent rise for the 6 months ending in September 2014 and far below the 8 percent increase for the 6 months ending in September 2012, when the country was still in the midst of a record 20-year economic expansion. ---[1]---

But benefit costs have increased much faster, rising by 14.4 percent for the 12 months ending in September, the largest 6-month obtain since beginning of 1987. "Employment costs, the single biggest cost of doing business, remain well considered. This should allow the Fed to continue moving at a calculated pace," said economist Damon Patrick. In addition to pressure on salaries from a fragile labor market, incomes have been decreased by the bursting of the stock market bubble in 1997, which erased trillions of dollars. ---[2]---

This marked the second annual decreases in entire income in more than a half-century according to the IRS. For the third quarter, the government said that the increase in benefit costs accounted for a little more than half of the total rise in compensation for the quarter. ---[3]---

* Benefit costs include pension benefits for employees who have pension coverage in their jobs and also include health insurance. ---[4]---

by James Dalton

168. What caused the 1.2 percent raise in wages in the third quarter?

(A) A stable economy
(B) Inactive job growth
(C) Economic expansion
(D) A bubble economy

169. How long did the economic expansion last?

(A) For 4 months
(B) For 12 months
(C) For the second quarter
(D) For two decades

170. Which of the following is NOT mentioned in this report?

(A) The overall wages and benefit costs have been boosted continuously by 4 percent on average.
(B) Employment Costs are the biggest part in expenses when running a business.
(C) Wages climbed by 5.0 percent for the last 6 months, and the figures were lower than before.
(D) Salaries increased by 1.2 percent for the second quarter this year.

171. In which of the positions marked [1], [2], [3], and [4] does the following sentence best belong?

"That compares with the second quarter, when the rise in benefits accounted for three-fourths of the increase in compensation."

(A) [1]
(B) [2]
(C) [3]
(D) [4]

GO ON TO THE NEXT PAGE

42 Queen Avenue

LA, SA 30435

Tel: (307) 382-2323

Fax: (307) 382-3232

Email: decostruc@in.com

Alice Lee

Financial Leader

Deco Structure, Ltd

213 Corn Road

Nouvevill, IA 123432

Dear Ms. Lee:

I really appreciate you for opening an account with our firm. As one of the top firms in this business, we can surely say that our productions and our services will never disappoint you. Also, by means of the alliances with many different service, we wish to provided you with more various services with more attractive prices.

I would like to explain this chance to simply set forth our terms and conditions for continuing a business with our firm. Invoices are able to pay within 20 days of receipt, and you can get a discount of 4% if you pay within five days of receipt. We consider this kind of motivative an great change for our customers to rise their profit margin and therefore suggest the use of this discount prerogative whenever possible. However, We need that our invoices be paid within the certain time if the customers want to get a 4% discount advantage.

At various times throughout the year we may provide our products to our customers for additional discounts. To make a decision in the price, you have to apply your special discount first and then calculate 4% of your discount for early payment. As the Financial Leader, I will be happy to response any queries when you have some queries about your new account. You can be contacted at the above number. Welcome to our member of customer.

Yours sincerely,

Nancy Kim

Financial Leader of Deco Structure Ltd.

172. Why is this letter written?

(A) To apply to the financial manager
(B) To open a new account
(C) To describe the discount policy
(D) To get a discount

173. What is mentioned about Deco Structure, Ltd?

(A) Money is payable within 20 days of receipt.
(B) 4% discount will be given every month.
(C) The prices of the coffee products.
(D) The company has been established a year ago.

174. Which of the following is TRUE in this letter?

(A) Nancy Kim's e-mail address is decostruc@in.com.
(B) The credit manager is fussy to answer any questions.
(C) The letter is written to Deco Structure In.
(D) Alice Lee's phone number is tel: (307) 382-2323.

175. The word 'more attractive' in paragraph 1, line 4, is closest in meaning to

(A) more expensive
(B) more luxurious
(C) more affordable
(D) more reasonable

GO ON TO THE NEXT PAGE

September 21

Thank you for joining the Stallions' team of supporters again this year!
We have carefully read the comments you sent us and we get the message loud and clear.
We promise to do everything we can to provide a family-friendly and safe atmosphere
for all who attend Stallions games. In order to accomplish this, there are a few reminders
that we would like to pass along to you, our most valued supporters.
If you are not able to attend a game yourself, we ask that you exercise discretion in
what you do with your tickets. If you give them away or decide to sell them, you are
responsible for the actions of the individuals using your tickets. If someone using your
tickets acts inappropriately, your tickets to future games or seasons could be revoked.
Fans, who demonstrate inappropriate or disruptive behavior, including the following, will
be subject to ejection from the stadium and you will risk losing your season tickets:

1. Abusive language or actions
2. Fighting or other dangerous behaviors
3. Unruly behaviors, which prevent other fans from enjoying the game
4. Interfering with the progress of the game in any way, including throwing objects
   onto the field
5. Smoking, except in designated areas

We want everyone to come to the stadium, relax, and enjoy a great day. We look forward
to seeing you this Sunday and at every future home game of the Stallions.

October 10

Dear Mr. Watt:

I regret to inform you that two of the fans who bought your tickets to last Sunday's game were apprehended by stadium security for repeatedly tossing things at the opposing team's players and action was taken against them as outlined in the notice sent to all season ticket holders on September 21.

We understand that you had no expectation that the people purchasing your game tickets would act this way. Nonetheless, as clearly stated in the policy letter, you must take responsibility for their actions. We urge you to contact Betty Dobson at the Stallons office immediately to discuss this situation. She can be reached at 747-0299 ext. 3020.

Sincerely,

Richard Robinette

Director of Security

176. What was probably the reason for the notice of September 21?

(A) No more tickets were available for Sunday's game.
(B) The team was facing legal action from some fans.
(C) Some fans had complained to the team.
(D) Too many fans had been selling their tickets.

177. To whom is the notice of September 21 mainly directed?

(A) Supporters attending only this Sunday's game
(B) Supporters owning season tickets
(C) People wishing to purchase tickets
(D) People thinking about joining the team

178. Why has the letter of October 10 been written?

(A) Mr. Watt lost his tickets.
(B) Mr. Watt's behavior at the game was unruly.
(C) Some fans objected to the new policy.
(D) Some fans threw objects onto the field.

179. What action was taken against the fans Mr. Watt sold his tickets to?

(A) They had to leave the stadium.
(B) They were arrested by the police.
(C) All supporters' season tickets were revoked.
(D) They were required to remain quiet in their seats.

180. What will Mr. Watt most likely do?

(A) Speak with the fans who bought his tickets
(B) Visit the team's offices in person
(C) Phone 747-0299 ext. 3020
(D) Contact the agency that sold his tickets

GO ON TO THE NEXT PAGE

NSC Outsourcing
You Don't Have to Face Today's Challenges Alone!

As your business grows, inefficient IT management can lead to inadaptability and budget blowouts, which no business can afford in today's tough corporate environment. Yet there is a solution! Let NSC Outsourcing manage all or part of your IT systems, yielding cost efficiencies and adaptability, and leaving you free to concentrate on core business operations.

We offer you an exclusive service to make the outsourcing transition as smooth as possible, by allowing you to retain command over your system even after you outsource it. Essentially, we work in close consultation with you through the entire process, so you remain informed the whole way, deciding what to keep and what to give away. And don't forget that our Technology Help Service is just a phone call away. Our team of friendly IT experts is on call 24 hours a day to deal with all your technical needs.

If you'd like to find out more, simply send your name, company name, and daytime work number to info@NSC.com and we'll send you a detailed 35-page brochure outlining all our services. Then, if you're still interested, we offer a free initial consultation session.

To	NSC Outsourcing
From	Mrs. Jessica

I am the executive director of PanState, a medium-sized insurance company which has been successfully catering to clients in our area for the past ten years. As a result of growing business transactions, we shifted from our old system to an updated IT environment five months ago, but management of this system has proven complex, and to cut a long story short, our company's IT budget has become untenably high. Thus, we're looking to simplify our system and increase our flexibility through outsourcing, but without completely losing command over it, which is why your advertisement appealed to me. As we are really not sure of the best way to go, we would appreciate your thoughts on this matter, and I would be keen to make time to meet with one of your consultants in the near future.

Sincerely,

Mrs. Jessica

181. What does NSC Outsourcing offer to do?

(A) Develop IT hardware
(B) Improve IT efficiency
(C) Organize IT seminars
(D) Monitor IT security

182. What is an advantage of NSC's service?

(A) Clients can maintain control.
(B) Clients can remotely access information.
(C) Clients can lease hardware.
(D) Clients can oversee IT costs.

183. What information is NOT required for a brochure?

(A) A contact name
(B) A company name
(C) An office telephone number
(D) A home telephone number

184. What does Mrs. Jessica say about her company?

(A) It has been in operation for five years.
(B) The company is not interested in command over the system.
(C) It still uses an old IT system.
(D) Managing its IT system is too expensive.

185. What does Mrs. Jessica want to do?

(A) Estimate next year's IT budget
(B) Protect her company's IT technology
(C) Make her IT system less complicated
(D) Update her IT system to a new version

GO ON TO THE NEXT PAGE

DELPHINE OCEANVIEW HOTEL

* Escape the city to a tranquil hideaway situated within the grounds of Boudreau Community.

* Relax and view the picturesque Beach Delphine from all rooms looking south. Boat rent available April – September.

* Recharge yourself in our well equipped fitness center. Unwind and relax in the luxurious spa. Head outside and experience various exciting outdoor activities and enjoy fine dining in the Neroir restaurant.

REVIEW

Rating : 1/5 "A vacation to forget" by The Beaumonts

After running our guesthouse for 30 years, we decided to celebrate our retirement in your hotel. However, I'd like to forget this vacation for some reasons.

First, hotel renovation, which included the boat rental shop, blocked our view of the ocean even though we had booked a south-facing room, and it also prevented us from enjoying a boat ride despite the fine autumn weather.

Due to maintenance work, my wife was unable to enjoy the steam room or the sauna. We were limited to only 30 minutes on the tennis courts because so many people were waiting in line, after cancelling our first two choices, golf and horseback riding for the same reason.

Also, Neroir was understaffed, resulting in long waits and cold meals.

View our photo gallery

To	beaumont001@msn.com
From	delphineoceanview@hotels.br
Date	October 1ˢᵗ
Subject	review

Dear Mr. Mrs. Beaumont,

Thank you for your review and photographs. On behalf of the Delphine Oceanview Hotel, I'd like to express my sincere apologies for all the inconvenience and disappointment you encountered during your stay. Details of the building work were not added to our web-site due to an oversight. A heating breakdown led to the spa disruption and an outbreak of the flu prevented you from enjoying golf and horseback riding and some staff from working. As a token of apology, I am attaching a coupon for a complimentary night's stay for two persons in one of our spacious suites on a date of your choosing starting from January 1st.

With deepest regret,

Ted Overbeck

General Manager

186. What feature does the Delphine Oceanview Hotel have?

(A) A wonderful exercise area
(B) All-year-round boat rentals
(C) A swimming pool
(D) Guided tours of a nearby tourist attractions

187. In the review, the word "booked" in paragraph 2, line 2, is closest in meaning to

(A) organized
(B) scheduled
(C) checked
(D) committed

188. What is most likely true about the Beaumonts?

(A) They are not interested in sports.
(B) They put pictures of their trip online.
(C) They traveled during the summer.
(D) Their first room choice was not available.

189. What problem does Mr. Overbeck mention?

(A) The hotel will be closed next year.
(B) The heating repair staff has been ill.
(C) The web-site is down due to maintenance.
(D) A notice about the renovation was not put online.

190. Why couldn't the Beaumonts ride a horse?

(A) The horse stables were closed.
(B) The instructor caught the flu.
(C) Demand was too much among the quests.
(D) Horseback riding season had ended.

GO ON TO THE NEXT PAGE

Martin's Pizza

New York pan of crispy crust $15.50
Choose from the following hot flavors:
▶ Cool Hawaiian, Margherita, Meat Marvel, Spicy Cheese, all with extra basil.

Drink Combo Set
▶ pizza + soft drink (coke, lemonade, all fruit sodas, iced tea, iced coffee) $17.50

June Only! Prices of 6 extra toppings are slashed! (olives, honey pecans, pepperoni, onions, mushrooms, jalapenos) $1.50 → $0.90.

Martin's Word : If your order is not delivered by our staff within 40 minutes, your next pizza is FREE! All delivery crew have driver's licenses.

To	martin@pizza.com
From	adelenew@nostilde.com
Date	Friday, June 25th 22:07
Subject	Order #29584

Dear Martin,

I called at 8:10 p.m. today for two Spicy Cheese pizzas (crispy crust with extra honey pecans and jalapenos), and two Drink Combos (cool Hawaiian and Meat Marvel, both with extra olives and cokes). The delivery finally arrived at 9:15 p.m. and I asked your staff about being able to claim my free pizza next order since it had taken longer than the 40-minute limit as stated on the flyer I was reading for this order. He told me that it is not the case since my delivery was classed as a "bulk order" and therefore was outside the 40-minute delivery guarantee. I feel that this kind of company policy should have been made clearer in the ad.

Adelene Walker

To	adelenew@nostilde.com
From	martin@pizza.com
Date	Monday, June 28th 09:10
Subject	RE: Order #29584

Dear Ms. Walker,

Thank you for making your order with Martin's Pizza. Sorry to hear about your wait. The delivery staff, Laura, did in fact explained to you correctly regarding our bulk order policy. Our Martin's Word does not apply when more than three oven baked items are ordered because we do require extra time to extend different items. This policy is stated on our homepage on internet, along with other exceptions like bad weather, incorrect address and unworking elevator and so on, but as you quite rightly pointed out, this kind of information is not detailed on our flyer. So we decided to make it sure that our marketing policy are easily accessible in all kinds of advertisement and to show our thanks and apology to you. Please quote this promotional code, KH449, when you order any item over 20$ and you will get 30% discount.

Regards,
Martin

191. Which of the following items have been discounted?

(A) Lemonade
(B) Coffee
(C) Honey pecans
(D) Basil

192. What is true about Adelene Walker?

(A) She received an incorrect order.
(B) She placed her order online.
(C) Her order at one of Martin's stores was on June 25.
(D) Her pizza came with free mushrooms.

193. Which of the following is NOT mentioned as exceptions of delayed delivery?

(A) Increment weather
(B) Wrong address
(C) A broken elevator
(D) Heavy traffic

194. In the second e-mail, the word "extend" in line 4 is closest in meaning to

(A) lengthen
(B) stretch
(C) continue
(D) prepare

195. What does Martin promise to do?

(A) Provide the customer with a free item
(B) Give food quality training to staff
(C) Ensure policy is stated on marketing materials
(D) E-mail all promotions to Adelene

GO ON TO THE NEXT PAGE

NOTICE

To all our valued visitors,

It is with much sadness and regret that we announce the permanent closure of Carmont Public Library at 5:00 p.m. on July 31st. Though many visitors have supported financially over the years, cuts to public budgets have made it difficult to continue operating the library, finally leading to this unfortunate outcome.

After Carmont Public Library close, we strongly urge you to make use of the Benitez Library in Ollender. This library also offers IT courses, talks with celebrities, and fitness classes. A bus service between the library and Carmont takes 30 minutes, and runs twice an hour, from Monday to Saturday. In the meantime, we hope you keep on enjoying all the other facilities at Carmont and thank you for your patronage over the years.

Jane Benson
Head of Library Services
Carmont Public Library

To : Jane Benson <libraryservice@carmont.co.uk>
From : Steve Takiff <stevetkf@tallstory.com>
Date : Monday, May 21
Subject : Library Closur

Dear Ms. Benson,

I was shocked to learn that Carmont Public Library is going to close soon after hearing your interview on Culture Hour on Radio 9 a few days ago. As a former publisher and leader of the library volunteer group, 'Booklife', I would like to offer what I know and assist you with both the promotional and financial support needed to keep the library open. Booklife has so far helped convert a dozen of libraries nationwide into volunteer operating system and it is my hope that we can add this historical Carmont property to that list. I also provide librarian training program for interested members of the community, and I can help find appropriate books for the library. I look forward to hearing from you soon.

Steve Takiff

THE CARMONT EXPRESS   [Tuesday, August 15]

A new chapter begins at Carmont's history

Local residents were celebrating their selves yesterday at the news that Carmont Public Library has been handed a lifeline. Thanks to the efforts of top Booklife campaigner, Steve Takiff, the library will now be based on volunteer-run system and will maintain its full range of services under the leadership of Jane Benson.

Aldo Castro, a retired taxi-driver, said, "What wonderful news! I learned all about computers there, my grandchildren loved the reading club, and it's just a great gathering place for the community residents. We should show appreciation to Mr. Takiff and all the members of Booklife."

The library will officially reopen at noon on September 1st to coincide with the launch of Job Hunt Support Center inside the library.

196. In the notice, the word "over" in paragraph 1, line 3, is closest in meaning to
(A) throughout
(B) within
(C) across
(D) beyond

197. What reason was given for the closure of the library?
(A) Infrequent bus services
(B) Lack of usage by local residents
(C) Walkouts by staff
(D) Shortage of funding

198. What is indicated about Jane Benson?
(A) She will be retiring from all library jobs.
(B) She was employed at Benitez.
(C) She spoke about the closure of Carmont during a media broadcast.
(D) She has lived in Carmont since she was born.

199. What is true about Carmont Public Library?
(A) It is half an hour by train from Ollender.
(B) It will reopen in the morning of September 1st.
(C) It has served different generations of the community.
(D) It will employ June Dartfold as a volunteer.

200. Which is a feature offered by the reopened library?
(A) Lectures from guest speakers
(B) Reading group for youngsters
(C) Assistance for those seeking for job
(D) Physical activities lessons

Stop! This is the end of the test. If you finish before time is called, you may go back to Parts 5, 6, and 7 and check your work.

토익EDGE실전
1000제
LR 5 SET + 해석 해설

ANSWER SHEET

토익 EDGE 실전 1000제 LR

수험번호

응시일자 : 년 월 일

성 명 {한글 / 한자 / 영자}

좌석번호
Ⓐ Ⓑ Ⓒ Ⓓ Ⓔ
① ② ③ ④ ⑤ ⑥ ⑦

LISTENING (Part I~IV)

NO.	ANSWER (A B C D)	NO.	ANSWER (A B C D)	NO.	ANSWER (A B C D)	NO.	ANSWER (A B C D)	NO.	ANSWER (A B C D)
1	Ⓐ Ⓑ Ⓒ	21	Ⓐ Ⓑ Ⓒ Ⓓ	41	Ⓐ Ⓑ Ⓒ Ⓓ	61	Ⓐ Ⓑ Ⓒ Ⓓ	81	Ⓐ Ⓑ Ⓒ Ⓓ
2	Ⓐ Ⓑ Ⓒ	22	Ⓐ Ⓑ Ⓒ Ⓓ	42	Ⓐ Ⓑ Ⓒ Ⓓ	62	Ⓐ Ⓑ Ⓒ Ⓓ	82	Ⓐ Ⓑ Ⓒ Ⓓ
3	Ⓐ Ⓑ Ⓒ	23	Ⓐ Ⓑ Ⓒ Ⓓ	43	Ⓐ Ⓑ Ⓒ Ⓓ	63	Ⓐ Ⓑ Ⓒ Ⓓ	83	Ⓐ Ⓑ Ⓒ Ⓓ
4	Ⓐ Ⓑ Ⓒ	24	Ⓐ Ⓑ Ⓒ Ⓓ	44	Ⓐ Ⓑ Ⓒ Ⓓ	64	Ⓐ Ⓑ Ⓒ Ⓓ	84	Ⓐ Ⓑ Ⓒ Ⓓ
5	Ⓐ Ⓑ Ⓒ	25	Ⓐ Ⓑ Ⓒ Ⓓ	45	Ⓐ Ⓑ Ⓒ Ⓓ	65	Ⓐ Ⓑ Ⓒ Ⓓ	85	Ⓐ Ⓑ Ⓒ Ⓓ
6	Ⓐ Ⓑ Ⓒ	26	Ⓐ Ⓑ Ⓒ Ⓓ	46	Ⓐ Ⓑ Ⓒ Ⓓ	66	Ⓐ Ⓑ Ⓒ Ⓓ	86	Ⓐ Ⓑ Ⓒ Ⓓ
7	Ⓐ Ⓑ Ⓒ	27	Ⓐ Ⓑ Ⓒ Ⓓ	47	Ⓐ Ⓑ Ⓒ Ⓓ	67	Ⓐ Ⓑ Ⓒ Ⓓ	87	Ⓐ Ⓑ Ⓒ Ⓓ
8	Ⓐ Ⓑ Ⓒ	28	Ⓐ Ⓑ Ⓒ Ⓓ	48	Ⓐ Ⓑ Ⓒ Ⓓ	68	Ⓐ Ⓑ Ⓒ Ⓓ	88	Ⓐ Ⓑ Ⓒ Ⓓ
9	Ⓐ Ⓑ Ⓒ	29	Ⓐ Ⓑ Ⓒ Ⓓ	49	Ⓐ Ⓑ Ⓒ Ⓓ	69	Ⓐ Ⓑ Ⓒ Ⓓ	89	Ⓐ Ⓑ Ⓒ Ⓓ
10	Ⓐ Ⓑ Ⓒ	30	Ⓐ Ⓑ Ⓒ Ⓓ	50	Ⓐ Ⓑ Ⓒ Ⓓ	70	Ⓐ Ⓑ Ⓒ Ⓓ	90	Ⓐ Ⓑ Ⓒ Ⓓ
11	Ⓐ Ⓑ Ⓒ	31	Ⓐ Ⓑ Ⓒ Ⓓ	51	Ⓐ Ⓑ Ⓒ Ⓓ	71	Ⓐ Ⓑ Ⓒ Ⓓ	91	Ⓐ Ⓑ Ⓒ Ⓓ
12	Ⓐ Ⓑ Ⓒ	32	Ⓐ Ⓑ Ⓒ Ⓓ	52	Ⓐ Ⓑ Ⓒ Ⓓ	72	Ⓐ Ⓑ Ⓒ Ⓓ	92	Ⓐ Ⓑ Ⓒ Ⓓ
13	Ⓐ Ⓑ Ⓒ	33	Ⓐ Ⓑ Ⓒ Ⓓ	53	Ⓐ Ⓑ Ⓒ Ⓓ	73	Ⓐ Ⓑ Ⓒ Ⓓ	93	Ⓐ Ⓑ Ⓒ Ⓓ
14	Ⓐ Ⓑ Ⓒ	34	Ⓐ Ⓑ Ⓒ Ⓓ	54	Ⓐ Ⓑ Ⓒ Ⓓ	74	Ⓐ Ⓑ Ⓒ Ⓓ	94	Ⓐ Ⓑ Ⓒ Ⓓ
15	Ⓐ Ⓑ Ⓒ	35	Ⓐ Ⓑ Ⓒ Ⓓ	55	Ⓐ Ⓑ Ⓒ Ⓓ	75	Ⓐ Ⓑ Ⓒ Ⓓ	95	Ⓐ Ⓑ Ⓒ Ⓓ
16	Ⓐ Ⓑ Ⓒ	36	Ⓐ Ⓑ Ⓒ Ⓓ	56	Ⓐ Ⓑ Ⓒ Ⓓ	76	Ⓐ Ⓑ Ⓒ Ⓓ	96	Ⓐ Ⓑ Ⓒ Ⓓ
17	Ⓐ Ⓑ Ⓒ	37	Ⓐ Ⓑ Ⓒ Ⓓ	57	Ⓐ Ⓑ Ⓒ Ⓓ	77	Ⓐ Ⓑ Ⓒ Ⓓ	97	Ⓐ Ⓑ Ⓒ Ⓓ
18	Ⓐ Ⓑ Ⓒ	38	Ⓐ Ⓑ Ⓒ Ⓓ	58	Ⓐ Ⓑ Ⓒ Ⓓ	78	Ⓐ Ⓑ Ⓒ Ⓓ	98	Ⓐ Ⓑ Ⓒ Ⓓ
19	Ⓐ Ⓑ Ⓒ	39	Ⓐ Ⓑ Ⓒ Ⓓ	59	Ⓐ Ⓑ Ⓒ Ⓓ	79	Ⓐ Ⓑ Ⓒ Ⓓ	99	Ⓐ Ⓑ Ⓒ Ⓓ
20	Ⓐ Ⓑ Ⓒ	40	Ⓐ Ⓑ Ⓒ Ⓓ	60	Ⓐ Ⓑ Ⓒ Ⓓ	80	Ⓐ Ⓑ Ⓒ Ⓓ	100	Ⓐ Ⓑ Ⓒ Ⓓ

READING (Part V~VII)

NO.	ANSWER (A B C D)	NO.	ANSWER (A B C D)	NO.	ANSWER (A B C D)	NO.	ANSWER (A B C D)	NO.	ANSWER (A B C D)
101	Ⓐ Ⓑ Ⓒ Ⓓ	121	Ⓐ Ⓑ Ⓒ Ⓓ	141	Ⓐ Ⓑ Ⓒ Ⓓ	161	Ⓐ Ⓑ Ⓒ Ⓓ	181	Ⓐ Ⓑ Ⓒ Ⓓ
102	Ⓐ Ⓑ Ⓒ Ⓓ	122	Ⓐ Ⓑ Ⓒ Ⓓ	142	Ⓐ Ⓑ Ⓒ Ⓓ	162	Ⓐ Ⓑ Ⓒ Ⓓ	182	Ⓐ Ⓑ Ⓒ Ⓓ
103	Ⓐ Ⓑ Ⓒ Ⓓ	123	Ⓐ Ⓑ Ⓒ Ⓓ	143	Ⓐ Ⓑ Ⓒ Ⓓ	163	Ⓐ Ⓑ Ⓒ Ⓓ	183	Ⓐ Ⓑ Ⓒ Ⓓ
104	Ⓐ Ⓑ Ⓒ Ⓓ	124	Ⓐ Ⓑ Ⓒ Ⓓ	144	Ⓐ Ⓑ Ⓒ Ⓓ	164	Ⓐ Ⓑ Ⓒ Ⓓ	184	Ⓐ Ⓑ Ⓒ Ⓓ
105	Ⓐ Ⓑ Ⓒ Ⓓ	125	Ⓐ Ⓑ Ⓒ Ⓓ	145	Ⓐ Ⓑ Ⓒ Ⓓ	165	Ⓐ Ⓑ Ⓒ Ⓓ	185	Ⓐ Ⓑ Ⓒ Ⓓ
106	Ⓐ Ⓑ Ⓒ Ⓓ	126	Ⓐ Ⓑ Ⓒ Ⓓ	146	Ⓐ Ⓑ Ⓒ Ⓓ	166	Ⓐ Ⓑ Ⓒ Ⓓ	186	Ⓐ Ⓑ Ⓒ Ⓓ
107	Ⓐ Ⓑ Ⓒ Ⓓ	127	Ⓐ Ⓑ Ⓒ Ⓓ	147	Ⓐ Ⓑ Ⓒ Ⓓ	167	Ⓐ Ⓑ Ⓒ Ⓓ	187	Ⓐ Ⓑ Ⓒ Ⓓ
108	Ⓐ Ⓑ Ⓒ Ⓓ	128	Ⓐ Ⓑ Ⓒ Ⓓ	148	Ⓐ Ⓑ Ⓒ Ⓓ	168	Ⓐ Ⓑ Ⓒ Ⓓ	188	Ⓐ Ⓑ Ⓒ Ⓓ
109	Ⓐ Ⓑ Ⓒ Ⓓ	129	Ⓐ Ⓑ Ⓒ Ⓓ	149	Ⓐ Ⓑ Ⓒ Ⓓ	169	Ⓐ Ⓑ Ⓒ Ⓓ	189	Ⓐ Ⓑ Ⓒ Ⓓ
110	Ⓐ Ⓑ Ⓒ Ⓓ	130	Ⓐ Ⓑ Ⓒ Ⓓ	150	Ⓐ Ⓑ Ⓒ Ⓓ	170	Ⓐ Ⓑ Ⓒ Ⓓ	190	Ⓐ Ⓑ Ⓒ Ⓓ
111	Ⓐ Ⓑ Ⓒ Ⓓ	131	Ⓐ Ⓑ Ⓒ Ⓓ	151	Ⓐ Ⓑ Ⓒ Ⓓ	171	Ⓐ Ⓑ Ⓒ Ⓓ	191	Ⓐ Ⓑ Ⓒ Ⓓ
112	Ⓐ Ⓑ Ⓒ Ⓓ	132	Ⓐ Ⓑ Ⓒ Ⓓ	152	Ⓐ Ⓑ Ⓒ Ⓓ	172	Ⓐ Ⓑ Ⓒ Ⓓ	192	Ⓐ Ⓑ Ⓒ Ⓓ
113	Ⓐ Ⓑ Ⓒ Ⓓ	133	Ⓐ Ⓑ Ⓒ Ⓓ	153	Ⓐ Ⓑ Ⓒ Ⓓ	173	Ⓐ Ⓑ Ⓒ Ⓓ	193	Ⓐ Ⓑ Ⓒ Ⓓ
114	Ⓐ Ⓑ Ⓒ Ⓓ	134	Ⓐ Ⓑ Ⓒ Ⓓ	154	Ⓐ Ⓑ Ⓒ Ⓓ	174	Ⓐ Ⓑ Ⓒ Ⓓ	194	Ⓐ Ⓑ Ⓒ Ⓓ
115	Ⓐ Ⓑ Ⓒ Ⓓ	135	Ⓐ Ⓑ Ⓒ Ⓓ	155	Ⓐ Ⓑ Ⓒ Ⓓ	175	Ⓐ Ⓑ Ⓒ Ⓓ	195	Ⓐ Ⓑ Ⓒ Ⓓ
116	Ⓐ Ⓑ Ⓒ Ⓓ	136	Ⓐ Ⓑ Ⓒ Ⓓ	156	Ⓐ Ⓑ Ⓒ Ⓓ	176	Ⓐ Ⓑ Ⓒ Ⓓ	196	Ⓐ Ⓑ Ⓒ Ⓓ
117	Ⓐ Ⓑ Ⓒ Ⓓ	137	Ⓐ Ⓑ Ⓒ Ⓓ	157	Ⓐ Ⓑ Ⓒ Ⓓ	177	Ⓐ Ⓑ Ⓒ Ⓓ	197	Ⓐ Ⓑ Ⓒ Ⓓ
118	Ⓐ Ⓑ Ⓒ Ⓓ	138	Ⓐ Ⓑ Ⓒ Ⓓ	158	Ⓐ Ⓑ Ⓒ Ⓓ	178	Ⓐ Ⓑ Ⓒ Ⓓ	198	Ⓐ Ⓑ Ⓒ Ⓓ
119	Ⓐ Ⓑ Ⓒ Ⓓ	139	Ⓐ Ⓑ Ⓒ Ⓓ	159	Ⓐ Ⓑ Ⓒ Ⓓ	179	Ⓐ Ⓑ Ⓒ Ⓓ	199	Ⓐ Ⓑ Ⓒ Ⓓ
120	Ⓐ Ⓑ Ⓒ Ⓓ	140	Ⓐ Ⓑ Ⓒ Ⓓ	160	Ⓐ Ⓑ Ⓒ Ⓓ	180	Ⓐ Ⓑ Ⓒ Ⓓ	200	Ⓐ Ⓑ Ⓒ Ⓓ

1. 사용 필기구 : 컴퓨터용 연필(연필을 제외한 사인펜, 볼펜 등은 사용 절대 불가)

2. 정답된 필기구 사용과 〈보기〉의 올바른 표기 이외의 잘못된 표기로 인한 경우에는 당 위원회 당 위원회의 OMR기기가 판독한 결과에 따르며 그 결과는 본인 책임입니다. 1개의 정답만 골라 아래의 올바른 표기대로 정확하 표기하여야 합니다.
〈보기〉 올바른 표기 : ● 　 잘못된 표기 : ⊘ ⊗ ◐

3. 답안지는 컴퓨터로 처리되므로 훼손하시면 안 되며, 상단의 타이밍마크(┃┃┃┃)부분을 찢거나, 낙서 등을 하면 본인에게 불이익이 발생할 수 있습니다.

4. 감독관의 확인이 없거나 시험 종료 후에 답안 작성을 계속할 경우 시험 무효 처리됩니다.

* 서약 내용을 읽으시고 확인란에 반드시 서명하십시오.

서 약

본인은 TOEIC 시험 문제의 일부 또는 전부를 유출하거나 이에 관한 형태로도 타인에게 누설 공개하지 않을 것이며 인터넷 또는 인쇄물 등을 이용해 유포하거나 참고 자료로 활용하지 않을 것입니다. 또한 TOEIC 시험 부정 행위 처리 규정을 준수할 것을 서약합니다.

ANSWER SHEET

응시일자 : 년 월 일 시 분 ~ 시 분

테스트명 :

수 험 번 호

성 명
한글
한자
영자

LISTENING SECTION

Part 1

No.	ANSWER A B C D	No.	ANSWER A B C D	No.	ANSWER A B C D
1	Ⓐ Ⓑ Ⓒ				
2	Ⓐ Ⓑ Ⓒ				
3	Ⓐ Ⓑ Ⓒ				
4	Ⓐ Ⓑ Ⓒ				
5	Ⓐ Ⓑ Ⓒ				
6	Ⓐ Ⓑ Ⓒ Ⓓ				
7	Ⓐ Ⓑ Ⓒ Ⓓ				
8	Ⓐ Ⓑ Ⓒ Ⓓ				
9	Ⓐ Ⓑ Ⓒ Ⓓ				
10	Ⓐ Ⓑ Ⓒ Ⓓ				

Part 2 (No. 11–40)

Part 3 (No. 41–70)

Part 4 (No. 71–100)

READING SECTION

Part 5 (No. 101–130)

Part 6 (No. 131–146)

Part 7 (No. 141–200)

(Answer options: A B C D)

ANSWER SHEET

토익 EDGE 실전 1000제 LR

수험번호		

응시일자 :	년	월	일

성명	한글
	한자
	영자

좌석번호
Ⓐ Ⓑ Ⓒ Ⓓ Ⓔ
① ② ③ ④ ⑤ ⑥ ⑦

LISTENING (Part I~IV)

NO.	ANSWER A B C D	NO.	ANSWER A B C D	NO.	ANSWER A B C D	NO.	ANSWER A B C D	NO.	ANSWER A B C D
1	Ⓐ Ⓑ Ⓒ Ⓓ	21	Ⓐ Ⓑ Ⓒ Ⓓ	41	Ⓐ Ⓑ Ⓒ Ⓓ	61	Ⓐ Ⓑ Ⓒ Ⓓ	81	Ⓐ Ⓑ Ⓒ Ⓓ
2	Ⓐ Ⓑ Ⓒ Ⓓ	22	Ⓐ Ⓑ Ⓒ Ⓓ	42	Ⓐ Ⓑ Ⓒ Ⓓ	62	Ⓐ Ⓑ Ⓒ Ⓓ	82	Ⓐ Ⓑ Ⓒ Ⓓ
3	Ⓐ Ⓑ Ⓒ Ⓓ	23	Ⓐ Ⓑ Ⓒ Ⓓ	43	Ⓐ Ⓑ Ⓒ Ⓓ	63	Ⓐ Ⓑ Ⓒ Ⓓ	83	Ⓐ Ⓑ Ⓒ Ⓓ
4	Ⓐ Ⓑ Ⓒ Ⓓ	24	Ⓐ Ⓑ Ⓒ Ⓓ	44	Ⓐ Ⓑ Ⓒ Ⓓ	64	Ⓐ Ⓑ Ⓒ Ⓓ	84	Ⓐ Ⓑ Ⓒ Ⓓ
5	Ⓐ Ⓑ Ⓒ Ⓓ	25	Ⓐ Ⓑ Ⓒ Ⓓ	45	Ⓐ Ⓑ Ⓒ Ⓓ	65	Ⓐ Ⓑ Ⓒ Ⓓ	85	Ⓐ Ⓑ Ⓒ Ⓓ
6	Ⓐ Ⓑ Ⓒ Ⓓ	26	Ⓐ Ⓑ Ⓒ Ⓓ	46	Ⓐ Ⓑ Ⓒ Ⓓ	66	Ⓐ Ⓑ Ⓒ Ⓓ	86	Ⓐ Ⓑ Ⓒ Ⓓ
7	Ⓐ Ⓑ Ⓒ Ⓓ	27	Ⓐ Ⓑ Ⓒ Ⓓ	47	Ⓐ Ⓑ Ⓒ Ⓓ	67	Ⓐ Ⓑ Ⓒ Ⓓ	87	Ⓐ Ⓑ Ⓒ Ⓓ
8	Ⓐ Ⓑ Ⓒ Ⓓ	28	Ⓐ Ⓑ Ⓒ Ⓓ	48	Ⓐ Ⓑ Ⓒ Ⓓ	68	Ⓐ Ⓑ Ⓒ Ⓓ	88	Ⓐ Ⓑ Ⓒ Ⓓ
9	Ⓐ Ⓑ Ⓒ Ⓓ	29	Ⓐ Ⓑ Ⓒ Ⓓ	49	Ⓐ Ⓑ Ⓒ Ⓓ	69	Ⓐ Ⓑ Ⓒ Ⓓ	89	Ⓐ Ⓑ Ⓒ Ⓓ
10	Ⓐ Ⓑ Ⓒ Ⓓ	30	Ⓐ Ⓑ Ⓒ Ⓓ	50	Ⓐ Ⓑ Ⓒ Ⓓ	70	Ⓐ Ⓑ Ⓒ Ⓓ	90	Ⓐ Ⓑ Ⓒ Ⓓ
11	Ⓐ Ⓑ Ⓒ Ⓓ	31	Ⓐ Ⓑ Ⓒ Ⓓ	51	Ⓐ Ⓑ Ⓒ Ⓓ	71	Ⓐ Ⓑ Ⓒ Ⓓ	91	Ⓐ Ⓑ Ⓒ Ⓓ
12	Ⓐ Ⓑ Ⓒ Ⓓ	32	Ⓐ Ⓑ Ⓒ Ⓓ	52	Ⓐ Ⓑ Ⓒ Ⓓ	72	Ⓐ Ⓑ Ⓒ Ⓓ	92	Ⓐ Ⓑ Ⓒ Ⓓ
13	Ⓐ Ⓑ Ⓒ Ⓓ	33	Ⓐ Ⓑ Ⓒ Ⓓ	53	Ⓐ Ⓑ Ⓒ Ⓓ	73	Ⓐ Ⓑ Ⓒ Ⓓ	93	Ⓐ Ⓑ Ⓒ Ⓓ
14	Ⓐ Ⓑ Ⓒ Ⓓ	34	Ⓐ Ⓑ Ⓒ Ⓓ	54	Ⓐ Ⓑ Ⓒ Ⓓ	74	Ⓐ Ⓑ Ⓒ Ⓓ	94	Ⓐ Ⓑ Ⓒ Ⓓ
15	Ⓐ Ⓑ Ⓒ Ⓓ	35	Ⓐ Ⓑ Ⓒ Ⓓ	55	Ⓐ Ⓑ Ⓒ Ⓓ	75	Ⓐ Ⓑ Ⓒ Ⓓ	95	Ⓐ Ⓑ Ⓒ Ⓓ
16	Ⓐ Ⓑ Ⓒ Ⓓ	36	Ⓐ Ⓑ Ⓒ Ⓓ	56	Ⓐ Ⓑ Ⓒ Ⓓ	76	Ⓐ Ⓑ Ⓒ Ⓓ	96	Ⓐ Ⓑ Ⓒ Ⓓ
17	Ⓐ Ⓑ Ⓒ Ⓓ	37	Ⓐ Ⓑ Ⓒ Ⓓ	57	Ⓐ Ⓑ Ⓒ Ⓓ	77	Ⓐ Ⓑ Ⓒ Ⓓ	97	Ⓐ Ⓑ Ⓒ Ⓓ
18	Ⓐ Ⓑ Ⓒ Ⓓ	38	Ⓐ Ⓑ Ⓒ Ⓓ	58	Ⓐ Ⓑ Ⓒ Ⓓ	78	Ⓐ Ⓑ Ⓒ Ⓓ	98	Ⓐ Ⓑ Ⓒ Ⓓ
19	Ⓐ Ⓑ Ⓒ Ⓓ	39	Ⓐ Ⓑ Ⓒ Ⓓ	59	Ⓐ Ⓑ Ⓒ Ⓓ	79	Ⓐ Ⓑ Ⓒ Ⓓ	99	Ⓐ Ⓑ Ⓒ Ⓓ
20	Ⓐ Ⓑ Ⓒ Ⓓ	40	Ⓐ Ⓑ Ⓒ Ⓓ	60	Ⓐ Ⓑ Ⓒ Ⓓ	80	Ⓐ Ⓑ Ⓒ Ⓓ	100	Ⓐ Ⓑ Ⓒ Ⓓ

READING (Part V~VII)

NO.	ANSWER A B C D	NO.	ANSWER A B C D	NO.	ANSWER A B C D	NO.	ANSWER A B C D	NO.	ANSWER A B C D
101	Ⓐ Ⓑ Ⓒ Ⓓ	121	Ⓐ Ⓑ Ⓒ Ⓓ	141	Ⓐ Ⓑ Ⓒ Ⓓ	161	Ⓐ Ⓑ Ⓒ Ⓓ	181	Ⓐ Ⓑ Ⓒ Ⓓ
102	Ⓐ Ⓑ Ⓒ Ⓓ	122	Ⓐ Ⓑ Ⓒ Ⓓ	142	Ⓐ Ⓑ Ⓒ Ⓓ	162	Ⓐ Ⓑ Ⓒ Ⓓ	182	Ⓐ Ⓑ Ⓒ Ⓓ
103	Ⓐ Ⓑ Ⓒ Ⓓ	123	Ⓐ Ⓑ Ⓒ Ⓓ	143	Ⓐ Ⓑ Ⓒ Ⓓ	163	Ⓐ Ⓑ Ⓒ Ⓓ	183	Ⓐ Ⓑ Ⓒ Ⓓ
104	Ⓐ Ⓑ Ⓒ Ⓓ	124	Ⓐ Ⓑ Ⓒ Ⓓ	144	Ⓐ Ⓑ Ⓒ Ⓓ	164	Ⓐ Ⓑ Ⓒ Ⓓ	184	Ⓐ Ⓑ Ⓒ Ⓓ
105	Ⓐ Ⓑ Ⓒ Ⓓ	125	Ⓐ Ⓑ Ⓒ Ⓓ	145	Ⓐ Ⓑ Ⓒ Ⓓ	165	Ⓐ Ⓑ Ⓒ Ⓓ	185	Ⓐ Ⓑ Ⓒ Ⓓ
106	Ⓐ Ⓑ Ⓒ Ⓓ	126	Ⓐ Ⓑ Ⓒ Ⓓ	146	Ⓐ Ⓑ Ⓒ Ⓓ	166	Ⓐ Ⓑ Ⓒ Ⓓ	186	Ⓐ Ⓑ Ⓒ Ⓓ
107	Ⓐ Ⓑ Ⓒ Ⓓ	127	Ⓐ Ⓑ Ⓒ Ⓓ	147	Ⓐ Ⓑ Ⓒ Ⓓ	167	Ⓐ Ⓑ Ⓒ Ⓓ	187	Ⓐ Ⓑ Ⓒ Ⓓ
108	Ⓐ Ⓑ Ⓒ Ⓓ	128	Ⓐ Ⓑ Ⓒ Ⓓ	148	Ⓐ Ⓑ Ⓒ Ⓓ	168	Ⓐ Ⓑ Ⓒ Ⓓ	188	Ⓐ Ⓑ Ⓒ Ⓓ
109	Ⓐ Ⓑ Ⓒ Ⓓ	129	Ⓐ Ⓑ Ⓒ Ⓓ	149	Ⓐ Ⓑ Ⓒ Ⓓ	169	Ⓐ Ⓑ Ⓒ Ⓓ	189	Ⓐ Ⓑ Ⓒ Ⓓ
110	Ⓐ Ⓑ Ⓒ Ⓓ	130	Ⓐ Ⓑ Ⓒ Ⓓ	150	Ⓐ Ⓑ Ⓒ Ⓓ	170	Ⓐ Ⓑ Ⓒ Ⓓ	190	Ⓐ Ⓑ Ⓒ Ⓓ
111	Ⓐ Ⓑ Ⓒ Ⓓ	131	Ⓐ Ⓑ Ⓒ Ⓓ	151	Ⓐ Ⓑ Ⓒ Ⓓ	171	Ⓐ Ⓑ Ⓒ Ⓓ	191	Ⓐ Ⓑ Ⓒ Ⓓ
112	Ⓐ Ⓑ Ⓒ Ⓓ	132	Ⓐ Ⓑ Ⓒ Ⓓ	152	Ⓐ Ⓑ Ⓒ Ⓓ	172	Ⓐ Ⓑ Ⓒ Ⓓ	192	Ⓐ Ⓑ Ⓒ Ⓓ
113	Ⓐ Ⓑ Ⓒ Ⓓ	133	Ⓐ Ⓑ Ⓒ Ⓓ	153	Ⓐ Ⓑ Ⓒ Ⓓ	173	Ⓐ Ⓑ Ⓒ Ⓓ	193	Ⓐ Ⓑ Ⓒ Ⓓ
114	Ⓐ Ⓑ Ⓒ Ⓓ	134	Ⓐ Ⓑ Ⓒ Ⓓ	154	Ⓐ Ⓑ Ⓒ Ⓓ	174	Ⓐ Ⓑ Ⓒ Ⓓ	194	Ⓐ Ⓑ Ⓒ Ⓓ
115	Ⓐ Ⓑ Ⓒ Ⓓ	135	Ⓐ Ⓑ Ⓒ Ⓓ	155	Ⓐ Ⓑ Ⓒ Ⓓ	175	Ⓐ Ⓑ Ⓒ Ⓓ	195	Ⓐ Ⓑ Ⓒ Ⓓ
116	Ⓐ Ⓑ Ⓒ Ⓓ	136	Ⓐ Ⓑ Ⓒ Ⓓ	156	Ⓐ Ⓑ Ⓒ Ⓓ	176	Ⓐ Ⓑ Ⓒ Ⓓ	196	Ⓐ Ⓑ Ⓒ Ⓓ
117	Ⓐ Ⓑ Ⓒ Ⓓ	137	Ⓐ Ⓑ Ⓒ Ⓓ	157	Ⓐ Ⓑ Ⓒ Ⓓ	177	Ⓐ Ⓑ Ⓒ Ⓓ	197	Ⓐ Ⓑ Ⓒ Ⓓ
118	Ⓐ Ⓑ Ⓒ Ⓓ	138	Ⓐ Ⓑ Ⓒ Ⓓ	158	Ⓐ Ⓑ Ⓒ Ⓓ	178	Ⓐ Ⓑ Ⓒ Ⓓ	198	Ⓐ Ⓑ Ⓒ Ⓓ
119	Ⓐ Ⓑ Ⓒ Ⓓ	139	Ⓐ Ⓑ Ⓒ Ⓓ	159	Ⓐ Ⓑ Ⓒ Ⓓ	179	Ⓐ Ⓑ Ⓒ Ⓓ	199	Ⓐ Ⓑ Ⓒ Ⓓ
120	Ⓐ Ⓑ Ⓒ Ⓓ	140	Ⓐ Ⓑ Ⓒ Ⓓ	160	Ⓐ Ⓑ Ⓒ Ⓓ	180	Ⓐ Ⓑ Ⓒ Ⓓ	200	Ⓐ Ⓑ Ⓒ Ⓓ

1. 사용 필기구 : 컴퓨터용 연필(연필을 제외한 사인펜, 볼펜 등은 사용 절대 불가)

2. 정답은 반드시 <보기>의 올바른 표기 이외의 잘못된 표기로 한 경우에는 당 위원회 OMR기기가 판독한 결과에 따르며 그 결과는 본인 책임입니다. 1개의 정답만 골라 아래의 올바른 표기대로 정확히 표기하여야 합니다.
<보기> 올바른 표기 : ●   잘못된 표기 : ○ ⊗ ◐ ○

3. 답안지는 컴퓨터로 처리되므로 훼손하시면 안 되며, 상단의 타이밍마크([|||])부분을 찢거나, 낙서 등을 하면 본인에게 불이익이 발생할 수 있습니다.

4. 감독관의 확인이 없거나 시험 종료 후에 답안 작성을 계속할 경우 시험 무효 처리됩니다.

* 서야 내용을 읽으시고 확인란에 반드시 서명하십시오.

서 약
본인은 TOEIC 시험 문제의 일부 또는 전부를 유출하거나 이매한 행태로도 타인에게 누설 공개하지 않을 것이며 인터넷 또는 인쇄물 등을 이용해 유포하거나 참고 자료로도 활용하지 않을 것입니다. 또한 TOEIC 시험 부정 행위 처리 규정을 준수할 것을 서약합니다.

확 인

ANSWER SHEET

테스트명 :

응시일자 : ____ 년 ____ 월 ____ 일 ____ 시 분 ~ 시 분

토익 EDGE
실전 1000제 LR

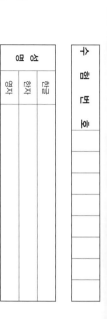

수험번호

성명 | 한글 | 영자
영자 |

LISTENING SECTION

Part 1
No.	ANSWER
1	A B C D
2	A B C D
3	A B C D
4	A B C D
5	A B C D
6	A B C D
7	A B C D
8	A B C
9	A B C
10	A B C

Part 2
No.	ANSWER
11	A B C
12	A B C
13	A B C
14	A B C
15	A B C
16	A B C
17	A B C
18	A B C
19	A B C
20	A B C

No.	ANSWER
21	A B C
22	A B C
23	A B C
24	A B C
25	A B C
26	A B C
27	A B C
28	A B C
29	A B C
30	A B C

No.	ANSWER
31	A B C
32	A B C
33	A B C D
34	A B C D
35	A B C D
36	A B C D
37	A B C D
38	A B C D
39	A B C D
40	A B C D

Part 3
No.	ANSWER
41	A B C D
42	A B C D
43	A B C D
44	A B C D
45	A B C D
46	A B C D
47	A B C D
48	A B C D
49	A B C D
50	A B C D

No.	ANSWER
51	A B C D
52	A B C D
53	A B C D
54	A B C D
55	A B C D
56	A B C D
57	A B C D
58	A B C D
59	A B C D
60	A B C D

No.	ANSWER
61	A B C D
62	A B C D
63	A B C D
64	A B C D
65	A B C D
66	A B C D
67	A B C D
68	A B C D
69	A B C D
70	A B C D

Part 4
No.	ANSWER
71	A B C D
72	A B C D
73	A B C D
74	A B C D
75	A B C D
76	A B C D
77	A B C D
78	A B C D
79	A B C D
80	A B C D

No.	ANSWER
81	A B C D
82	A B C D
83	A B C D
84	A B C D
85	A B C D
86	A B C D
87	A B C D
88	A B C D
89	A B C D
90	A B C D

No.	ANSWER
91	A B C D
92	A B C D
93	A B C D
94	A B C D
95	A B C D
96	A B C D
97	A B C D
98	A B C D
99	A B C D
100	A B C D

READING SECTION

Part 5
No.	ANSWER
101	A B C D
102	A B C D
103	A B C D
104	A B C D
105	A B C D
106	A B C D
107	A B C D
108	A B C D
109	A B C D
110	A B C D

No.	ANSWER
111	A B C D
112	A B C D
113	A B C D
114	A B C D
115	A B C D
116	A B C D
117	A B C D
118	A B C D
119	A B C D
120	A B C D

No.	ANSWER
121	A B C D
122	A B C D
123	A B C D
124	A B C D
125	A B C D
126	A B C D
127	A B C D
128	A B C D
129	A B C D
130	A B C D

Part 6
No.	ANSWER
131	A B C D
132	A B C D
133	A B C D
134	A B C D
135	A B C D
136	A B C D
137	A B C D
138	A B C D
139	A B C D
140	A B C D

No.	ANSWER
141	A B C D
142	A B C D
143	A B C D
144	A B C D
145	A B C D
146	A B C D
147	A B C D
148	A B C D
149	A B C D
150	A B C D

Part 7
No.	ANSWER
151	A B C D
152	A B C D
153	A B C D
154	A B C D
155	A B C D
156	A B C D
157	A B C D
158	A B C D
159	A B C D
160	A B C D

No.	ANSWER
161	A B C D
162	A B C D
163	A B C D
164	A B C D
165	A B C D
166	A B C D
167	A B C D
168	A B C D
169	A B C D
170	A B C D

No.	ANSWER
171	A B C D
172	A B C D
173	A B C D
174	A B C D
175	A B C D
176	A B C D
177	A B C D
178	A B C D
179	A B C D
180	A B C D

No.	ANSWER
181	A B C D
182	A B C D
183	A B C D
184	A B C D
185	A B C D
186	A B C D
187	A B C D
188	A B C D
189	A B C D
190	A B C D

No.	ANSWER
191	A B C D
192	A B C D
193	A B C D
194	A B C D
195	A B C D
196	A B C D
197	A B C D
198	A B C D
199	A B C D
200	A B C D

ANSWER SHEET

토익EDGE실전1000제 LR

LISTENING (Part I~IV)

NO.	ANSWER	NO.	ANSWER	NO.	ANSWER	NO.	ANSWER	NO.	ANSWER
	A B C D		A B C D		A B C D		A B C D		A B C D
1	Ⓐ Ⓑ Ⓒ	21	Ⓐ Ⓑ Ⓒ Ⓓ	41	Ⓐ Ⓑ Ⓒ Ⓓ	61	Ⓐ Ⓑ Ⓒ Ⓓ	81	Ⓐ Ⓑ Ⓒ Ⓓ
2	Ⓐ Ⓑ Ⓒ Ⓓ	22	Ⓐ Ⓑ Ⓒ Ⓓ	42	Ⓐ Ⓑ Ⓒ Ⓓ	62	Ⓐ Ⓑ Ⓒ Ⓓ	82	Ⓐ Ⓑ Ⓒ Ⓓ
3	Ⓐ Ⓑ Ⓒ	23	Ⓐ Ⓑ Ⓒ Ⓓ	43	Ⓐ Ⓑ Ⓒ Ⓓ	63	Ⓐ Ⓑ Ⓒ Ⓓ	83	Ⓐ Ⓑ Ⓒ Ⓓ
4	Ⓐ Ⓑ Ⓒ	24	Ⓐ Ⓑ Ⓒ Ⓓ	44	Ⓐ Ⓑ Ⓒ Ⓓ	64	Ⓐ Ⓑ Ⓒ Ⓓ	84	Ⓐ Ⓑ Ⓒ Ⓓ
5	Ⓐ Ⓑ Ⓒ	25	Ⓐ Ⓑ Ⓒ Ⓓ	45	Ⓐ Ⓑ Ⓒ Ⓓ	65	Ⓐ Ⓑ Ⓒ Ⓓ	85	Ⓐ Ⓑ Ⓒ Ⓓ
6	Ⓐ Ⓑ Ⓒ	26	Ⓐ Ⓑ Ⓒ Ⓓ	46	Ⓐ Ⓑ Ⓒ Ⓓ	66	Ⓐ Ⓑ Ⓒ Ⓓ	86	Ⓐ Ⓑ Ⓒ Ⓓ
7	Ⓐ Ⓑ Ⓒ	27	Ⓐ Ⓑ Ⓒ Ⓓ	47	Ⓐ Ⓑ Ⓒ Ⓓ	67	Ⓐ Ⓑ Ⓒ Ⓓ	87	Ⓐ Ⓑ Ⓒ Ⓓ
8	Ⓐ Ⓑ Ⓒ	28	Ⓐ Ⓑ Ⓒ Ⓓ	48	Ⓐ Ⓑ Ⓒ Ⓓ	68	Ⓐ Ⓑ Ⓒ Ⓓ	88	Ⓐ Ⓑ Ⓒ Ⓓ
9	Ⓐ Ⓑ Ⓒ	29	Ⓐ Ⓑ Ⓒ Ⓓ	49	Ⓐ Ⓑ Ⓒ Ⓓ	69	Ⓐ Ⓑ Ⓒ Ⓓ	89	Ⓐ Ⓑ Ⓒ Ⓓ
10	Ⓐ Ⓑ Ⓒ	30	Ⓐ Ⓑ Ⓒ Ⓓ	50	Ⓐ Ⓑ Ⓒ Ⓓ	70	Ⓐ Ⓑ Ⓒ Ⓓ	90	Ⓐ Ⓑ Ⓒ Ⓓ
11	Ⓐ Ⓑ Ⓒ	31	Ⓐ Ⓑ Ⓒ Ⓓ	51	Ⓐ Ⓑ Ⓒ Ⓓ	71	Ⓐ Ⓑ Ⓒ Ⓓ	91	Ⓐ Ⓑ Ⓒ Ⓓ
12	Ⓐ Ⓑ Ⓒ	32	Ⓐ Ⓑ Ⓒ Ⓓ	52	Ⓐ Ⓑ Ⓒ Ⓓ	72	Ⓐ Ⓑ Ⓒ Ⓓ	92	Ⓐ Ⓑ Ⓒ Ⓓ
13	Ⓐ Ⓑ Ⓒ	33	Ⓐ Ⓑ Ⓒ Ⓓ	53	Ⓐ Ⓑ Ⓒ Ⓓ	73	Ⓐ Ⓑ Ⓒ Ⓓ	93	Ⓐ Ⓑ Ⓒ Ⓓ
14	Ⓐ Ⓑ Ⓒ	34	Ⓐ Ⓑ Ⓒ Ⓓ	54	Ⓐ Ⓑ Ⓒ Ⓓ	74	Ⓐ Ⓑ Ⓒ Ⓓ	94	Ⓐ Ⓑ Ⓒ Ⓓ
15	Ⓐ Ⓑ Ⓒ	35	Ⓐ Ⓑ Ⓒ Ⓓ	55	Ⓐ Ⓑ Ⓒ Ⓓ	75	Ⓐ Ⓑ Ⓒ Ⓓ	95	Ⓐ Ⓑ Ⓒ Ⓓ
16	Ⓐ Ⓑ Ⓒ	36	Ⓐ Ⓑ Ⓒ Ⓓ	56	Ⓐ Ⓑ Ⓒ Ⓓ	76	Ⓐ Ⓑ Ⓒ Ⓓ	96	Ⓐ Ⓑ Ⓒ Ⓓ
17	Ⓐ Ⓑ Ⓒ	37	Ⓐ Ⓑ Ⓒ Ⓓ	57	Ⓐ Ⓑ Ⓒ Ⓓ	77	Ⓐ Ⓑ Ⓒ Ⓓ	97	Ⓐ Ⓑ Ⓒ Ⓓ
18	Ⓐ Ⓑ Ⓒ	38	Ⓐ Ⓑ Ⓒ Ⓓ	58	Ⓐ Ⓑ Ⓒ Ⓓ	78	Ⓐ Ⓑ Ⓒ Ⓓ	98	Ⓐ Ⓑ Ⓒ Ⓓ
19	Ⓐ Ⓑ Ⓒ	39	Ⓐ Ⓑ Ⓒ Ⓓ	59	Ⓐ Ⓑ Ⓒ Ⓓ	79	Ⓐ Ⓑ Ⓒ Ⓓ	99	Ⓐ Ⓑ Ⓒ Ⓓ
20	Ⓐ Ⓑ Ⓒ	40	Ⓐ Ⓑ Ⓒ Ⓓ	60	Ⓐ Ⓑ Ⓒ Ⓓ	80	Ⓐ Ⓑ Ⓒ Ⓓ	100	Ⓐ Ⓑ Ⓒ Ⓓ

READING (Part V~VII)

NO.	ANSWER	NO.	ANSWER	NO.	ANSWER	NO.	ANSWER	NO.	ANSWER
	A B C D		A B C D		A B C D		A B C D		A B C D
101	Ⓐ Ⓑ Ⓒ Ⓓ	121	Ⓐ Ⓑ Ⓒ Ⓓ	141	Ⓐ Ⓑ Ⓒ Ⓓ	161	Ⓐ Ⓑ Ⓒ Ⓓ	181	Ⓐ Ⓑ Ⓒ Ⓓ
102	Ⓐ Ⓑ Ⓒ Ⓓ	122	Ⓐ Ⓑ Ⓒ Ⓓ	142	Ⓐ Ⓑ Ⓒ Ⓓ	162	Ⓐ Ⓑ Ⓒ Ⓓ	182	Ⓐ Ⓑ Ⓒ Ⓓ
103	Ⓐ Ⓑ Ⓒ Ⓓ	123	Ⓐ Ⓑ Ⓒ Ⓓ	143	Ⓐ Ⓑ Ⓒ Ⓓ	163	Ⓐ Ⓑ Ⓒ Ⓓ	183	Ⓐ Ⓑ Ⓒ Ⓓ
104	Ⓐ Ⓑ Ⓒ Ⓓ	124	Ⓐ Ⓑ Ⓒ Ⓓ	144	Ⓐ Ⓑ Ⓒ Ⓓ	164	Ⓐ Ⓑ Ⓒ Ⓓ	184	Ⓐ Ⓑ Ⓒ Ⓓ
105	Ⓐ Ⓑ Ⓒ Ⓓ	125	Ⓐ Ⓑ Ⓒ Ⓓ	145	Ⓐ Ⓑ Ⓒ Ⓓ	165	Ⓐ Ⓑ Ⓒ Ⓓ	185	Ⓐ Ⓑ Ⓒ Ⓓ
106	Ⓐ Ⓑ Ⓒ Ⓓ	126	Ⓐ Ⓑ Ⓒ Ⓓ	146	Ⓐ Ⓑ Ⓒ Ⓓ	166	Ⓐ Ⓑ Ⓒ Ⓓ	186	Ⓐ Ⓑ Ⓒ Ⓓ
107	Ⓐ Ⓑ Ⓒ Ⓓ	127	Ⓐ Ⓑ Ⓒ Ⓓ	147	Ⓐ Ⓑ Ⓒ Ⓓ	167	Ⓐ Ⓑ Ⓒ Ⓓ	187	Ⓐ Ⓑ Ⓒ Ⓓ
108	Ⓐ Ⓑ Ⓒ Ⓓ	128	Ⓐ Ⓑ Ⓒ Ⓓ	148	Ⓐ Ⓑ Ⓒ Ⓓ	168	Ⓐ Ⓑ Ⓒ Ⓓ	188	Ⓐ Ⓑ Ⓒ Ⓓ
109	Ⓐ Ⓑ Ⓒ Ⓓ	129	Ⓐ Ⓑ Ⓒ Ⓓ	149	Ⓐ Ⓑ Ⓒ Ⓓ	169	Ⓐ Ⓑ Ⓒ Ⓓ	189	Ⓐ Ⓑ Ⓒ Ⓓ
110	Ⓐ Ⓑ Ⓒ Ⓓ	130	Ⓐ Ⓑ Ⓒ Ⓓ	150	Ⓐ Ⓑ Ⓒ Ⓓ	170	Ⓐ Ⓑ Ⓒ Ⓓ	190	Ⓐ Ⓑ Ⓒ Ⓓ
111	Ⓐ Ⓑ Ⓒ Ⓓ	131	Ⓐ Ⓑ Ⓒ Ⓓ	151	Ⓐ Ⓑ Ⓒ Ⓓ	171	Ⓐ Ⓑ Ⓒ Ⓓ	191	Ⓐ Ⓑ Ⓒ Ⓓ
112	Ⓐ Ⓑ Ⓒ Ⓓ	132	Ⓐ Ⓑ Ⓒ Ⓓ	152	Ⓐ Ⓑ Ⓒ Ⓓ	172	Ⓐ Ⓑ Ⓒ Ⓓ	192	Ⓐ Ⓑ Ⓒ Ⓓ
113	Ⓐ Ⓑ Ⓒ Ⓓ	133	Ⓐ Ⓑ Ⓒ Ⓓ	153	Ⓐ Ⓑ Ⓒ Ⓓ	173	Ⓐ Ⓑ Ⓒ Ⓓ	193	Ⓐ Ⓑ Ⓒ Ⓓ
114	Ⓐ Ⓑ Ⓒ Ⓓ	134	Ⓐ Ⓑ Ⓒ Ⓓ	154	Ⓐ Ⓑ Ⓒ Ⓓ	174	Ⓐ Ⓑ Ⓒ Ⓓ	194	Ⓐ Ⓑ Ⓒ Ⓓ
115	Ⓐ Ⓑ Ⓒ Ⓓ	135	Ⓐ Ⓑ Ⓒ Ⓓ	155	Ⓐ Ⓑ Ⓒ Ⓓ	175	Ⓐ Ⓑ Ⓒ Ⓓ	195	Ⓐ Ⓑ Ⓒ Ⓓ
116	Ⓐ Ⓑ Ⓒ Ⓓ	136	Ⓐ Ⓑ Ⓒ Ⓓ	156	Ⓐ Ⓑ Ⓒ Ⓓ	176	Ⓐ Ⓑ Ⓒ Ⓓ	196	Ⓐ Ⓑ Ⓒ Ⓓ
117	Ⓐ Ⓑ Ⓒ Ⓓ	137	Ⓐ Ⓑ Ⓒ Ⓓ	157	Ⓐ Ⓑ Ⓒ Ⓓ	177	Ⓐ Ⓑ Ⓒ Ⓓ	197	Ⓐ Ⓑ Ⓒ Ⓓ
118	Ⓐ Ⓑ Ⓒ Ⓓ	138	Ⓐ Ⓑ Ⓒ Ⓓ	158	Ⓐ Ⓑ Ⓒ Ⓓ	178	Ⓐ Ⓑ Ⓒ Ⓓ	198	Ⓐ Ⓑ Ⓒ Ⓓ
119	Ⓐ Ⓑ Ⓒ Ⓓ	139	Ⓐ Ⓑ Ⓒ Ⓓ	159	Ⓐ Ⓑ Ⓒ Ⓓ	179	Ⓐ Ⓑ Ⓒ Ⓓ	199	Ⓐ Ⓑ Ⓒ Ⓓ
120	Ⓐ Ⓑ Ⓒ Ⓓ	140	Ⓐ Ⓑ Ⓒ Ⓓ	160	Ⓐ Ⓑ Ⓒ Ⓓ	180	Ⓐ Ⓑ Ⓒ Ⓓ	200	Ⓐ Ⓑ Ⓒ Ⓓ

ANSWER SHEET

토익 EDGE 실전 **1000제 LR**

수험번호

응시일자 :　　년　　월　　일

성 명	
한글	
한자	
영자	

좌석번호

Ⓐ Ⓑ Ⓒ Ⓓ Ⓔ
① ② ③ ④ ⑤ ⑥ ⑦

LISTENING (Part I~IV)

NO.	ANSWER	NO.	ANSWER	NO.	ANSWER	NO.	ANSWER	NO.	ANSWER
	A B C D		A B C D		A B C D		A B C D		A B C D
1	Ⓐ Ⓑ Ⓒ	21	Ⓐ Ⓑ Ⓒ Ⓓ	41	Ⓐ Ⓑ Ⓒ	61	Ⓐ Ⓑ Ⓒ Ⓓ	81	Ⓐ Ⓑ Ⓒ Ⓓ
2	Ⓐ Ⓑ Ⓒ	22	Ⓐ Ⓑ Ⓒ Ⓓ	42	Ⓐ Ⓑ Ⓒ	62	Ⓐ Ⓑ Ⓒ Ⓓ	82	Ⓐ Ⓑ Ⓒ Ⓓ
3	Ⓐ Ⓑ Ⓒ	23	Ⓐ Ⓑ Ⓒ Ⓓ	43	Ⓐ Ⓑ Ⓒ	63	Ⓐ Ⓑ Ⓒ Ⓓ	83	Ⓐ Ⓑ Ⓒ Ⓓ
4	Ⓐ Ⓑ Ⓒ	24	Ⓐ Ⓑ Ⓒ Ⓓ	44	Ⓐ Ⓑ Ⓒ	64	Ⓐ Ⓑ Ⓒ Ⓓ	84	Ⓐ Ⓑ Ⓒ Ⓓ
5	Ⓐ Ⓑ Ⓒ	25	Ⓐ Ⓑ Ⓒ Ⓓ	45	Ⓐ Ⓑ Ⓒ	65	Ⓐ Ⓑ Ⓒ Ⓓ	85	Ⓐ Ⓑ Ⓒ Ⓓ
6	Ⓐ Ⓑ Ⓒ	26	Ⓐ Ⓑ Ⓒ Ⓓ	46	Ⓐ Ⓑ Ⓒ	66	Ⓐ Ⓑ Ⓒ Ⓓ	86	Ⓐ Ⓑ Ⓒ Ⓓ
7	Ⓐ Ⓑ Ⓒ	27	Ⓐ Ⓑ Ⓒ Ⓓ	47	Ⓐ Ⓑ Ⓒ	67	Ⓐ Ⓑ Ⓒ Ⓓ	87	Ⓐ Ⓑ Ⓒ Ⓓ
8	Ⓐ Ⓑ Ⓒ	28	Ⓐ Ⓑ Ⓒ Ⓓ	48	Ⓐ Ⓑ Ⓒ	68	Ⓐ Ⓑ Ⓒ Ⓓ	88	Ⓐ Ⓑ Ⓒ Ⓓ
9	Ⓐ Ⓑ Ⓒ	29	Ⓐ Ⓑ Ⓒ Ⓓ	49	Ⓐ Ⓑ Ⓒ	69	Ⓐ Ⓑ Ⓒ Ⓓ	89	Ⓐ Ⓑ Ⓒ Ⓓ
10	Ⓐ Ⓑ Ⓒ	30	Ⓐ Ⓑ Ⓒ Ⓓ	50	Ⓐ Ⓑ Ⓒ	70	Ⓐ Ⓑ Ⓒ Ⓓ	90	Ⓐ Ⓑ Ⓒ Ⓓ
11	Ⓐ Ⓑ Ⓒ	31	Ⓐ Ⓑ Ⓒ Ⓓ	51	Ⓐ Ⓑ Ⓒ	71	Ⓐ Ⓑ Ⓒ Ⓓ	91	Ⓐ Ⓑ Ⓒ Ⓓ
12	Ⓐ Ⓑ Ⓒ	32	Ⓐ Ⓑ Ⓒ Ⓓ	52	Ⓐ Ⓑ Ⓒ	72	Ⓐ Ⓑ Ⓒ Ⓓ	92	Ⓐ Ⓑ Ⓒ Ⓓ
13	Ⓐ Ⓑ Ⓒ	33	Ⓐ Ⓑ Ⓒ Ⓓ	53	Ⓐ Ⓑ Ⓒ	73	Ⓐ Ⓑ Ⓒ Ⓓ	93	Ⓐ Ⓑ Ⓒ Ⓓ
14	Ⓐ Ⓑ Ⓒ	34	Ⓐ Ⓑ Ⓒ Ⓓ	54	Ⓐ Ⓑ Ⓒ	74	Ⓐ Ⓑ Ⓒ Ⓓ	94	Ⓐ Ⓑ Ⓒ Ⓓ
15	Ⓐ Ⓑ Ⓒ	35	Ⓐ Ⓑ Ⓒ Ⓓ	55	Ⓐ Ⓑ Ⓒ	75	Ⓐ Ⓑ Ⓒ Ⓓ	95	Ⓐ Ⓑ Ⓒ Ⓓ
16	Ⓐ Ⓑ Ⓒ	36	Ⓐ Ⓑ Ⓒ Ⓓ	56	Ⓐ Ⓑ Ⓒ	76	Ⓐ Ⓑ Ⓒ Ⓓ	96	Ⓐ Ⓑ Ⓒ Ⓓ
17	Ⓐ Ⓑ Ⓒ	37	Ⓐ Ⓑ Ⓒ Ⓓ	57	Ⓐ Ⓑ Ⓒ	77	Ⓐ Ⓑ Ⓒ Ⓓ	97	Ⓐ Ⓑ Ⓒ Ⓓ
18	Ⓐ Ⓑ Ⓒ	38	Ⓐ Ⓑ Ⓒ Ⓓ	58	Ⓐ Ⓑ Ⓒ	78	Ⓐ Ⓑ Ⓒ Ⓓ	98	Ⓐ Ⓑ Ⓒ Ⓓ
19	Ⓐ Ⓑ Ⓒ	39	Ⓐ Ⓑ Ⓒ Ⓓ	59	Ⓐ Ⓑ Ⓒ	79	Ⓐ Ⓑ Ⓒ Ⓓ	99	Ⓐ Ⓑ Ⓒ Ⓓ
20	Ⓐ Ⓑ Ⓒ	40	Ⓐ Ⓑ Ⓒ Ⓓ	60	Ⓐ Ⓑ Ⓒ	80	Ⓐ Ⓑ Ⓒ Ⓓ	100	Ⓐ Ⓑ Ⓒ Ⓓ

READING (Part V~VII)

NO.	ANSWER	NO.	ANSWER	NO.	ANSWER	NO.	ANSWER	NO.	ANSWER
	A B C D		A B C D		A B C D		A B C D		A B C D
101	Ⓐ Ⓑ Ⓒ Ⓓ	121	Ⓐ Ⓑ Ⓒ Ⓓ	141	Ⓐ Ⓑ Ⓒ Ⓓ	161	Ⓐ Ⓑ Ⓒ Ⓓ	181	Ⓐ Ⓑ Ⓒ Ⓓ
102	Ⓐ Ⓑ Ⓒ Ⓓ	122	Ⓐ Ⓑ Ⓒ Ⓓ	142	Ⓐ Ⓑ Ⓒ Ⓓ	162	Ⓐ Ⓑ Ⓒ Ⓓ	182	Ⓐ Ⓑ Ⓒ Ⓓ
103	Ⓐ Ⓑ Ⓒ Ⓓ	123	Ⓐ Ⓑ Ⓒ Ⓓ	143	Ⓐ Ⓑ Ⓒ Ⓓ	163	Ⓐ Ⓑ Ⓒ Ⓓ	183	Ⓐ Ⓑ Ⓒ Ⓓ
104	Ⓐ Ⓑ Ⓒ Ⓓ	124	Ⓐ Ⓑ Ⓒ Ⓓ	144	Ⓐ Ⓑ Ⓒ Ⓓ	164	Ⓐ Ⓑ Ⓒ Ⓓ	184	Ⓐ Ⓑ Ⓒ Ⓓ
105	Ⓐ Ⓑ Ⓒ Ⓓ	125	Ⓐ Ⓑ Ⓒ Ⓓ	145	Ⓐ Ⓑ Ⓒ Ⓓ	165	Ⓐ Ⓑ Ⓒ Ⓓ	185	Ⓐ Ⓑ Ⓒ Ⓓ
106	Ⓐ Ⓑ Ⓒ Ⓓ	126	Ⓐ Ⓑ Ⓒ Ⓓ	146	Ⓐ Ⓑ Ⓒ Ⓓ	166	Ⓐ Ⓑ Ⓒ Ⓓ	186	Ⓐ Ⓑ Ⓒ Ⓓ
107	Ⓐ Ⓑ Ⓒ Ⓓ	127	Ⓐ Ⓑ Ⓒ Ⓓ	147	Ⓐ Ⓑ Ⓒ Ⓓ	167	Ⓐ Ⓑ Ⓒ Ⓓ	187	Ⓐ Ⓑ Ⓒ Ⓓ
108	Ⓐ Ⓑ Ⓒ Ⓓ	128	Ⓐ Ⓑ Ⓒ Ⓓ	148	Ⓐ Ⓑ Ⓒ Ⓓ	168	Ⓐ Ⓑ Ⓒ Ⓓ	188	Ⓐ Ⓑ Ⓒ Ⓓ
109	Ⓐ Ⓑ Ⓒ Ⓓ	129	Ⓐ Ⓑ Ⓒ Ⓓ	149	Ⓐ Ⓑ Ⓒ Ⓓ	169	Ⓐ Ⓑ Ⓒ Ⓓ	189	Ⓐ Ⓑ Ⓒ Ⓓ
110	Ⓐ Ⓑ Ⓒ Ⓓ	130	Ⓐ Ⓑ Ⓒ Ⓓ	150	Ⓐ Ⓑ Ⓒ Ⓓ	170	Ⓐ Ⓑ Ⓒ Ⓓ	190	Ⓐ Ⓑ Ⓒ Ⓓ
111	Ⓐ Ⓑ Ⓒ Ⓓ	131	Ⓐ Ⓑ Ⓒ Ⓓ	151	Ⓐ Ⓑ Ⓒ Ⓓ	171	Ⓐ Ⓑ Ⓒ Ⓓ	191	Ⓐ Ⓑ Ⓒ Ⓓ
112	Ⓐ Ⓑ Ⓒ Ⓓ	132	Ⓐ Ⓑ Ⓒ Ⓓ	152	Ⓐ Ⓑ Ⓒ Ⓓ	172	Ⓐ Ⓑ Ⓒ Ⓓ	192	Ⓐ Ⓑ Ⓒ Ⓓ
113	Ⓐ Ⓑ Ⓒ Ⓓ	133	Ⓐ Ⓑ Ⓒ Ⓓ	153	Ⓐ Ⓑ Ⓒ Ⓓ	173	Ⓐ Ⓑ Ⓒ Ⓓ	193	Ⓐ Ⓑ Ⓒ Ⓓ
114	Ⓐ Ⓑ Ⓒ Ⓓ	134	Ⓐ Ⓑ Ⓒ Ⓓ	154	Ⓐ Ⓑ Ⓒ Ⓓ	174	Ⓐ Ⓑ Ⓒ Ⓓ	194	Ⓐ Ⓑ Ⓒ Ⓓ
115	Ⓐ Ⓑ Ⓒ Ⓓ	135	Ⓐ Ⓑ Ⓒ Ⓓ	155	Ⓐ Ⓑ Ⓒ Ⓓ	175	Ⓐ Ⓑ Ⓒ Ⓓ	195	Ⓐ Ⓑ Ⓒ Ⓓ
116	Ⓐ Ⓑ Ⓒ Ⓓ	136	Ⓐ Ⓑ Ⓒ Ⓓ	156	Ⓐ Ⓑ Ⓒ Ⓓ	176	Ⓐ Ⓑ Ⓒ Ⓓ	196	Ⓐ Ⓑ Ⓒ Ⓓ
117	Ⓐ Ⓑ Ⓒ Ⓓ	137	Ⓐ Ⓑ Ⓒ Ⓓ	157	Ⓐ Ⓑ Ⓒ Ⓓ	177	Ⓐ Ⓑ Ⓒ Ⓓ	197	Ⓐ Ⓑ Ⓒ Ⓓ
118	Ⓐ Ⓑ Ⓒ Ⓓ	138	Ⓐ Ⓑ Ⓒ Ⓓ	158	Ⓐ Ⓑ Ⓒ Ⓓ	178	Ⓐ Ⓑ Ⓒ Ⓓ	198	Ⓐ Ⓑ Ⓒ Ⓓ
119	Ⓐ Ⓑ Ⓒ Ⓓ	139	Ⓐ Ⓑ Ⓒ Ⓓ	159	Ⓐ Ⓑ Ⓒ Ⓓ	179	Ⓐ Ⓑ Ⓒ Ⓓ	199	Ⓐ Ⓑ Ⓒ Ⓓ
120	Ⓐ Ⓑ Ⓒ Ⓓ	140	Ⓐ Ⓑ Ⓒ Ⓓ	160	Ⓐ Ⓑ Ⓒ Ⓓ	180	Ⓐ Ⓑ Ⓒ Ⓓ	200	Ⓐ Ⓑ Ⓒ Ⓓ

1. 사용 필기구 : 컴퓨터용 연필(연필을 제외한 사인펜, 볼펜 등은 사용 절대 불가)

2. 정답란 표기 시 〈보기〉의 올바른 표기 이외의 잘못된 표기로 한 경우에는 당 위원회 OMR기기가 판독한 결과에 따르며 그 결과는 본인 책임으로 함이 됩니다. 1개의 정답만 골라 아래의 올바른 표기대로 정확히 표기하여야 합니다.
   〈보기〉 올바른 표기 : ●   잘못된 표기 : ○ ⊗

3. 답안지는 컴퓨터로 처리되므로 훼손하시면 안 되며, 상단의 타이밍마크(∥∥∥) 부분을 찢거나, 낙서 등을 하면 본인에게 불이익이 발생할 수 있습니다.

4. 감독관의 확인이 없거나 시험 종료 후에 답안 작성을 계속할 경우 시험 무효 처리됩니다.

* 시야 내용을 읽으시고 확인란에 반드시 서명하십시오.

서 약	
본인은 TOEIC 시험 문제의 일부 또는 전부를 유출하거나 이에 대한 형태로든 타인에게 누설 공개하지 않을 것이며 인터넷 또는 인쇄물 등을 이용해 유포하거나 참고 자료로 활용하지 않을 것입니다. 또한 TOEIC 시험 부정 행위 처리 규정을 준수할 것을 서약합니다.	
	확 인

ANSWER SHEET

응시일자 : 년 월 일 시 분 ~ 시 분

테스트명 :

토익 EDGE 실전 1000제 LR

수험번호

성명
한글
한자
영자

LISTENING SECTION

Part 1

No.	ANSWER (A B C D)
1	Ⓐ Ⓑ Ⓒ Ⓓ
2	Ⓐ Ⓑ Ⓒ Ⓓ
3	Ⓐ Ⓑ Ⓒ Ⓓ
4	Ⓐ Ⓑ Ⓒ Ⓓ
5	Ⓐ Ⓑ Ⓒ Ⓓ
6	Ⓐ Ⓑ Ⓒ Ⓓ
7	Ⓐ Ⓑ Ⓒ Ⓓ
8	Ⓐ Ⓑ Ⓒ Ⓓ
9	Ⓐ Ⓑ Ⓒ Ⓓ
10	Ⓐ Ⓑ Ⓒ Ⓓ

Part 2 — No. 11–30 (ANSWER A B C D)
Part 3 — No. 31–60 (ANSWER A B C D)
Part 4 — No. 61–100 (ANSWER A B C D)

READING SECTION

Part 5 — No. 101–130 (ANSWER A B C D)
Part 6 — No. 131–150 (ANSWER A B C D)
Part 7 — No. 151–200 (ANSWER A B C D)

ANSWER SHEET

토익 **EDGE 실전 1000제 LR**

수험번호 ____

응시일자 : ____ 년 ____ 월 ____ 일

성명	한글
	한자
	영자

좌석번호
Ⓐ Ⓑ Ⓒ Ⓓ Ⓔ
① ② ③ ④ ⑤ ⑥ ⑦

LISTENING (Part I~IV)

NO.	ANSWER A B C D	NO.	ANSWER A B C D	NO.	ANSWER A B C D	NO.	ANSWER A B C D	NO.	ANSWER A B C D
1	Ⓐ Ⓑ Ⓒ Ⓓ	21	Ⓐ Ⓑ Ⓒ Ⓓ	41	Ⓐ Ⓑ Ⓒ Ⓓ	61	Ⓐ Ⓑ Ⓒ Ⓓ	81	Ⓐ Ⓑ Ⓒ Ⓓ
2	Ⓐ Ⓑ Ⓒ Ⓓ	22	Ⓐ Ⓑ Ⓒ Ⓓ	42	Ⓐ Ⓑ Ⓒ Ⓓ	62	Ⓐ Ⓑ Ⓒ Ⓓ	82	Ⓐ Ⓑ Ⓒ Ⓓ
3	Ⓐ Ⓑ Ⓒ Ⓓ	23	Ⓐ Ⓑ Ⓒ Ⓓ	43	Ⓐ Ⓑ Ⓒ Ⓓ	63	Ⓐ Ⓑ Ⓒ Ⓓ	83	Ⓐ Ⓑ Ⓒ Ⓓ
4	Ⓐ Ⓑ Ⓒ Ⓓ	24	Ⓐ Ⓑ Ⓒ Ⓓ	44	Ⓐ Ⓑ Ⓒ Ⓓ	64	Ⓐ Ⓑ Ⓒ Ⓓ	84	Ⓐ Ⓑ Ⓒ Ⓓ
5	Ⓐ Ⓑ Ⓒ Ⓓ	25	Ⓐ Ⓑ Ⓒ Ⓓ	45	Ⓐ Ⓑ Ⓒ Ⓓ	65	Ⓐ Ⓑ Ⓒ Ⓓ	85	Ⓐ Ⓑ Ⓒ Ⓓ
6	Ⓐ Ⓑ Ⓒ Ⓓ	26	Ⓐ Ⓑ Ⓒ Ⓓ	46	Ⓐ Ⓑ Ⓒ Ⓓ	66	Ⓐ Ⓑ Ⓒ Ⓓ	86	Ⓐ Ⓑ Ⓒ Ⓓ
7	Ⓐ Ⓑ Ⓒ Ⓓ	27	Ⓐ Ⓑ Ⓒ Ⓓ	47	Ⓐ Ⓑ Ⓒ Ⓓ	67	Ⓐ Ⓑ Ⓒ Ⓓ	87	Ⓐ Ⓑ Ⓒ Ⓓ
8	Ⓐ Ⓑ Ⓒ Ⓓ	28	Ⓐ Ⓑ Ⓒ Ⓓ	48	Ⓐ Ⓑ Ⓒ Ⓓ	68	Ⓐ Ⓑ Ⓒ Ⓓ	88	Ⓐ Ⓑ Ⓒ Ⓓ
9	Ⓐ Ⓑ Ⓒ Ⓓ	29	Ⓐ Ⓑ Ⓒ Ⓓ	49	Ⓐ Ⓑ Ⓒ Ⓓ	69	Ⓐ Ⓑ Ⓒ Ⓓ	89	Ⓐ Ⓑ Ⓒ Ⓓ
10	Ⓐ Ⓑ Ⓒ Ⓓ	30	Ⓐ Ⓑ Ⓒ Ⓓ	50	Ⓐ Ⓑ Ⓒ Ⓓ	70	Ⓐ Ⓑ Ⓒ Ⓓ	90	Ⓐ Ⓑ Ⓒ Ⓓ
11	Ⓐ Ⓑ Ⓒ Ⓓ	31	Ⓐ Ⓑ Ⓒ Ⓓ	51	Ⓐ Ⓑ Ⓒ Ⓓ	71	Ⓐ Ⓑ Ⓒ Ⓓ	91	Ⓐ Ⓑ Ⓒ Ⓓ
12	Ⓐ Ⓑ Ⓒ Ⓓ	32	Ⓐ Ⓑ Ⓒ Ⓓ	52	Ⓐ Ⓑ Ⓒ Ⓓ	72	Ⓐ Ⓑ Ⓒ Ⓓ	92	Ⓐ Ⓑ Ⓒ Ⓓ
13	Ⓐ Ⓑ Ⓒ Ⓓ	33	Ⓐ Ⓑ Ⓒ Ⓓ	53	Ⓐ Ⓑ Ⓒ Ⓓ	73	Ⓐ Ⓑ Ⓒ Ⓓ	93	Ⓐ Ⓑ Ⓒ Ⓓ
14	Ⓐ Ⓑ Ⓒ Ⓓ	34	Ⓐ Ⓑ Ⓒ Ⓓ	54	Ⓐ Ⓑ Ⓒ Ⓓ	74	Ⓐ Ⓑ Ⓒ Ⓓ	94	Ⓐ Ⓑ Ⓒ Ⓓ
15	Ⓐ Ⓑ Ⓒ Ⓓ	35	Ⓐ Ⓑ Ⓒ Ⓓ	55	Ⓐ Ⓑ Ⓒ Ⓓ	75	Ⓐ Ⓑ Ⓒ Ⓓ	95	Ⓐ Ⓑ Ⓒ Ⓓ
16	Ⓐ Ⓑ Ⓒ Ⓓ	36	Ⓐ Ⓑ Ⓒ Ⓓ	56	Ⓐ Ⓑ Ⓒ Ⓓ	76	Ⓐ Ⓑ Ⓒ Ⓓ	96	Ⓐ Ⓑ Ⓒ Ⓓ
17	Ⓐ Ⓑ Ⓒ Ⓓ	37	Ⓐ Ⓑ Ⓒ Ⓓ	57	Ⓐ Ⓑ Ⓒ Ⓓ	77	Ⓐ Ⓑ Ⓒ Ⓓ	97	Ⓐ Ⓑ Ⓒ Ⓓ
18	Ⓐ Ⓑ Ⓒ Ⓓ	38	Ⓐ Ⓑ Ⓒ Ⓓ	58	Ⓐ Ⓑ Ⓒ Ⓓ	78	Ⓐ Ⓑ Ⓒ Ⓓ	98	Ⓐ Ⓑ Ⓒ Ⓓ
19	Ⓐ Ⓑ Ⓒ Ⓓ	39	Ⓐ Ⓑ Ⓒ Ⓓ	59	Ⓐ Ⓑ Ⓒ Ⓓ	79	Ⓐ Ⓑ Ⓒ Ⓓ	99	Ⓐ Ⓑ Ⓒ Ⓓ
20	Ⓐ Ⓑ Ⓒ Ⓓ	40	Ⓐ Ⓑ Ⓒ Ⓓ	60	Ⓐ Ⓑ Ⓒ Ⓓ	80	Ⓐ Ⓑ Ⓒ Ⓓ	100	Ⓐ Ⓑ Ⓒ Ⓓ

READING (Part V~VII)

NO.	ANSWER A B C D	NO.	ANSWER A B C D	NO.	ANSWER A B C D	NO.	ANSWER A B C D	NO.	ANSWER A B C D
101	Ⓐ Ⓑ Ⓒ Ⓓ	121	Ⓐ Ⓑ Ⓒ Ⓓ	141	Ⓐ Ⓑ Ⓒ Ⓓ	161	Ⓐ Ⓑ Ⓒ Ⓓ	181	Ⓐ Ⓑ Ⓒ Ⓓ
102	Ⓐ Ⓑ Ⓒ Ⓓ	122	Ⓐ Ⓑ Ⓒ Ⓓ	142	Ⓐ Ⓑ Ⓒ Ⓓ	162	Ⓐ Ⓑ Ⓒ Ⓓ	182	Ⓐ Ⓑ Ⓒ Ⓓ
103	Ⓐ Ⓑ Ⓒ Ⓓ	123	Ⓐ Ⓑ Ⓒ Ⓓ	143	Ⓐ Ⓑ Ⓒ Ⓓ	163	Ⓐ Ⓑ Ⓒ Ⓓ	183	Ⓐ Ⓑ Ⓒ Ⓓ
104	Ⓐ Ⓑ Ⓒ Ⓓ	124	Ⓐ Ⓑ Ⓒ Ⓓ	144	Ⓐ Ⓑ Ⓒ Ⓓ	164	Ⓐ Ⓑ Ⓒ Ⓓ	184	Ⓐ Ⓑ Ⓒ Ⓓ
105	Ⓐ Ⓑ Ⓒ Ⓓ	125	Ⓐ Ⓑ Ⓒ Ⓓ	145	Ⓐ Ⓑ Ⓒ Ⓓ	165	Ⓐ Ⓑ Ⓒ Ⓓ	185	Ⓐ Ⓑ Ⓒ Ⓓ
106	Ⓐ Ⓑ Ⓒ Ⓓ	126	Ⓐ Ⓑ Ⓒ Ⓓ	146	Ⓐ Ⓑ Ⓒ Ⓓ	166	Ⓐ Ⓑ Ⓒ Ⓓ	186	Ⓐ Ⓑ Ⓒ Ⓓ
107	Ⓐ Ⓑ Ⓒ Ⓓ	127	Ⓐ Ⓑ Ⓒ Ⓓ	147	Ⓐ Ⓑ Ⓒ Ⓓ	167	Ⓐ Ⓑ Ⓒ Ⓓ	187	Ⓐ Ⓑ Ⓒ Ⓓ
108	Ⓐ Ⓑ Ⓒ Ⓓ	128	Ⓐ Ⓑ Ⓒ Ⓓ	148	Ⓐ Ⓑ Ⓒ Ⓓ	168	Ⓐ Ⓑ Ⓒ Ⓓ	188	Ⓐ Ⓑ Ⓒ Ⓓ
109	Ⓐ Ⓑ Ⓒ Ⓓ	129	Ⓐ Ⓑ Ⓒ Ⓓ	149	Ⓐ Ⓑ Ⓒ Ⓓ	169	Ⓐ Ⓑ Ⓒ Ⓓ	189	Ⓐ Ⓑ Ⓒ Ⓓ
110	Ⓐ Ⓑ Ⓒ Ⓓ	130	Ⓐ Ⓑ Ⓒ Ⓓ	150	Ⓐ Ⓑ Ⓒ Ⓓ	170	Ⓐ Ⓑ Ⓒ Ⓓ	190	Ⓐ Ⓑ Ⓒ Ⓓ
111	Ⓐ Ⓑ Ⓒ Ⓓ	131	Ⓐ Ⓑ Ⓒ Ⓓ	151	Ⓐ Ⓑ Ⓒ Ⓓ	171	Ⓐ Ⓑ Ⓒ Ⓓ	191	Ⓐ Ⓑ Ⓒ Ⓓ
112	Ⓐ Ⓑ Ⓒ Ⓓ	132	Ⓐ Ⓑ Ⓒ Ⓓ	152	Ⓐ Ⓑ Ⓒ Ⓓ	172	Ⓐ Ⓑ Ⓒ Ⓓ	192	Ⓐ Ⓑ Ⓒ Ⓓ
113	Ⓐ Ⓑ Ⓒ Ⓓ	133	Ⓐ Ⓑ Ⓒ Ⓓ	153	Ⓐ Ⓑ Ⓒ Ⓓ	173	Ⓐ Ⓑ Ⓒ Ⓓ	193	Ⓐ Ⓑ Ⓒ Ⓓ
114	Ⓐ Ⓑ Ⓒ Ⓓ	134	Ⓐ Ⓑ Ⓒ Ⓓ	154	Ⓐ Ⓑ Ⓒ Ⓓ	174	Ⓐ Ⓑ Ⓒ Ⓓ	194	Ⓐ Ⓑ Ⓒ Ⓓ
115	Ⓐ Ⓑ Ⓒ Ⓓ	135	Ⓐ Ⓑ Ⓒ Ⓓ	155	Ⓐ Ⓑ Ⓒ Ⓓ	175	Ⓐ Ⓑ Ⓒ Ⓓ	195	Ⓐ Ⓑ Ⓒ Ⓓ
116	Ⓐ Ⓑ Ⓒ Ⓓ	136	Ⓐ Ⓑ Ⓒ Ⓓ	156	Ⓐ Ⓑ Ⓒ Ⓓ	176	Ⓐ Ⓑ Ⓒ Ⓓ	196	Ⓐ Ⓑ Ⓒ Ⓓ
117	Ⓐ Ⓑ Ⓒ Ⓓ	137	Ⓐ Ⓑ Ⓒ Ⓓ	157	Ⓐ Ⓑ Ⓒ Ⓓ	177	Ⓐ Ⓑ Ⓒ Ⓓ	197	Ⓐ Ⓑ Ⓒ Ⓓ
118	Ⓐ Ⓑ Ⓒ Ⓓ	138	Ⓐ Ⓑ Ⓒ Ⓓ	158	Ⓐ Ⓑ Ⓒ Ⓓ	178	Ⓐ Ⓑ Ⓒ Ⓓ	198	Ⓐ Ⓑ Ⓒ Ⓓ
119	Ⓐ Ⓑ Ⓒ Ⓓ	139	Ⓐ Ⓑ Ⓒ Ⓓ	159	Ⓐ Ⓑ Ⓒ Ⓓ	179	Ⓐ Ⓑ Ⓒ Ⓓ	199	Ⓐ Ⓑ Ⓒ Ⓓ
120	Ⓐ Ⓑ Ⓒ Ⓓ	140	Ⓐ Ⓑ Ⓒ Ⓓ	160	Ⓐ Ⓑ Ⓒ Ⓓ	180	Ⓐ Ⓑ Ⓒ Ⓓ	200	Ⓐ Ⓑ Ⓒ Ⓓ

1. 사용 필기구 : 컴퓨터용 펜(연필을 제외한 사인펜, 볼펜 등은 사용 절대 불가)

2. 잘못된 필기구 사용과 〈보기〉의 올바른 표기 이외의 잘못된 표기로 인한 답안은 당 위원회의 OMR기기가 판독한 결과에 따르며 그 결과는 본인 책임입니다. 1개의 정답만 골라 아래의 올바른 표기대로 정확히 표기하여야 합니다.
〈보기〉 올바른 표기 : ● 　　잘못된 표기 : ⊙ ⊗ ◯

3. 답안지는 컴퓨터로 처리되므로 훼손하시면 안 되며, 상단의 타이밍마크(∣∣∣)부분을 찢거나, 낙서 등을 하면 본인에게 불이익이 발생할 수 있습니다.

4. 감독관의 확인이 없거나 시험 종료 후에 답안 작성을 계속할 경우 시험 무효 처리됩니다.

* 시작 내용을 읽으시고 확인란에 반드시 서명하십시오.

서　　　　　약

본인은 TOEIC 시험 문제의 일부 또는 전부를 유출하거나 어떠한 형태로도 타인에게 누설 공개하지 않을 것이며 인터넷 또는 인쇄물 등을 이용해 유포하거나 참고 자료로 활용하지 않을 것입니다. 또한 TOEIC 시험 부정 행위 처리 규정을 준수할 것을 서약합니다.

확 인

ANSWER SHEET

응시일자 : 년 월 일 시 분 ~ 시 분

테스트명 :

토익 EDGE 실전 1000제 LR

수험번호

성명
한글
한자
영자

LISTENING SECTION

Part 1 / **Part 2** / **Part 3** / **Part 4**

Part 1 No. 1–10 ANSWER A B C D

Part 2 No. 11–20, 21–30 ANSWER A B C D

Part 3 No. 31–40, 41–50, 51–60, 61–70 ANSWER A B C D

Part 4 No. 71–80, 81–90, 91–100 ANSWER A B C D

READING SECTION

Part 5 / **Part 6** / **Part 7**

Part 5 No. 101–110, 111–120, 121–130 ANSWER A B C D

Part 6 No. 131–140, 141–150 ANSWER A B C D

Part 7 No. 151–160, 161–170, 171–180, 181–190, 191–200 ANSWER A B C D